UPON THESE THREE THINGS

Jewish Perspectives on Loving God

Jeff Levin

To Mike and Dara —
With great appreciation for your
friendship and continued service
to our country.

Jeff

ISR BOOKS
WACO, TX
2014

Cover designed by Neil S. Luft
Proofread by Mark Bast, MB Ink
Packaged by Wish Publishing

Printed in the United States of America
10 9 8 7 6 5 4 3 2

Published by ISR Books
One Bear Place #97236
Baylor University
Waco, TX 76798

For Lea, my love

ALSO BY JEFF LEVIN

JUDAISM AND HEALTH:
A Handbook of Practical, Professional and Scholarly Resources
(Edited with M. F. Prince)

HEALING TO ALL THEIR FLESH:
Jewish & Christian Perspectives on Spirituality, Theology, & Health
(Edited with K. G. Meador)

DIVINE LOVE:
Perspectives from the World's Religious Traditions
(Edited with S. G. Post)

FAITH, MEDICINE, AND SCIENCE:
A Festschrift in Honor of Dr. David B. Larson
(Edited with H. G. Koenig)

RELIGION IN THE LIVES OF AFRICAN AMERICANS:
Social, Psychological, and Health Perspectives
(with R. J. Taylor and L. M. Chatters)

GOD, FAITH, AND HEALTH:
Exploring the Spirituality-Healing Connection

ESSENTIALS OF COMPLEMENTARY AND ALTERNATIVE MEDICINE
(Edited with W. B. Jonas)

RELIGION IN AGING AND HEALTH:
Theoretical Foundations and Methodological Frontiers
(Edited)

TABLE OF

CONTENTS

FOREWORD

The author of this book has entered my life in two disparate ways. I had the privilege of being Jeff Levin's rabbi and teacher during the primary period of his religious education, and I have encountered him as a distinguished epidemiologist through his research and writings on the relationship between religious observance and health.

Through his enduringly productive career, Jeff Levin remains both a respected social scientist and a religiously committed Jew. The two parts of his life converge in this volume. Searching for the possible mediating factors that produce the correlation between serious religious commitment and health, Levin has focused on the presence of a loving relationship with God and how that functions in a person's life as the possible mediating link.

In this book, the author does not seek to demonstrate the link through epidemiologic research. Rather, he explores what the love of God means in Judaism and in his own life as a Jew. On one level, this is the personal witness of one who has discovered the deepest meaning of his life through his Judaism; on another, it is the fruit of his extensive immersion in the classic biblical and rabbinic texts as well as the thought of contemporary Jewish scholars.

What emerges from this extended essay on the love of God in Jewish tradition is a major unifying theme: the most authentic expression of the love of God is a love of God's children. Even the most profound personal mystical experience of God is ultimately validated when it prompts us to help repair that tiny corner of God's world that has been entrusted to our care. The author contends that a commitment to *tikkun olam* (mending God's world) is not only the keynote of liberal Judaism but an authentic rendering of traditional Jewish sources. He also finds that a purely secular commitment to social justice and love of neighbor lacks the depth dimension of a life that embodies worship of God and a discipline of religious observance.

Jeff Levin takes seriously the Jewish religious story. He believes in a God who is the Source of all being and who has revealed the divine self in a unique way to the Jewish people. He believes that God and the world need the witness of the faithful Jew. Therefore, a Jew who attempts to distance himself or herself from the Jewish heritage is repudiating a sacred mission.

By the same token, Judaism remains the Jew's lens to the world. The faithful Jew's concerns should embrace all God's children and respect the spiritual paths charted by other great religious movements. Jeff Levin is a liberal Jew who rejects the intolerance that stems from some forms of religious orthodoxy.

The reader of this volume will enjoy the company of a social scientist who not only has discovered positive correlations between religion and health but also has fervently appropriated the gifts of a religious perspective for his own life.

Rabbi Samuel E. Karff, DHL

Past President, Central Conference of American Rabbis

Rabbi Emeritus, Congregation Beth Israel

Houston, Texas

PREFACE

L oving God—what could be simpler yet more profound? It is the striving within the heart that draws billions of people around the world to worship, to serve others, to reach an understanding of their life's purpose. Yet for many of us in today's world, the idea of an intimate connection with the divine is a remote concept, all but forgotten in our workaday lives—even in our religious practice.

I am an epidemiologist and have conducted scholarly research for over thirty years on the consequences of religious observance for our well-being—mentally, emotionally, and even physically.[1] Several years ago, in an interview with a leading medical journal, I was asked to discuss a new research project that I was conducting on the health impact of love, funded by the Institute of Noetic Sciences, a California think tank devoted to the investigation of consciousness and healing.

The interview soon turned to the topic of God, specifically the concept of loving God. I described how two decades of investigation had led me to begin searching for underlying explanations for a connection between religious practice and health. I had begun considering possible "mediating factors"— technical jargon for links in a chain from a potential cause (e.g., religious participation) to an ultimate outcome or effect (e.g., well-being or health). Just what was it, I speculated, that makes sense of the thousand-plus published studies suggesting a link between aspects of one's religious life and subsequent physical or emotional well-being? What function or expression of being religious might best account for its ostensibly salutary impact?

A good candidate, I suggested, was love—or, more specifically, the presence of a loving relationship with God. I was asked on what basis I could say this. My conclusion, I admitted, was not based on any published research on the topic; there was practically none. All I could claim for support were some preliminary, unpublished findings from my study and my own subjective feelings about God and love as a husband, a Jew, and a human being.

I suspect that the interviewer was looking for something scholarly and pithy and profound, but the best that I could come up with was this:

As I reflect on how I have experienced love in my own life, the thing that comes to mind is the love I feel for Lea [my wife] and the love I receive from her. It is an essential part of my life and sometimes it is hard for me to differentiate loving God from loving Lea. We also joke that sometimes we feel so much love it is hard to tell if it is love I am giving her or love she is giving me. It all blends together.

I think love is the most fundamental human experience and expression. It is the stuff out of which reality is made. It is the actual substance, if you will, from which all of creation is manifested. I think that when we activate it, when we feel it or think about it or express it, we call into being the same forces that lovingly created the universe and all of us. It is like a positive feedback loop. The more love we give out, the more love there is and the more we feel.[2]

The interview continued on for several more pages, touching on a bunch of topics far more provocative than loving God. But since its publication, whenever I have heard from someone who read the interview the one feature that stood out the most, without exception, is my brief soliloquy on God, love, and Lea.

In a way, I am not surprised. On the basis of my own reading and exploring over the past decades, I have begun to conclude that the presence of a meaningful and loving relationship with God or the divine is at the root of research findings pointing to an instrumental value of religious faith or spirituality—that is, a value or good above and beyond the "in and of itself" sense that many believe ought to drive religious observance. With this in mind, in an essay published many years ago, I encouraged researchers seeking to understand the impact of spirituality in individual human lives to look to "even seemingly ineffable psychospiritual phenomena such as love."[3]

This was just speculation on my part. But I imagined that perhaps the experience of love—of giving it and receiving it in return from one's family or friends, one's partner, oneself—provides a conduit for a salutary force or energy or power. By extension, the ultimate expression of love—between the Creator and the created—might be the most nurturing and healing of all. Perhaps understanding how people feel about God, I thought, could be the key to making sense of the burgeoning (and confusing and controversial) scientific literature that seems to link religious pursuits to greater well-being. How we conceive of God, what it means to love God, how our faith traditions instruct us to establish a loving relationship with God, whether we love God, how and why we love God, whether we feel that God loves us or cares about us, how this love inspires us to be who we are—could how each of us answers questions like these have consequences for each of our lives or for our world?

This is a far-out question, admittedly, especially for an epidemiologist. Moreover, its consideration is beyond the scope of a single study or a single book. Contemplating how best to seek answers has led me in two divergent directions.

One direction is through science: wearing my epidemiologist's hat, I have continued to pursue research on whether and how our relationship with God may serve to affect physical and psychological dimensions of well-being. More recently, I have explored how researchers might begin to think about transcendent, mystical, and unitive states of consciousness and how these might possibly influence our well-being or health. My wife, Lea, also an epidemiologist, has become a collaborator with me in this work.[4]

But this has little to do with why I chose to write *Upon These Three Things*. This book does not involve epidemiology or science, nor is it explicitly about any putative connections among God, love, and health, nor is it a medical book in any way. It addresses more fundamental issues about normative Jewish beliefs that allow me to make use of my other background: as a religious scholar and a Jew. This book explores Jewish moral and theological perspectives on what it means to love God: how Jews think about God, how we relate to and experience God, and how this affects us.

To this end, I have posed four questions. These are not to be confused with the *mah nishtanah* that we recite in the Passover *seder*, of course, but like those other four questions they serve a heuristic function. Answers to these questions, to the extent to which such answers are knowable, can help to inform a mature understanding of the breadth and diversity of Jewish approaches to loving God. These questions are:

- What does it mean to love God?

- How do we love God?

- How does loving God affect our lives?

- How does loving God affect our world?

All of us relate to God in distinctive ways, according to our own upbringing, preferences, and experiences. One recalls the old joke that where there are two Jews, there are three opinions. This holds true when it comes to what Jews think about God, what we do about it, and how this affects us, individually and collectively. But this should not discourage efforts to find common threads or at least to document the diversity that exists within Judaism.

Naturally, my perspectives on these issues are colored by my own beliefs and experiences as a Jew and by my own style of Jewish observance. But I have tried to be representative in capturing what our patriarchs and prophets and our sages and scholars have had to say. In this book, I have attempted to draw upon a wide range of Jewish sources and texts, both canon and commentary, both traditional and contemporary. I have sought to be both descriptive and interpretive.

Each chapter is organized around specific issues that arise in characterizing Jewish responses to each respective question. These discussions are not exhaustive. For one, I am not a rabbinic scholar. I have tried to reference important Jewish texts and commentaries, but no doubt I have left out many works that others more learned than I am would include. I have endeavored to be scholarly but have tried not to write a purely academic tome with citations that would be obscure to a layperson or to someone without a *y'shivah* education. Moreover, my intention is not simply to catalog everything that every significant Jewish thinker or text has ever said in response to these four questions. That would be impossible, and, anyway,

I am not someone with the requisite skills to do that. Rather, I hope to provide a representative selection of salient themes that have emerged over the course of Jewish history and that shape how we engage God—in our thoughts and feelings and actions.

At the same time, this book advances a thesis: that despite the value that our tradition places "upon these three things" (*Pirke Avot* 1:2)—upon learning (*torah*), worship (*avodah*), and acts of lovingkindness (*g'milut chasadim*)—the latter is first among equals. That is, while our minds and hearts and actions are all required to serve God, to repair the world, the ethical *mitzvot* are most important of all. Compassion takes precedence over learning and worship.

Make no mistake, each of these elements is required if one is to become a fully engaged Jew. Each provides something indispensable for our *n'shamah*, or soul, and each may bring benefit to humankind. A person living the fullest Jewish life experiences God through use of the mind, by way of *talmud torah*, or study of the scriptures; the heart, by way of *t'fillah*, or prayer; and the body, by way of *tz'dakah*, or pursuit of justice. For Jews, as for the Christian theologian Paul Tillich, the most complete expression of *emunah*, or faith, contains a balance of all three things.[5] But Jewish tradition seems clear in its judgment that better one should pursue "justice, justice" (Deuteronomy 16:20) and not be formally or institutionally religious than be otherwise religiously observant to a tee and ignore the needs of the disadvantaged or suffering.

In the *haftarah* to *Parashat D'varim*, God rebukes a ritually observant yet "sinful nation" (Isaiah 1:4) in the strongest, most unequivocal terms:

> *"What need have I of all your sacrifices?" says the Lord. "I am sated with burnt offerings of rams, and suet of fatlings, and blood of bulls; and I have no delight in lambs and he-goats. That you come to appear before Me—who asked that of you? Trample My courts no more; bringing oblations is futile, incense is offensive to Me. New moon and sabbath, proclaiming of solemnities, assemblies with iniquity, I cannot abide. Your new moons and fixed seasons fill Me with loathing; they are become a burden to Me, I cannot endure them. And when you lift up your hands, I will turn My eyes away from you; though you pray at length, I will not*

listen. Your hands are stained with crime—wash yourselves clean; put your evil doings away from My sight. Cease to do evil; learn to do good. Devote yourselves to justice; aid the wronged. Uphold the rights of the orphan; defend the cause of the widow." (Isaiah 1:11–17)

This theme is ever-present in the Torah and in the writings of the prophets (e.g., Amos 5:21–24; Zechariah 7:8–13; Isaiah 58:2–7). There must be a reason for this, grounded in human nature, to which both gentile and Jew are subject. I believe that God has made clear that while all of the *mitzvot* revealed to us require our engagement—however each Jewish movement and each individual Jew may wish to define "engagement"—nonetheless, social justice and attention to the needs of the oppressed and less fortunate trump the rest. Lest we miss the point, God reiterates later in the *haftarah*: "But if you refuse and disobey, you will be devoured by the sword. . . . and those who forsake the Lord shall perish" (Isaiah 1:20, 28).

The moral: one may be a good Jew without being a student of the Torah or a synagogue member and while entertaining doubts and questions about God, as long as one attends diligently to acts of *tz'dakah*, *chesed* (mercy), and *tikkun olam* (repair of the world). If one is just the opposite, God forbid, then one has failed God and Judaism in the most basic way and is guilty of *chilul Hashem*, a desecration of God's name.

The theological earthquakes that attended to debates over the social gospel among our Protestant Christian friends beginning over a century ago are fundamentally alien to Jewish thought. For Jews, no choice is inherent between religious observance and social consciousness. The latter is a principal fruit of the former and indeed largely defines it. In my opinion, the primary value of *talmud torah* and *avodah* is to nourish our soul and strengthen our character to where the practice of *g'milut chasadim* in its fullness becomes second nature. Expressing compassion and love for others is, ultimately, how we best love God.

This book therefore focuses on both the substance and the consequences of loving God. I am hopeful that the material presented in this book will provide guidance, support, and inspiration for all Jews and for people of other faiths and religious traditions who are enriched by their own loving relationship with the divine or who are seeking the peace and contentment that such a connection can bring.

For me, writing *Upon These Three Things* has been a blessed undertaking but nonetheless an intellectual challenge. This book has nothing to do, of course, with science or public health or medical research in any way. This project has been a welcome respite from three decades of doing epidemiology: gathering data, crunching numbers, drawing up tables, and writing reports. It has enabled me to take off my scientist's hat and put on my religious scholar's hat, retrieved from a dusty old storage box on a shelf in an attic closet. Many of my colleagues may not be aware of this, but my original academic training was in religious studies, at Duke University, beginning in the 1970s. It has always been a special joy for me to pursue scholarly writing on the topic of religion. This has mostly taken the form of empirical research and writing about religion and health, religion and science, religion and aging, and other of religion's wider consequences, as I have done for so many years. By contrast, this project has afforded an opportunity to write about the religious life of the people that I know best: Jews seeking a fuller expression of their love for God and, one hopes, for all sentient beings.

Whether I am successful is for the reader to decide. Perhaps I should not admit it, but I was plagued by anxiety as I began to work on this book. Who am I to attempt to summarize and interpret the works of our people's sages and scholars and of Jewish canon, armed with a secular university education in religion? I did not possess the confidence going into this project that I have carried into my other academic books and articles on the topic of religion written over the past thirty years. But perhaps this was a good thing. It forced me to "let go and let God," as the saying goes—to operate from my passion and my reverence, open to inspiration, and not wholly from within my left brain, as per my background as a scientist. Lea lovingly prodded me to surround my writing sessions with meditation, prayer, and *kavvanah*, with loving thoughts and positive intentions. She constantly reminded me to remain open to what God wished to speak to me. Lea prayed that the experience would both change me and bless others. I can attest that her first prayer was answered. I remain hopeful that the second prayer will be, too.

Several people deserve my heartfelt thanks for their assistance and support as I researched and wrote *Upon These Three Things*.

Stephen Post, professor of preventive medicine and director of the Center for Medical Humanities, Compassionate Care, and Bioethics at SUNY Stony Brook, generously funded my work on this project through a grant from the Institute for Research on Unlimited Love (IRUL), which he serves as president. I have enjoyed serving as IRUL's research area consultant for public health and medicine and am truly humbled that Stephen, a world-renowned religious scholar and bioethicist trained at the University of Chicago Divinity School, believed in the ability of an academic biomedical scientist to produce a work of Jewish scholarship. I have cherished our recent collaboration, which produced an edited book entitled *Divine Love: Perspectives from the World's Religious Traditions.*[6] The present book, *Upon These Three Things*, is a companion piece to the work that Stephen and I undertook together.

I am also grateful to my colleagues Linda Chatters and Robert Taylor of the University of Michigan for providing me with office space during my annual week-long visits to Ann Arbor to collaborate on our various research projects over the years. This book is a dramatic departure, to say the least, from our collaborative work of the past twenty-five years—empirical life-course research on religious participation among minority populations. Yet Robert and Linda did not seem to mind that I spent a portion of one of my annual visits several years ago working on the proposal and outline for *Upon These Three Things*. They have been wonderful friends and always so supportive of my work.

Thanks also go out to my faculty colleagues at the Institute for Studies of Religion at Baylor University. Rod Stark, Byron Johnson, Philip Jenkins, David Jeffrey, Gordon Melton, and Tommy Kidd have been good friends and have supported and encouraged my work, as have our wonderful administrative staff: Frances Malone, Cameron Andrews, and Leone Moore. Rod, especially, has been instrumental in seeing this book through to publication.

I must also acknowledge my earliest mentor in religious studies at Duke, the late C. Eric Lincoln. Dr. Lincoln's vision of religion as an instrument for applied social ethics and his encouraging me to pursue a scholarly career in religious studies helped to define my life's path and contributed to a professional and personal evolvement that has culminated in this book. *Zich'rono liv'rachah.*

Besides these individuals, many Jewish colleagues provided me with valuable feedback at various stages of this project. If *Upon These Three Things* reads like a work of Jewish scholarship, or close to it, and not like the writing of an epidemiology professor, then it is due in no small part to the counsel and direction of so many kind friends.

Finally, that I might have any personal insights to contribute on the topic of loving God is owed entirely to my beloved wife, Lea. I experience God's love every day through the person of Lea and God's mercy through her presence in my life. "A woman of valor who can find? for her worth is far above rubies. The heart of her husband doth safely trust in her, and he hath no lack of gain" (Proverbs 31:10–11).

Jeff Levin

Woodway, Texas

CHAPTER ONE
THREE THINGS, MANY QUESTIONS

"Shimon the Just used to say, 'Upon these three things the world stands: on learning (torah), on worship (avodah), and on acts of lovingkindness (g'milut chasadim).'" (Pirke Avot 1:2)

Torah. Avodah. G'milut chasadim.

What is it about these three things that merits their designation as the foundations of our world?

When I first encountered this verse decades ago, upon reading the words of *Pirke Avot*, I was struck by the beauty and simplicity of the imagery. Like the wooden posts of a three-legged stool, all of existence was declared to rest upon the collective merit of the Jewish people with respect to three *mitzvot*. By dint of a mutual commitment to learning God's word, to serving God through worship, and to performing acts of lovingkindness, Jews may ensure the perpetuation of life on earth. I also detected, as subtext, an unspoken but obvious hint of the consequences of neglecting these commandments.

The English word "things," translated from the Hebrew *d'varim*, does not do justice to what seems to be implied here. According to most Hebrew-English dictionaries, *d'var* may also be translated as "word" or "saying" or "matter." The same three-letter root (*dalet-bet-resh*) with different vocalizations and/or suffixes yields words that are translated as divergently as "speech" (*divrah*) and "leader" (*dabar*). This root is probably most familiar to Jews in a couple of variations: as the phrase *d'var torah*, a *d'rash* or teaching on a Torah verse or *parashah*, and in *Sefer D'varim*, or the Book of Deuteronomy, the fifth book of the Torah, in which Moses gives his final three speeches summarizing the teachings that God revealed to him and through his leadership.

Still another vocalization results in a more ominous word, *deber*, the term for plague or pestilence, most familiar to us from its presence in the Passover *haggadah*. Further, in a couple of its variant verb forms, the root becomes variations of *hidbir* or *hadbar*, implying subduing or being subdued.

Taken together, all of these words and meanings help elucidate the passage in *Pirke Avot*. Rabbi Shimon's instructions to pursue Torah learning and worship and kind acts are at once a guide to living and a warning. We can do these three things, and the world will survive. Or we can fail to do so and thus unleash a pestilence, so to speak, that will subdue the world and unleash it from its moorings. The moral entreaty and the imprecation exist side by side and are inseparable.

Subtleties in translating *Pirke Avot* into English provide additional insight into this passage. The second of the three things that sustain the world is often translated not as "worship" but as "Temple service" or, more generally, as "divine service" or "service to God." In Rabbi Rami M. Shapiro's modern interpretive reading of this passage, the world stands "Upon Reality. Upon self-emptying prayer and meditation. Upon acts of love and kindness."[1] His take on the first pillar, *torah*, as "Reality" itself is neither fanciful nor *sui generis*; the thirteenth-century sage Rabbi Yonah ben Avraham suggests that the world does not merely stand upon these three things but was actually created for the sake of them.[2]

Another clue as to the function or utility of these three things may be found in a prior passage of *Pirke Avot*. As the tractate begins, the traditional accounting of the oral transmission of the Torah is narrated—from God, on Sinai, to Moses to Joshua to the elders to the prophets and finally to the men of the Great Assembly. This is followed immediately by the first substantive lesson in *Pirke Avot*—by extension, the "users' manual" for all subsequent recipients of the oral Torah:

> *They [the men of the Great Assembly] said three things: "Be prudent in judgment. Raise up many disciples. Make a fence for the Torah." (Pirke Avot 1:1)*

It is no coincidence that one list of three things should precede another such list. This alerts the reader to something of a correlation or correspondence between the two lists. A careful reading suggests that the three things upon which the world stands serve to fulfill each respective directive from the Great Assembly. How do we become prudent in judgment? By learning Torah. How do we raise up disciples? By maintaining synagogues and teaching the rituals of worship and about our duty to serve to God. How do we make a fence around the Torah? By performing acts of lovingkindness.

Deconstructing the specific actions encapsulated in and defined by each of these three *mitzvot* reveals all of the possible actions of a human psyche in its fullest expression. These three things upon which the world stands and for which the world was created together constitute the three basic psychological functions of human beings. *Torah* implies studying and learning from Jewish canonical writings and involves cognition, the act of thinking—use of the mind or soul. *Avodah* implies serving and worshipping God, whether alone or in the presence of fellow Jews and involves affect, the act of feeling—use of the heart, metaphorically speaking, or, in religious terms, the spirit. *G'milut chasadim* implies fulfilling acts of *chesed* or kindness and involves the act of doing—use of the body.

Rabbi Shimon's statement on the ultimate implications of *torah*, *avodah*, and *g'milut chasadim* is thus a reminder of the ultimate potential of a life lived to its fullest using all of our essential human capacities. Through our mental and emotional and physical actions directed toward spiritual ends, the world itself will be sustained. In the *Sh'ma*, recited each morning by Jews as we set our intentions for the day, we see these three things come together clearly and for a specific purpose "You shall love the Lord your God with all your heart and with all your soul and with all your might" (Deuteronomy 6:5)—and for a clearly articulated end—"in order that you may live" (Deuteronomy 30:6). In case this is not clear enough, the Talmud weighs in on the consequences of ignoring each element of this prayer's charge:

> *Rab Judah also said: "Three things shorten a man's days and years: To be given a scroll of the Law to read from and to refuse, to be given a cup of benediction to say grace over and to refuse, and to assume airs of authority." (B'rakhot 55a)*

Each of these three transgressions, in order, equals an obvious negation of a respective one of Rabbi Shimon's three *mitzvot*.

At the risk of hyperbole, the "three things" of *Pirke Avot* read like no less than a definitive Jewish take on the elusive key to life. They are clearly intended to be taken to heart and acted upon. It may be confusing, or disconcerting, to discover then that they are not the only litany of three such things enumerated by canon or the sages. In fact, they are not the only "three things" upon which the "world stands" listed in *Pirke Avot*.

THREE THINGS OR MANY THINGS

Later on in *Pirke Avot*, we find this:

Rabban Shimon ben Gamliel said: "The world stands upon three things: Upon justice (din; literally "judgment") and upon truth (emet) and upon peace (shalom)." (Pirke Avot 1:18)

This is a different Rabbi Shimon and a different three things. These particular three things, though, carry the authority of Torah, as they recall the words of the Prophet Zechariah:

These are the things you are to do: Speak the truth to one another, render true and perfect justice [some translations state "peace"] in your gates. And do not contrive evil against one another. (Zechariah 8:16–17)

Moreover, the Yerushalmi declares, "And the three of them are really one thing. If justice is carried out, truth is realized....peace is made" (*Y. Taanit* 4:2).

I suppose that it is possible, on the surface, to see a conflict between these two expositions of the three things upon which the world stands. For one, the wording is distinctive. Yet these two lists can be reconciled—and quite easily. Shimon ben Gamliel's three things elegantly describe a world in which Shimon the Just's three things are fulfilled. Where there is Torah learning, there is truth. Where there are worship and service to God, there is peace. Where acts of lovingkindness prevail in the affairs of human beings, there is justice.

The three things of Shimon ben Gamliel represent a kind of ideal—the end result of Jewish lives committed to fulfilling the *mitzvot* spoken of by Shimon the Just. Truth, peace, and justice are goals that every human should endorse. But merely stating this fact does not tell us how to get there. It describes the end but does not reveal the means to that end.

The first list of three things—*torah, avodah,* and *g'milut chasadim*—contains actions that each of us can perform regularly. We know that the Torah was given to engender in us the wisdom to serve God through acting ethically (*B'rakhot* 17a) and, further, that the greatness of Torah learning is that "it leads to action" (*Kiddushin* 40b). Little wonder that it is the three things of Shimon the Just—not Shimon ben Gamliel—that are enshrined, for example, in the *al shloshah d'varim* ("upon three things") chant in the *hakafah* (procession) section of the Torah service in some *siddurim,* or prayer books. Meditating on an ideal is well and good, but it is far better to focus our energies on doing what we can to attain it.

Variations on this theme of three things essential to an observant and ethically lived life are found elsewhere in Jewish writings. Although the constituent elements may differ, it is always more or less the same three things—that is, some combination of mental or intellectual pursuit, heartfelt religious activity, and ethical behavior in the cause of some ideal.

The nineteenth-century Chasidic master, Rabbi Yehuda Leib Alter, known as the S'fat Emet, reflected on the verse in Deuteronomy that "the thing," meaning the Torah, "is very close to you, in your mouth and in your heart, to observe it" (Deuteronomy 30:14). According to Professor Victor Cohen, the S'fat Emet taught that

> [t]here are three things that are needed to open the well of wisdom: speech, thought, and action. All of these emanate from the mouth as we related the fervor and desires of the heart.[3]

Here, we get a glimpse of the self-reflexive beauty of the S'fat Emet's three things combined with the two Shimons' three things touched on earlier and how self-referentially they all intertwine and relate back to each other like a kind of sacred Möbius strip: the Torah is wisdom. It was given to impel us to action. Through learning Torah, worshipping God, and performing acts of lovingkindness, we may further the cause of truth, peace, and justice. This great work, in turn, involving the thoughts we think upon learning scripture, the words we speak when we pray and convene with others for reverencing God, and the actions we undertake that qualify as *g'milut chasadim,* brings us ever closer to the Torah and unlocks for us its wisdom—which encourages further ethical action, and so on.

Like a cosmic positive feedback loop, by committing our minds, hearts, and bodies to sacred work, we may help to achieve *tikkun olam*, thus elevating ourselves and engendering even more insight that can spur us to even more action. The end result: evermore *k'dusah*, or holiness, spread throughout the world. It is no surprise that the three things of Shimon the Just are referred to by Rabbi Yisrael Meir Kagan, the Chofetz Chaim, the great apostle of lovingkindness, as "three pathways to holiness."[4]

Another "three things" are found among the letters of Rabbi Nathan Sternharz, known as Reb Noson of Breslov, disciple of the legendary eighteenth-century Chasidic storyteller Rebbe Nachman of Breslov. Reb Noson's list of essentials is similar to that of Shimon the Just:

> *Please, my son, look carefully at what your purpose is....Our days are like a passing shadow, and time rushes by. Nothing but the Torah, prayer and good deeds that you manage to seize each day will remain with you. Everything else is fleeting.*[5]

From this, we see that fulfillment of these three things is not just ethically commanded. Rather, they are the only things in life that make sense and are the only actions we may undertake that are truly lasting. The enduring nature of our good deeds, especially, is endorsed by the Torah: "his beneficence lasts forever" (Psalms 112:9), even "[preceding] him for the world to come" (*Sotah* 3b). This is because, according to the Chofetz Chaim, "As a person practices this art, he perfects it; at the same time, it perfects him."[6]

Perhaps the most familiar exposition of three essential things, besides the lists in *Pirke Avot*, is found in the *machzor*, or High Holy Days prayer book, taken from a passage in the Yerushalmi (*Y. Taanit* 2:1) and later referenced in the Midrash (Genesis *Rabbah* 44:12). On Rosh Hashanah and Yom Kippur, the *piyyut* (liturgical poem) known as the *u'netaneh tokef* ("let us proclaim the power") culminates in this great declaration, often capitalized or boldfaced in translation for emphasis: "But repentance (*t'shuvah*), prayer (*t'fillah*), and charity (*tz'dakah*) remove the evil of the decree!"[7] The English translation differs only slightly across the *machzorim* of respective Jewish movements. In this prayer, we are reminded that God alone decides "who will live and who will die"[8] and that we are so inscribed and then sealed in the book of life, or are not, between Rosh Hashanah and Yom Kippur.

On the surface, these "three T's" represent our way to annul this decree and ensure another year of prospering. But, at a deeper level, they are akin to a sacred formula that, chanted in unison within a congregation, sets a collective intention to perform a great and sacred work. This work involves specific actions making use of our minds (for *t'shuvah*), our hearts (for *t'fillah*), and our bodies (for *tz'dakah*). This list of three things is thus not dissimilar—in fact, is almost equivalent—to the *torah*, *avodah*, and *g'milut chasadim* of Shimon the Just. The prayer book's three things are actually special cases of each of the respective three things found in *Pirke Avot*, elevated to a high moral plane.

THE MEANING OF THESE THREE THINGS

As I have reflected and meditated upon these three things, I have wondered at length about just what exactly God intends to communicate to us through this taxonomy and its associated commentaries. The words of Shimon the Just and the words of the various others that constitute a *d'rash* on his teaching, including those found in the prayer book, loom large in the Jewish canon and Jewish liturgy. There must be important reasons.

In trying to deduce the ultimate meaning of these three things, I have been struck by several possibilities. Each of these presents my own subjective take on how the three pillars of *Pirke Avot* might serve to enlighten, enrich, or inspire us to live better Jewish lives.

First, Rabbi Shimon's declaration on *torah*, *avodah*, and *g'milut chasadim* represents a kind of covenant between Jews and God. If we follow Rabbi Hillel's famous imperative to "go and learn it" (*Shabbat* 31a), obey Moses' plea that "only Him shall you worship" (Deuteronomy 10:20), and hearken to the prophet's call to "practice goodness and justice" (Hosea 12:7), then our world will survive and flourish.

Contemporary sensibilities may flinch at taking this literally—that is, as a veiled threat by an omnipotent deity to destroy the physical earth should we fail to follow through on our obligations. But other interpretations are possible, such as considering the words of *Pirke Avot* as being akin to a social contract in Rousseau's sense—specifically, one that promises political and economic consequences to a society that are commensurate with the moral behavior of its citizens. Liberty, prosperity, and justice may be sustained only where a people is committed to translating a love of Torah and God into acts of lovingkindness to all human beings. At the same time, given the precarious state of our planet's physical environment and innumerable not-so-future threats stemming in large part from our own immorality and arrogance—nuclear war, bioterrorism, depletion of natural resources, endangered species, habitat destruction—perhaps a literal take on how our moral actions ensure whether "the world stands" is indeed justified.

Second, Rabbi Shimon's statement in *Pirke Avot*—the statements of both Rabbi Shimons, actually, along with the prayer book declaration—constitutes a profound meditation on redemption, both collective and personal. For Jews, redemption, or salvation, is not conceived of as in other monotheistic traditions—that is, as a confessional, soteriological drama played out between an individual "fallen" soul that must become reconciled or restored to its Creator through some external means—sacraments, grace, vicarious atonement—and that has supernatural implications for that individual's eschatology.

In Judaism, by contrast, there is no such doctrine purporting, in the famous words of Rabbi Abba Hillel Silver, "that men need to be saved."[9] Humans are not fallen or beset by an inherent sinfulness. After God created the first humans, He "saw all that He had made, and found it very good" (Genesis 1:31). The work of redemption, for Jews, is collective, a group effort, in which all of us are charged by God, as was Abram, to "go forth" (Genesis 12:1), or, more precisely, to "go forth to clear the roads of thorns" (*Moed Katan* 5a). What is demanded of us is ethical action in service to the greater good "in order that the equity of God's justice may be verified in the world" (Genesis *Rabbah* 55:1).

In other words, the principal drama of Jewish existence is not a work of self-actualization that, successfully negotiated over millions of lives, may lead in the end to social transformation. Rather, it is the heavenly command "Justice, justice shall you pursue" (Deuteronomy 16:20), directed to all of *k'lal yisrael*, or the Jewish people as a whole, and with real-world consequences: "that you may thrive" (Deuteronomy 16:20). The protagonist in this drama is not a lone individual whose reward is to come, through grace, in the next life. Instead, all of us together in the here and now, through our translation of *emunah*, or faith, into *tzedek*, or acts of justice or righteousness (Isaiah 11:5), have a hand in remaking our world. This is what God expects of us as Jews and what Judaism values most about faith.

The various collections of "three things" offer precise guidance as to what this work of redemption is to consist of and how it will take place. Through a commitment to Torah learning, we may experience *t'shuvah* and thenceforth be led to live a life committed to *emet*. This life can be enriched by *avodah*, highlighted by *t'fillah*, that ideally will lead us to go forth and spread shalom. This we may best accomplish through *g'milut chasadim*, such as *tz'dakah*, that define and eventually help to create a world where justice prevails. In so doing, we spread holiness and healing that, God willing, may touch all other humans and human institutions. If some of this goodness reflects back on us and touches any of us individually, then that is an extra blessing. But that is not our principal objective or our motivation. We are focused outward, not inward; on all people, not just on our individual selves; and on this world, not on the world to come. In a nutshell, this is the Jewish religious path—our Way, our *tao*, our *dharma*.

Third, this essentially outward-looking charge notwithstanding, the path of social transformation, as captured in *Pirke Avot*, is also a road map to personal transformation. A commitment to *torah*, *avodah*, and *g'milut chasadim* is a blueprint for a fully engaged Jewish life. Moreover, this is our key to securing a full and mature relationship with God.

According to the Talmud, Rav Simlai explained that the 248 positive *mitzvot* correspond "to the number of the members of man's body" (*Makkot* 23b). This tells us that we are to serve God with all of our parts, with our full self—body, mind, and spirit. Rabbi Shimon has provided us with a guide to doing just that.

For reading, studying, and learning Torah and sacred writings, alone and in groups, and then acting on what we have learned, we must use all of our cognitive faculties. We must use our eyes and ears and other senses.

For serving God, including through praying to Him, celebrating sacred rituals, and participating in congregational life in its fullness, with *kavvanah*, we must be engaged in our hearts and spirits if we wish our supplications to be heard, as Rabbi Yehudah stated: "Prayer offered with true devotion is directed on high to the supernal recess, from whence issue all blessings and all freedom, to support the universe" (*Zohar* 1:229a).

For going forth in *chesed*, intent on working acts of *tz'dakah* in order to bring emotional and tangible blessings to our fellow humans, we need our physical bodies to carry us to where we are going. We need our arms and legs, if we are blessed to have them in working order, and our full complement of strength and energy to complete the labor our deeds require.

By each of us using "all my bones" (Psalms 35:10) to serve God, we can get more done and at the same time grow more quickly as Jews. God wants us to use all of our gifts in His service and to righteous ends. Skipping over one or the other of "these three things" means that we are giving less than a full effort to use the resources available to us. We can accomplish more when the mind, heart, and body are working together than if we leave one or two of these to wither on the vine. Anything less than full devotion is a waste of precious opportunities to be of service to others and to grow ever closer to God.

A caveat about this particular perspective on "these three things": as Jews, we must be ever vigilant not to fall prey to the modern therapeutic sensibility that transforms redemption into an individualistically defined and experienced state. As noted earlier, this is not the Jewish way. For us, redemption is collectively sought and communally experienced, and it is about ever evolving and ever progressing, not reaching some final, static stopping place. Likewise with respect to fulfilling *mitzvot*—any *mitzvot*—we should not focus on how they benefit the doer but rather on how they may serve to bring a blessing to others or to all humans.

Mitzvot such as *talmud torah*, *avodah* and *t'fillah*, pursuing *emet*, acts of *tz'dakah* or *chesed*—these were not given to us solely for our own (carnal) ends, for material reward or worldly success or happiness or health, although these may indeed be an outcome (Exodus 15:26). We would do far better to consider these acts as redemption in action, however each of us or each Jewish movement may wish to conceive of the pursuit of redemption.

Historically, Jews have found many ways to embrace this concept, whether we take it literally or metaphorically. But the commonality is identification of an ultimate purpose for *mitzvot* far beyond our personal, nonce concerns—one that serves, in the final analysis, to add to the holiness of the world: creating angels (*Pirke Avot* 4:11), redeeming the sparks,[10] "[hastening] thereby the coming of King Messiah" (Deuteronomy *Rabbah* 6:7), furthering the causes of charity and justice in the world until "the earth is full of the lovingkindness of the Lord" (*Sukkah* 49b), laboring "to turn darkness into light" (*Zohar* 1:4a), or simply bringing nearer the day when all beings will acknowledge, as the *Aleinu* prayer pleads, that "the Lord shall be One and His name One" (Zechariah 14:9).

Fourth, accordingly, we can begin to understand what the Chofetz Chaim had in mind when he referenced the three pillars of Rabbi Shimon as three distinct "pathways to holiness," as noted earlier. His *Sefer Ahavat Chesed* is replete with great wisdom and helpful life instructions for developing these pathways to their fullness. Three themes keep repeating, echoing sentences expressed earlier: our charge as Jews is to attend to the needs of others; the three pathways "are the only three real nutrients for a Jew's *neshamah*"[11] and define how we go about serving; and the surest way to accomplish this end is through acts of *chesed*. In other words, there may be three things, and all may be requisite, but one is first among equals.

This is a complicated issue for Jews and may seem controversial. The Mishnah instructs us, concerning the *mitzvot*, "but the study of Torah is as important as all of them together" (*M. Peah* 1:1). However, the Chofetz Chaim teaches, "An act of chesed…renders protection that even the learning of Torah cannot match."[12] This is not to be construed as referring just to the doer of the *mitzvah* or its recipient: "The benefits accrue not only to the individual, but to the Jewish people as a whole, with each act of kindness performed."[13] This is because "the work of righteousness shall be peace ... forever" (Isaiah 32:17).

This theme has been taken up repeatedly by medieval and contemporary rabbis. For example, Rabbi Silver explains, "Judaism is a summons not so much to ethical knowledge as to ethical action and mission,"[14] and "however exalted the study of the Torah was regarded, it was not enough."[15] It is not sufficient that we learn Torah and commit the words of the commandments to memory; we must "do them" (Deuteronomy 29:8). This is not a slight on the Torah, of course, but rather recognition that the *mitzvot ben adam l'chavero*, or so-called "horizontal" commandments—our acts of *chesed* and *tz'dakah* involving others—are a natural outgrowth of diligence in performing the *mitzvot ben adam l'makom*, or "vertical" commandments, namely, those involving *talmud torah* and *avodah*. These two commandments fuel the performance of our ethical actions.

Once again, *Pirke Avot* is a source of great clarification:

Rabbi Chaninah ben Dosa says, "Anyone whose deeds are more than his wisdom—his wisdom will endure. And anyone whose wisdom is more than his deeds—his wisdom will not endure." (Pirke Avot 3:9)

In other words, right action, as a Buddhist might say, trumps the pursuit of wisdom for wisdom's sake.

It is my firm belief that *talmud torah* and *avodah* (in the sense of ritual worship) can become idolatry—a clear violation of the second commandment—if practiced to the exclusion of actions in furtherance of *chesed* or *tz'dakah* or *tikkun olam*. I do not know whether many rabbis would couch this issue as starkly, but I am confident in this assessment. The Talmud seems to concur: "Rabbi Yehoshua ben Korchah said, 'Any one who shuts his eye against charity is like one who worships idols'" (*K'tubot* 68a). "These three things" constitute a concise primer on spreading holiness, but we must not confuse the prologue with the main text.

Finally, most of all, Rabbi Shimon's famous words appear to be a formula for righteous living, for engaging the divine, for loving God. For me, this is the most electric, most profound implication of "these three things." God, in His great mercy, has revealed to us a precise means of "loving the Lord your

God, walking in all His ways, and holding fast to Him" (Deuteronomy 11:22). We know that we are to love God, and in the *al shloshah d'varim* declaration and the commentaries that it has inspired, we have an unimpeachable statement as to what we are expected to do.

This is not to say that Jewish sources are unanimous as to what exactly constitutes loving God. We know that to fully encounter God, we must use our minds, hearts, and bodies to produce the requisite learning, spiritual growth, and action. But there is considerable diversity in how we tend to go about these three things. The various Jewish movements, traditions, and philosophical schools have various emphases, and different Jewish people of course have different preferences. All have their valid points, as long as they are consonant with our charge to pursue *torah*, *avodah*, and, ultimately, *g'milut chasadim*.

We all are free to find the best ways for ourselves to seek after God in hopes of encountering Him "face to face" (Genesis 32:31). Jewish scriptures and the commentaries of our great sages and rabbis are replete with instructions, exhortations, admonitions, and suggestions as to how this may be accomplished. Some of us are scholarly and revel in poring over sacred texts. Some of us are more emotional and spiritually inclined, drawn to prayer or meditation at home or in a *minyan*. Some of us have little use for the trappings of institutional religion but glory in the opportunity to do good deeds for other people. Others of us look for ways to incorporate some of each of these actions into our walk with God. These are all valid and nourishing ways to practice Judaism, to engage the divinity we discover before us, and to express our love and reverence for God's holiness.

If there is any kind of a universal in religious discourse on the many ways in which Jews love God, maybe it is found only in the acknowledged consequence of failing to try. This is no more starkly depicted than in the hellish vision captured in Bildad the Shuhite's lecture to Job, which concludes with "here was the place of him who knew not God" (Job 18:21). Notwithstanding that Bildad was being quite uncharitable to Job, who had endured great suffering and did not deserve the criticism, the substance of the charge is revealing. We may take this verse literally, or we may interpret it psychodynamically, but the dreadful legacy for the human spirit is the same. However it is that we are drawn to seek God, whatever it is we expect to find when we get there, and whether we ever fully succeed in this life, we must begin. There is no more inspiring passage in *Pirke Avot* than the famous words of Rabbi Tarfon: "It is not your job to finish the work, but you are not free to walk away from it" (*Pirke Avot* 2:16).

JEWISH PERSPECTIVES ON LOVING GOD

Conceiving of loving God as a human necessity may or may not be difficult, depending upon our understanding of Who God is and what it means to love Him. But conceiving of loving God as a directive or commandment seems to chafe against our modern, libertarian sensibilities. Indeed, this issue has occupied Jewish commentators for many centuries.

For example, in *Sefer HaChinnuch*, a sixteenth-century compilation of the 613 *mitzvot* ascribed to the thirteenth-century Rabbi Pinchas HaLevi, *mitzvah* number 418 is denoted "The precept of love for the eternal Lord" (*mitzvah ahavah Hashem*).[16] The commentary is unequivocal: "It applies in every place, at every time, for both men and women….This is one of the constant precepts for a man, forever imposed on him [to observe]."[17]

Yet how can we be commanded to love, to feel the emotion of love, whether toward God or toward other humans?

We all recognize the *Sh'ma*'s familiar words, "You shall love the Lord your God" (Deuteronomy 6:5). In *Kinyan Torah*, the *baraita* (extra-Mishnaic text) that constitutes the sixth chapter of *Pirke Avot*, the consequences of fulfilling this command are implicit. Included among a list of prerequisites for successfully learning Torah is to be a person "who loves God" (*ohev et haMakom*; literally "who loves the Place") (*Pirke Avot* 6:6). Referring to God as "the Place" is a metaphoric way to emphasize God's attribute as the Creator and Source of all space and time—the ever-present One Who exists everywhere and permeates and transcends all things.

For the sixteenth-century Italian sage Rabbi Ovadiah S'forno, this description of God's omnipresence is the key to understanding the passage. In his commentary, the S'forno interprets the passage to mean "You shall rejoice to do that which is good in His eyes once you discern that there is no nobler goal than this."[18] The S'forno interprets the word "*v'ahavta*" ("and you shall love") not as a command to love

God but rather as a prediction that we will do so, inevitably, upon contemplating God's majesty and greatness. This he reiterates in his commentary on *Parashat Ekev*, in which Moses reminds us "to love Him" (Deuteronomy 10:12). The S'forno explains, "And this (love) you shall attain when you consider His Goodness."[19]

Inevitable or not, two questions remain: just what does it mean, from a Jewish standpoint, to love God? Moreover, how are we to accomplish this?

For one, despite the words of the Torah and the Mishnah, expressing our relationship with the Creator of the universe in terms of "love" may strike some Jews as not typically Jewish. To truly love God—to feel the emotion that we usually associate with another person, such as a spouse or child or parent, in connection with a discarnate Being Whom we cannot perceive with our five gross senses—this may strike some Jews as improbable or not a Jewish priority. After all, we usually hear references to the phrase "loving God" or "loving the Lord" in the idioms of other faith traditions, such as Christianity. In that idiom, the descriptor is typically applied to a personal relationship with an incarnated human being who is believed to represent a physical manifestation of God Himself. These trinitarian and incarnational assertions are, of course, rejected by normative Jewish belief.[20] For us, God must remain ever One, unseen, and thus not easily or casually approached.

Yet the extent to which "loving God" thus seems like a reasonable objective for other religions but not for us simply evinces how thoroughly many Western Jews have become detached from historic Jewish understandings of God. Many of us, through assimilation, nonobservance, or lack of formal Jewish education, have surrendered our tradition's sense of Whom God is to what we tacitly presume to be the common beliefs of other faiths. The images and attributes that we thus associate with God may, for some secular or unaffiliated Jews, originate more in what the late sociologist Robert Bellah referred to as the common "civil religion"[21] than in Jewish canon and tradition.

Alternatively, some Jews may subscribe to the false distinction proffered by some writers who purport to differentiate between a New Testament God of love and a stern God of judgment Who is characteristic, we are assured, of the Hebrew Bible. If we reject God—our God—because we believe that such a default "god" is not for us, or at least not a being for whom we could muster emotions such as warmth and devotion, then I believe we are guilty of having "roused Him to jealousy with strange gods" (Deuteronomy 32:16), whether or not we choose to take part in their worship.

I am reminded of a story I was told many years ago by a kindly Lubavitch rabbi. He had been confronted by a Jewish atheist who complained that he could not possibly ever believe in God. When the rabbi asked him why, the man gave a variety of reasons corresponding, the rabbi told me later, to a typical American child's simplistic conceptions of God, fueled mostly by non-Jewish values and ideas. "That god you don't believe in," the rabbi assured the man, "well, I don't believe in him either."

More than other Jewish traditions, the Chasidic movement has valued a conception of God as a beloved Being in Whose arms we may find nurture and sustenance and feel that our emotional yearning for the experience of love, given and received, is quenched in the most intimate way. In *Tanya*, Rabbi Schneur Zalman describes two types of love of God. Professor Cohen elaborates. The first type of love of God involves reflecting and meditating on God's majesty "in such detail that the intellect can grasp it."[22] The second type involves the "natural yearning"[23] for God—the longing of a soul for its Creator. The late Lubavitcher Rebbe, Menachem Mendel Schneerson, extended this typology in his discussion of the "two phases" of our love for God: "*ratzu*, a powerful yearning for connection with Him; and *shuv*, a commitment to return and express G-d's will by making this world a dwelling for Him."[24]

Taken together, we once again see manifest the three things of Rabbi Shimon, this time in the Chasidic perspective on loving God. There is a mental or intellectual component ("reflecting") and an emotional or spiritual component ("yearning") that find their culmination in action ("returning") in the form of *tikkun olam*. By now, this theme should be familiar. Moreover, according to Rebbe Schneerson, our love of God and our love of others are inseparable, as are our love of God and our charge to make this manifest in our behavior:

> *True love is transcendence, linking our physical selves to G-d and, therefore, to everyone else around us....[This] re-*

sponsibility is one of the greatest gifts G-d gave us—the gift of being active participants in the dynamic unfolding of the world's destiny. We must never ignore this gift.[25]

In this way, we may truly cause "that the Name of Heaven be beloved" (*Yoma* 86a).

On this point, traditional Orthodoxy is in accord. In the authoritative *Encyclopedia Talmudica*, in an essay entitled *"'Ahabath Hashem"* (The Love of God), the indivisibility of mind, heart, and body in the cause of loving God is apparent. The authors assert, "For it is by pondering on the words of the Torah that the love of God must inevitably find abode in the human heart,"[26] which means the subsequent translation of "service out of love."[27] "This standard is a very high one," the *Encyclopedia* continues. "Not every Sage can attain it."[28]

In *Derech Hashem*, Rabbi Moshe Chaim Luzzatto, eighteenth century Italian expositor of a systematic approach to Jewish theology and piety, ties together the same three elements. Love and awe of God are what "bring a person nearer to his Creator and form a bond of attachment to Him."[29] These, in turn, fall under the category of observance (*hamaaseh*), which along with study (*hatalmud*) makes up the larger category of serving God (*avodah*). According to Rabbi Luzzatto, known as the Ramchal, "The main element of such love is the joy in one's heart."[30] While these concepts interrelate differently than described by Rabbi Shimon, more or less the same components are present—study, service, observance; mind, heart, body—and they are intimately tied up with the love of God.

Modern Orthodoxy, as well, acknowledges and values the inseparability of "these three things" in defining what it means to love God. The movement's founder, Rabbi S. R. Hirsch provides a *d'rash* on *Parashat Vaetchannan* that details the implications of the word *"v'ahavta"* (Deuteronomy 6:5): "Seek the nearness of God by surrendering all your heart, all your soul and all your means to this end."[31] By "soul" and "heart," Rabbi Hirsch explains, he is referring to "All your thoughts and emotions"; by "means," he refers to "all your assets" used in good actions in service to God.[32]

The late Rabbi Leo Jung concurs. In *Knowledge and Love in Rabbinic Lore*, he asserts,

One will never know God through either more intellectual endeavor, or through more emotional identification with His spirit. It is only by passionate love of and work for the widow and orphan, the alien and every one else who is underprivileged that one's knowledge of Him may reach the human peak....[33]

Liberal Jewish sources also naturally evince a predilection for endorsements of the salience of righteous action as a marker for loving God. *Shaarei T'fillah*, a Reform prayer book, features this quotation from Martin Buber:

To love God truly, one must first love people. And if anyone tells you that he loves God and does not love his fellow humans, you will know that he is lying.[34]

Etz Hayim, the Conservative *chumash*, or Torah commentary, is just as direct. In its *d'rash* on a familiar verse (Deuteronomy 6:5), the authors state, "Israel's duty to love God is inseparable from action"[35] and "Love is more than an emotion."[36]

Finding God: Ten Jewish Responses,[37] by Rabbis Rifat Sonsino and Daniel B. Syme, is a comprehensive and provocative summary of a variety of more heterodox perspectives on what Jews believe about God. Alongside consideration of biblical and rabbinic perspectives, for example, are encapsulations of the pantheism, naturalism, and humanism of Spinoza, Kaplan, and Fromm, respectively. The authors' review demonstrates conclusively that even within Jewish tradition, there is a wide divergence of viewpoints on how we are to know God, what He wants from us, and what His ideal relationship is with the world.

At the same time, even the apostate Baruch Spinoza weighs in on the topic of loving God with a taxonomy that seems to revisit the familiar three pillars of Rabbi Shimon. The fascinating insights of the famous seventeenth-century Jewish philosopher are not widely known among Jewish laity, but he had much to say about the love of God. Spinoza distinguished among "rational love," a purely self-determined intellectual pursuit seeking union with God; "intuitive love," a less dualistic pursuit in which humans' love of God and God's love of humans is experienced as converging; and what he termed "imaginative love," a sensory-based expression that is independent of thoughts, presupposes God to be a supernatural judge, and thus is capable of a social utility by motivating kindness and tolerance.[38]

On occasion, historians seek simple ways to characterize the essential differences between the three major Jewish movements. Alongside the obvious and universally recognized differences derived from divergent understandings of the authority and mutability of *halakhah*, which were seminal for these movements, more elementary descriptions are sometimes put forth. The body-mind-spirit typology often comes into play, resulting in familiar stereotypes: Orthodox Judaism, especially the Chasidic varieties, is Torah Judaism, heart-centered, focused on precise rituals that arouse spirituality and *devekut*, or divine union. Conservative Judaism is rabbinic Judaism, intellectually oriented and focused on negotiating the dance between Jewish law and modernity. Reform Judaism is post-*halakhic* Judaism, grounded in an ideal of ethical monotheism and focused on social action and social justice.

These depictions are overstated and overgeneralized—more caricatures than representative of reality. While historically and phenomenologically, there may be some threads of truth in such characterizations, each Jewish movement explicitly values these important facets and expressions of Judaism and Jewishness: learning, spirituality, and faith in action. Traditional Jews, as well as liberal Jews, are committed to externalizing their love of God through performance of actions that seek to spread the ideals of charity, justice, and lovingkindness. The "three things" of Rabbi Shimon are the birthright of all Jews.

In a nutshell, the meaning of "these three things" in the context of loving God is manifest. As Jews, we are in a covenantal relationship with the Creator of the universe—an "everlasting covenant (*b'rit olam*)" (Genesis 9:16), a phrase so important that it appears sixteen times in the Hebrew Bible. We have responsibilities to God, just as He does to us. He needs us, just as we need Him. To fulfill our obligations, we are to love God, Who in turn will enable that "the world stands" (*Pirke Avot* 1:2). For this to be so—for this covenant to be fully realized on both sides—we must exercise all the innate pieces of our self that God gave us: our minds, for learning the Torah that we were given; our hearts, for worshipping the One Who gave us this gift; and our bodies, for putting into action the precepts that we learn from the Torah and wish to enact because of our gratitude to God. We are thus to occupy ourselves with *mitzvot* while placing our trust in God to "bless you and protect you" (Numbers 6:24), as He promised.

LOVING GOD: WHY, HOW, WHEREFORE

Pirke Avot tells us why, or to what end, we are to love God: in order that "the world stands" (*Pirke Avot* 1:2). The *Sh'ma* is explicit as to how we are to love God: "with all your heart and with all your soul and with all your might" (Deuteronomy 6:5). These three means by which we are to love God correspond neatly with the three pillars of Rabbi Shimon: "with all your heart" (*b'chol-l'vav'cha*) is how we are to practice *avodah*; "and with all your soul" (*u'v'chol-naf'sh'cha*) is how we are to learn Torah; "and with all your might" (*u'v'chol-m'odecha*) is how we are to pursue acts of *g'milut chasadim*.[39]

These two issues—the why and how of loving God—are taken up in greater detail in Chapters 2 and 3, respectively. There, I explore further what it means to love God—specifically, what Jewish tradition has to say, especially in light of the many attributes of God that may resonate differently in different Jews and thus elicit different responses in different people. This is followed by discussion of how individual Jews may choose to respond to the commandments regarding *torah*, *avodah*, and *g'milut chasadim*. These are the means to two inseparable ends: to know that "I the Lord am your God" (Ezekiel 20:19) and thus that we must "follow My laws and be careful to observe My rules" (Ezekiel 20:19). They are inseparable because, together, they both result from and indeed define the act of loving God.

Even nonreligious Jews are aware of Moses' famous call to "Dedicate yourselves to the Lord today" (Exodus 32:29) and the promised outcome: "that He may bestow a blessing upon you today" (Exodus 32:29). What, then, is that blessing?

To answer this question requires us to delve into the complicated task of reconciling the interconnectedness and interdependence of *k'lal yisrael* with the distinctive psychological needs of every individual Jewish person. The Jewish view of redemption, as described earlier, is a collectively realized and experienced phenomenon. When God speaks through the

Prophet Isaiah, "Come back to Me, for I redeem you" (Isaiah 44:22), He is speaking to all of Israel, the people, to all of us. When we seek to obey God by fulfilling His commandments, we are to do so for such larger ends, not solely to benefit ourselves.

But the issue is not that easily resolved.

As Jews, we are at once both sovereign individuals and part of a greater whole. We have obligations as a whole, and God has obligations to us as a whole. We also have individual obligations to God and to the whole, and as individuals we may receive blessings from God. These blessings consist of both those that we share in as part of the whole and those that are distinctly our own. This may seem paradoxical, but only if we see ourselves through a non-Jewish lens. Identification of the self solely with one's own singular physical being—or with one's body-mind-spirit complex—is alien to Judaism. The Jewish self is defined communally and self-identifies with the whole. When our ancestors were called to take up the yoke of the law, on Sinai with Moses, the Torah proclaims, "All the people answered as one" (Exodus 19:8). Since our beginnings as a people, God has seen us as one, even when our sometimes foolish actions obscure this identity.

At the same time, taking part in this great mass work of redemption—through Jewish learning, worship of God, and acts of goodness to others—does promise its blessings. While it is as a whole people that we are redeemed, each of us is capable of receiving blessings from God directly. The Torah describes many such worthy recipients: those who "obey the commandments of the Lord your God" (Deuteronomy 11:27), those with "clean hands and a pure heart" (Psalms 24:4), those who are "of the upright" (Proverbs 11:11)—the familiar three-fold reference to the written law enshrined in the Torah, the emotional life of the heart, and morally inspired action.

So we are to consecrate ourselves to God, to love Him, and to further His cause on the earth. What then will be the result—the promised blessings to each of us that labors to fulfill this "great work" (Nehemiah 6:3)? By this, I mean both us as individuals and the Jewish people as a whole. It should be self-evident that more charity, more justice, more mercy, and more acts of lovingkindness on the part of Jews will exert a societal impact that touches both Jew and gentile. But it is also true that following through on the charge to "love the Lord thy God, and to walk in all His ways" (Joshua 22:5), in the manner made clear in *Pirke Avot* and elsewhere, can serve as a conduit of blessings—a means to transform Jewish hearts and Jewish lives and, in so doing, God willing, produce more socially responsive, and thus better, Jews.

Rabbi Hirsch, in his commentary on the "three things" of *Pirke Avot*, makes clear where all this leads:

> *These are the three things which shape and perfect the world of man and all that pertains to it in accordance with the measure and way of its destiny. Whenever and wherever any of these three are inadequate or altogether lacking there is a gap which cannot be filled and there is no manifest destiny.*[40]

These issues—consider them the wherefore of loving God— are taken up in Chapters 4 and 5. After having discussed in earlier chapters what it means for Jews to love God and how we may go about doing so, I explore the implications of loving the One Who the psalmist assures us "watches over all who love Him" (Psalms 145:20). This translates into two additional questions: how does loving God affect our lives, and how does it affect our world?

The first question has to do with our self-image and self-identity as Jews and how this in turn serves to define our unique spiritual path and our efforts to renew and redeem ourselves and our world. The second question addresses the influence that Jews loving God and acting in accord with a God-given standard of morality can exert, collectively, on the transformation of social institutions and of our culture.

Our physical world can seem a cold and cruel place. The dominant ethos of our so-called modern civilization seems to depend upon and reinforce our identity as separated beings and our focus on the accumulation of material goods as a means to both self-identity and well-being. These are lies that every important stream of Jewish thought rejects. Without the buffer of a Jewishly lived life, this conditioning accomplishes its dirty work of alienating Jews from what is real, what matters, what is our highest calling, our true self—our identity as beings created "in the image of God" (Genesis 1:27).

This is no small matter and not one to dismiss as mere metaphor or unworthy of learned discourse. Our scriptures and sages gave considerable attention to this verse and to related verses (e.g., Genesis 9:6). The Talmud, Midrash, *Zohar*, and other sources all weigh in on its significance. In *Pirke Avot*, Rabbi Akiva is quoted:

> *Precious is the human being, who was created in the image of God. It was an act of still greater love that it was made known to him that he was created in the image of God.* (Pirke Avot 3:14)

Not only were we created in God's image, but it was an even more loving act (of "superabundant love," in the Soncino translation) for God to let us know. There must be a reason that God wished us to receive this information and for Rabbi Akiva to consider this act even greater than the initial act of being created in His image.

It is hard to conceive of a more empowering piece of knowledge than that God knowingly made us in His image and desires that we be fully aware of this source of our identity. It makes clever folk wisdom such as "we are co-creators with God" take on more profound and literal possibilities. At the least, it should cause us to ponder the teleological purpose of human life—to ask, "Why are we here?" God's destiny as God, if you will, appears intimately linked to our destiny as His creations. To fulfill His own charge for Himself, God needs us to grow in holiness and to spread that holiness to others and to the institutions of the world—to help Him prepare "the way of holiness" (Isaiah 35:8).

To love God means to be precisely the person that God would have us to be, acting on our highest, God-given instincts for the benefit of all our fellow beings, human and nonhuman, Jew and gentile. I would assert that being generous and just and kind and loving and philanthropic and charitable and responsive to the needs of others is the truest way for a Jew to express love for God. This path defines the uniqueness and genius of Jewish spirituality. Following it devotedly is our surest way to bring *tikkun*, in its fullest sense, both to the world and to ourselves.

CHAPTER TWO

WHAT DOES IT MEAN TO LOVE GOD?

"There is none like our God (ein keloheinu), *there is none like our Lord* (ein kadoneinu), *there is none like our King* (ein k'malkeinu), *there is none like our Savior* (ein k'moshienu)."*[1]*

Before we can identify in earnest all of the myriad ways that we Jews have found to express our love for God, we first have to understand the multiple meanings that we ascribe to our relationship or connection with the divine. Some of these meanings derive from how God is defined and described in scripture and in rabbinic writings. Some of these derive from our special identity as a people in a unique covenantal relationship with God. Some emerge from particular historical and cultural circumstances that have served to shape what we think about God and about why we must show Him reverence.

Is there any consensus in Jewish thinking and in the Jewish religion? Yes and no. There is unanimity, of course, that we ought to love God—that He is worthy of our devotion. The Hebrew Bible tells us this repeatedly: in the Torah (Deuteronomy 6:5; Deuteronomy 30:16), in the Prophets (Joshua 23:11; Isaiah 56:6), and in the Writings (Psalms 31:24). But how we have come to interpret this directive is deeply contextualized by how Jews have viewed God over the course of Jewish history; how we have experienced His love for us, personally and as a people; and what we have felt drawn to do about this in return and why. Moreover, different Jewish intellectual traditions have proffered distinct sets of expectations as to what the faithful are to believe about the responsibility to love God and why this is important.

For sure, there is a uniquely Jewish perspective on what it means to have a relationship with God—different even from those of other faiths with which we have much in common. For us, loving God means something quite distinct from what it means in the perspectives of other monotheistic religions (such as Christianity and Islam), other religions of national identity or peoplehood (such as Hinduism or Shinto), and other religions that place a premium on right action over and above doctrine and sentiment (such as Buddhism).

At the same time, within Judaism, there is a divergence of opinion as to why loving God matters and what obligations a Jew has to love God. The reasons given by rationalists are un-like those of mystics; those of traditionalists are not those of reformers or modernists; and those of pietists are different from those of cultural or secular Jews. We have assurance that "this is the whole duty of man" (Ecclesiastes 12:13), but what is "this"? Just what does it mean for a Jew to say that he or she has a relationship with God, ostensibly a relationship charac-terized by the word "love"?

To propose an answer, we must first explore several other questions that will serve to clarify the parameters of this larger question:

First, who is God? The Torah and rabbis provide answers. Some come from God Himself, as in His famous declaration to Moses: "I am that I am" (*Ehyeh-asher-Ehyeh*) (Exodus 3:14). Others are deductions from scripture or canonical commen-tary, such as the *sh'losh esrei middot*, or thirteen attributes of God (Exodus 34:6–7). The prayer book and liturgy also offer perspectives on God's identity, some of which, such as the *Ein Keloheinu* prayer, have shaped both our personal conceptions of God and our vernacular ways of referring to God.

Second, what are our obligations to God? The whole of Jewish history—our origins as a people, the reasons for our existence, our collective destiny—is captured in Moses' words: "The Lord our God made a covenant with us at Horeb" (Deuteronomy 5:2). A covenant implies a set of mutual obliga-tions, in this case obligations of God to human beings, specifi-cally the Jewish people, and our obligations to God. The former are plain, recorded throughout Jewish sacred writings and elu-cidated by the rabbis. The latter have been subject to considerable debate—an understatement, of course, attested to throughout the Talmud.

Third, how is loving God different? That is, what is it about loving God that is different from other ways of relating to Him? And what is it about God that makes loving Him different from loving a person, another living being, a material thing, or an ideal? In our approach to God, there is ideally an element of faith, of absolute belief coupled with implicit trust. The faith that we might possess in relation to "your Holy One, the Lord, Your King, the Creator of Israel" (Isaiah 43:15) naturally is not the same as what we might feel toward a fellow human, even a parent or friend or a great rabbi or mentor. At the same time, our relationship with the One Who created our flesh and breathed life into us is more profound than can be characterized by the word "faith"; there is or should be something more, something more intimate.

Jewish tradition provides insights into the meanings that people attach to their relationship with what is godly, holy, or sacred in their lives. While these meanings emerge as filtered through varied life circumstances, perceptions, and experiences, the uniqueness of our history as Jews, of our covenant with God, and especially of our magnificent revelation from God in the form of Torah, in its most inclusive sense, makes it possible to identify a uniquely Jewish perspective on what it means to love God.

WHO IS GOD?

Jewish sacred writings, beginning with the Torah, tell us Who God is in no uncertain terms. This is not to say that all of these identities and monikers are simply comprehended. God is at once obvious yet inscrutable. He is ever-present yet unapproachable. He is explicitly described to us, yet we do not fully know Him. If we know Him at all, it is not because we have seen or heard or touched Him in person but because of His actions on our behalf.

Referring to the miracles that liberated us from Pharaoh, Moses declared, "Know, therefore, that only the Lord your God is God, the steadfast God...never slow with those who reject Him, but requiting them instantly" (Deuteronomy 7:9–10). Yet, still, we do not entirely understand. According to the psalmist,

The Lord looks down from heaven on mankind to find a man of understanding, a man mindful of God. All have turned bad, altogether foul; there is none who does good, not even one. (Psalms 14:2–3)

One of the most explicit yet unfathomable characterizations of God comes from God Himself. As Moses tended to his flocks in the desert at the foot of Horeb, God made Himself manifest in the form of a burning bush. He called out to Moses, identifying Himself in several ways. These verses are insightful. They depict God revealing Himself to Moses and thus, in a sense, to all of us for the first time through a progressive sequence of Self-disclosure.

To begin, God stated, "Here I am" (Exodus 3:4). God is the One Who is present—Who, though unrecognizable in anthropomorphized form, is ever here. Apparently, this was beyond Moses' comprehension. So God continued.

Next, God described Himself as "the God of your father, the God of Abraham, the God of Isaac, the God of Jacob" (Exodus 3:6). Here is God as Heavenly Father, as Creator and Progenitor of the Jewish people. This time, Moses understood, and he responded accordingly: he "hid his face, for he was afraid to look at God" (Exodus 3:6). This was a start, but it was not what God was hoping for. So again He continued.

God then launched into a lengthy discourse in which He identified Himself as the One Who "marked well the plight of My people in Egypt and ha[s] heeded their outcry" (Exodus 3:7), Who has plans "to rescue them from the Egyptians and to bring them out of that land" (Exodus 3:8), and Who intends to dispatch a reluctant Moses to Pharaoh so that "you shall free My people, the Israelites, from Egypt" (Exodus 3:10). God is now a God of history—a God Who feels empathy for the past, Who has a plan for the future, and Who requires human actors to fulfill this plan. Moses was overwhelmed by these prospects but apparently now accepted God's presence, because he engaged Him in conversation. In fact, Moses felt familiar enough with God that he was emboldened to express doubts about God's plan: "Who am I that I should go to Pharaoh and free the Israelites from Egypt?" (Exodus 3:11).

So God assured Moses, "I will be with you" (Exodus 3:12). God is now a personal God, a comforter and companion. This identity, God explained to Moses, "shall be your sign that it was I that sent you" (Exodus 3:12). Moses was still plagued by doubts but no longer about God's wisdom in formulating His plan. Furthermore, he was soothed by God's promise to stand by him. But Moses was still worried about his credibility among the Israelites. After all, who would believe a story such as Moses would soon relate to them? Moses begged that when "they ask me, 'What is His name?' what shall I say to them?" (Exodus 3:13).

Finally, God was satisfied that Moses knew that He was, that He was there, that He was God of the Jewish people, that He would be their liberator, and that He would be their personal God. God also recognized, finally, that Moses had accepted his mission and would do as God wished. So He revealed His identity in full: "And God said to Moses, 'Ehyeh-Asher-Ehyeh'" (Exodus 3:14). Then, to clarify, "He continued, 'Thus shall you say to the Israelites, "Ehyeh sent me to you"'" (Exodus 3:14). Finally, just to be sure that there would be no confusion, God told Moses to reiterate that He was the One Who created the Jewish patriarchs—the Father of fathers (Exodus 3:15).

This episode occupies a prime chapter in the life story of our people. The progressive revelation of God to Moses is both a record of critical events in Jewish history—those passed and those foreseen—and an elegant model for how an individual being opens to the Divine Presence. At first, Moses did not recognize God—he did not see or hear or feel Him, despite His presence and proximity. The existence of God was so outside of Moses' realm of experience that He could not be perceived. Slowly, as God revealed aspects of Himself to Moses, the bonds of trust grew until Moses felt comfortable speaking with Him. Finally, they were companions and compatriots, planning together how to best advance the cause that God had set before Moses and that he had willingly accepted.

Just as Moses had revealed his most intimate fears to God, owning up to them before One Who had moments earlier been a complete stranger, God, too, revealed Himself to Moses—in the form of His name—and empowered Moses to share this name with all of the people. What for Moses began in mystery, as complete separation, passed through stages of fear, trepidation, and acceptance, finally culminating in love and collegiality.

Throughout the Torah, God is referred to by other names and descriptors. These describe important features of "the lustre of His majesty" (Genesis *Rabbah* 3:4) and were familiar enough to the Jewish people that they recognized them as references to God. Among the most prominent of these Godly identities is *El Shaddai*, or "God Almighty" (Genesis 17:1). This name was revealed to Abram, in much the same way that "I am that I am" was revealed to Moses four centuries later. Abram's reaction was not much different from his revered descendant's: he "threw himself on his face" (Genesis 17:3).

So God, as He did later with Moses, identified Himself by a combination of promises regarding what He would do for Abram's people and expectations that He had for Abram personally (Genesis 17:4–22). When God was finished speaking, Abram, now renamed Abraham, was on board. The Talmud records that, thenceforth, those who followed knew God "by the name of *El Shaddai*, and they did not question my character nor say to Me, 'What is Thy Name?'" (*Sanhedrin* 111a).

The next time God and Abraham met was at the start of *Parashat Vayyera*, the next episode in the Torah. Tellingly, it was not "God" that came to Abraham. Rather, "the Lord appeared to him by the terebinths of Mamre" (Genesis 18:1). The Torah here uses God's holy name, *Yud-He-Vav-He*, the tetragrammaton, rather than His station or title, God. This implies a degree of familiarity and personal connection that was not present earlier, before the first encounter with Abraham. Why is that?

Rabbi S. R. Hirsch suggests an answer. In his *d'rash* on this verse, he notes that this is "the first time we see Abraham standing before God as a true *navi* [prophet] to whom God 'reveals His secret to His servants the prophets' [Amos 3:7]."[2] To be a prophet is to be a servant of the people, consecrated to calling us out of idolatry and wickedness (Zechariah 5:8) and to a higher level of service to others. Only if we successfully negotiate this change in behavior are we worthy of knowing God as Who He really is, as Lord. By his comments in *Mikra'ot Gedolot*, the thirteenth-century Spanish sage Rabbi Moshe Ben Nachman, known as the Ramban, concurred. According to the Ramban, "God's appearance to him [Moses] was a reward for his obedience and indicated that He was pleased with him."[3]

Use of these two respective names, God and Lord, has implications for the potential personal relationships they imply. The same could be said for any of the myriad other forms of God's name or descriptors of God that populate Jewish sacred writings. Every such word exists to teach us something about Who God is, intrinsically as well as in relation to the Jewish people. The *Ein Keloheinu* prayer is a representative exemplar of a liturgical element created for just such a heuristic purpose. It represents a composite of several God identities that, transposed into the form of an acrostic and a hymn, has become a familiar feature of the *shabbat* and High Holy Days services (its precise location dependent upon respective *nusachim*, or liturgical styles and customs).[4]

Ein Keloheinu is one of the most familiar and beloved hymns in the Jewish liturgy. It consists of five stanzas of four lines apiece, each following a common repetitive pattern that invokes, respectively, God's identities as God, Lord, King, and Savior. These stanzas begin with, in order, "There is none like," "Who is like," "Let us praise," "Blessed be," and, "Lo, Thou art."[5] Combining the first letter of each of the Hebrew words that begins each of the first three respective stanzas—*ein, mi,* and *nodah*—produces the word "amen," the close of every Jewish prayer. Combining the first Hebrew word of each of the last two respective stanzas—*barukh* and *atah*—produces the phrase *"barukh atah,"* which begins every prayer. *Ein Keloheinu* is thus not just a summary of God's important identities, it is also a kind of primer on Jewish prayer. Moreover, we could also say that the recounting of Who God is and our affirmation that He merits our praise make up the template and ideal for all Jewish prayer.

According to the *Ein Keloheinu*, God is at once both "our God" (*Eloheinu*) and "our Lord" (*Adoneinu*) as well as much more, namely, "our King" (*Malkeinu*) and "our Savior" (*Moshienu*). Each of these titles, each of God's praiseworthy identities, tells us something distinct about Him and about His nature. Each name also speaks to us about our relationship with God and tells us something unique and wonderful about our birthright as His chosen creations. It is worth noting that in the prayer, each of these words stands not alone but takes the first-person plural possessive form: He is *our* God, Lord, King, and Savior. God is Who He is because of and through our relationship with Him.

He is our God (*Eloheinu*). He is our Creator, our Maker. He, our God, is One, as the *Sh'ma* reminds us (Deuteronomy 6:4). He is the great I Am. We owe Him gratitude and should hearken to His directives for our life. After all, He knows best, as He crafted us and our world. Our love for Him is the love of a child for a father, or parent, full of respect mixed with fear or awe. This is on account of His power, as well as of the trust we are compelled to place in Him because of His loyalty to us, demonstrated repeatedly throughout Jewish history. Because He made us, He can unmake us, although we have His promise that "I will preserve you" (Isaiah 49:8) and thus our unmaking will never come to pass.

He is our Lord (*Adoneinu*). We use the word "Lord" as a proxy for God's holy name, which is unpronounceable and unknowable, but the word that we have chosen has great significance. He is the One Who is Sovereign and Eternal—God over all space and time. He is a personal Being or Presence. He is our friend, our intimate companion. We appreciate His faithfulness to Israel despite our continued apostasy. He merits our faithfulness in return. Thus, it is as Lord that we can truly know God, as it was said, "I will betroth you to me in faithfulness; and you shall know the Lord" (Hosea 2:22). Loving God involves acknowledging our gratitude toward our Source of being. Loving the Lord is a matter of acknowledging our mutuality and partnership with God. In our relationship with the Lord, we become co-creators.

He is our King (*Malkeinu*). We are His subjects. We are obliged to be obedient to Him. We are His vassals, as we exist to carry out His will for His possessions, which we only lease for a season. Ultimately, God is "the Lord of all the earth" (Micah 4:13). We are duty-bound to Him, which is an implicit part of our covenant, as it is written, "Fear God, and keep His commandments; for this is the whole duty of man" (Ecclesiastes 12:13). Modern sensibilities may bristle at this identity and implied relationship, but it is necessary for the preservation of the world and for our well-being. Left to our devices, to our natural instincts and inclinations, we would soon be at the mercy of our *yetzer hara*, our lower nature, our evil inclination, much as a nation without strong, moral leadership will soon deteriorate into a chaotic assemblage of competing fiefs motivated by the basest of motives. Water seeks its own level; any human civilization that does not elevate itself by voluntarily subjecting itself to the supervision of the King of Kings—by way of following His precepts—will eventually expire.

He is our Savior (*Moshienu*). He redeems us. Why is He called Savior? Because He "shall preserve you from all evil; He shall preserve your soul" (Psalms 121:7). Not only does He save and preserve the Jewish nation, He saves us each of us from ourselves, spiritually, from our *yetzer hara*, which, unchecked, would destroy our will to fulfill *mitzvot*. He vanquishes our enemies, both external and internal—both internal to us as a people and internal to our own psyches. He knows us more and better than anyone else, yet He forgives us. He is our protector and our shield, our agent of supernatural blessing. Because He is our Savior, He can alter history and transcend the laws of nature that He engineered, for the same reason that He created them and His *mitzvot* in the first place: in order "that you may live" (Amos 5:14). He is thus worthy of our adoration and praise.

Clearly, there exists some overlap in these identities. In places, too, they even appear linked together, as in the psalm that states, "O Lord of hosts, my king and my God" (Psalms 84:4). God, Lord, King, and Savior do not, of course, refer to discrete Beings; after all, God is One. Any description of His identities is, by definition, a diminution or diminishment of His Oneness and represents a dualistic separation into elements of what is inseparable and elemental.

Across these identities, there are also both correspondences and contradictions. Both God-as-God and God-as-King evoke a quality of judgment. Likewise, God-as-Lord and God-as Savior are both evocative of God as merciful. Together, these meta-identities elicit a combination of fear (or awe) and love. Is this a paradox? Not really. Our simultaneous fear and love of God go hand in hand in defining and sketching out a complicated relationship that is, at once, eternal and unchanging for the Jewish people yet dynamic and complex across the course of each of our lives.

Another such seeming paradox involves God's role as an Actor in the affairs of the world and His "location" in relation to the world. This is the ancient philosophical dilemma of God's immanence or transcendence. This debate has polarized theologians in many other religious traditions for centuries and into the present day, for example, in liberal and neo-reformed Protestant Christianity.[6] Is God wholly or partly in or of the world? Is He entirely "outside" of or beyond the manifested world that He created? Is He near or present here with us, indwelling in our hearts or otherwise close by? Did He create our world and then step away? Is He intimately concerned with the affairs of human beings? Is He responsive to our needs? Can we truly know Him, fully or partially?

These concepts have not been debated with the same gravity within Judaism. Nor have they produced irreparable schisms among groups of adherents. There is good reason for this. Ours is not a religion divided into competing sects over discrete points of theology. Our divisions, rather, have originated in disputes over how and whether *halakhah*, traditionally viewed as revealed law, is to be translated into human action. For us, these latter differences are not discrete and have had the force of earthquakes. We have been much more willing to confront seeming paradoxes involving more ethereal matters, such as God's nature, by embracing the (apparent) paradox while searching for some rational resolution.

Rabbi Solomon Schechter, founding father of the Conservative movement, eloquently explained that, for Judaism, God is both immanent and transcendent. "To the Jew, God was at one and the same time above, beyond, and within the world, its soul and its life,"[7] he wrote. Further, "we must note that the fact of God's abiding in a heaven ever so high does not prevent him from being at the same time also on earth."[8] For Schechter, our own behavior is paramount in locating God's presence: "The fact is, that the nearness of God is determined by the conduct of man, and by his realisation of this nearness, that is, by his knowledge of God."[9]

Compared to us, who are fully immanent in physical bodies in a physical world, God surely seems like an infinitely transcendent Being Who exists mysteriously in some portion "outside" of the material realm that He created. However, we can be assured that He still occupies this realm, if in no other way than through having created us, and still needing us, to do work for Him in this concrete world of "images and forms"

(*Zohar* 2:150a). This was the whole purpose and point of God's having established covenants with humankind, beginning with Noah (Genesis *Rabbah* 31:12). If we feel that distance or separation has arisen between us and the One Who created us, we understand that we alone are to blame—that "your sins have hidden His face from you" (Isaiah 59:2).

WHAT ARE OUR OBLIGATIONS TO GOD?

Covenants between God and humankind consist, by definition, of two parts. There is God's part—His obligations to us—and our part—our obligations to God. In Judaism, these latter obligations translate invariably into duties and responsibilities that we owe to each other. If we are truly to be called children of the covenant, it will be because we have met our obligations to act ethically among each other and in our dealings with non-Jews. God cited the fate of our "covenant of life and well-being" (Malachi 2:5) when our leaders "made the many stumble through your rulings" (Malachi 2:8): "You have corrupted the covenant of the Levites—said the Lord of Hosts. And I, in turn, have made you despicable and vile in the eyes of all the people, because you disregard My ways" (Malachi 2:8). What are these "ways"?

Unlike certain Christian denominations and Islam, Judaism has never recognized a formal creedal statement or confession of faith as requisite or binding. This is not to say that such statements have not been proposed, but they have primarily been intellectual deductions devised to educate, inspire, and encourage greater observance among Jews. These have taken the form of litanies of descriptors of God or of our obligations as Jews. The most famous of the latter such statements is Maimonides' *shloshah asar ikkarim*, or thirteen principles of faith. The most famous of the former are the *sh'losh esrei middot*, or thirteen attributes of God, derived from the revelation to Moses (Exodus 34:6–7).

After God instructed Moses as to the second set of tablets and Moses had finished his work, he ascended Sinai, and the Lord descended to meet him. God then proceeded to describe Himself to Moses: He is the Lord (*Adonai*), both before and after we have sinned and repented. He is God (*El*). He is compassionate (*rachum*). He is gracious (*channun*). He is slow to anger (*erekh apayim*). He is abounding in kindness (*rav chesed*).

He is truth (*emet*). He extends kindness for thousands of generations (*notser chesed laalafim*). He forgives iniquity, transgression, and sin (*nose avon vafesha v'chattaah*). And He does not remit all punishment (*v'nakeh lo y'nakeh*).

This list is notable not in that it provides an exhaustive catalog of all of God's characteristics—that in itself is doubtful—but rather in that it provides a glimpse into how God wishes that Moses, and by extension all Jews, are to recognize Him. These attributes, if nothing else, paint a portrait of a Being Who is exceedingly ethical and merciful. We are to know God through His righteous and loving actions.

Our covenant, then, is with an ethical Being who wants us not to "disregard My ways" (Malachi 2:9) but to emulate them. These "ways" are precisely His attributes, as spoken to Moses. The Talmud refers to these attributes implicitly when Rabbi Yochanan says of God's speech to Moses, "He said to him: 'Whenever Israel sin, let them carry out this service before Me, and I will forgive them'" (*Rosh Hashanah* 17b). Are we really expected to be like God, to share His attributes and thus recapitulate His actions?

In no uncertain terms, yes. Rav Yehudah makes this explicit: "A covenant has been made with the thirteen attributes" (*Rosh Hashanah* 17b). In other words, according to Moses, "After the Lord your God shall ye walk" (Deuteronomy 13:5). Rabbi Chama b. Rabbi Chanina expounded on the connection between this verse and the thirteen attributes. Moses was saying that we are "to walk after the attributes of the Holy One, blessed be He. As He clothes the naked . . . visited the sick . . . comforted mourners . . . buried the dead" (*Sotah* 14a). None of this is outside of our capabilities; moreover, it is requisite if we are to fulfill our covenant with God.

The Rambam's thirteen principles are the closest thing to a recognized (although far from universally accepted) creedal statement that has emerged in Judaism. They are most familiar to religious Jews in the form of the thirteen couplets of the *Yigdal* hymn,[10] found among the *Birkhot Hashachar* devotions that precede *Shacharit*[11] or toward the close of the *Erev Shabbat* service or not at all, depending up which prayer book one uses.[12] The principles originated in the Rambam's commentary on the Mishnah, in his discussion of tractate *Sanhedrin*. The tenth chapter begins, "All Israelites have a share in the world to come" (*M. Sanhedrin* 10:1), and later on adds, "And these are the ones who have no portion in the world to come" (*M. Sanhedrin* 10:1), followed by a brief elaboration. For the Rambam, this was a stepping-off point to derive his thirteen principles.

The principles are typically translated as thirteen statements, each beginning with, "I believe with perfect faith" (*ani maamin b'emunah shleimah*).[13] They comprise belief that God created the universe; that God is One; that God is incorporeal, without a material body or a form; that God is eternal; that God is the only One to Whom we should pray; that all of the words of the prophets are true; that Moses is the greatest of all prophets; that the Torah that we have now is the same one given to Moses; that the Torah is immutable and will remain so forever; that God is omniscient of all of our future deeds and thoughts; that God rewards observance of *mitzvot* and punishes transgression; that a messiah will someday come; and that God will someday resurrect the dead.

Interestingly, the Rambam's thirteen principles seem to exhibit some correlation with the thirteen attributes given in the Torah. While not widely elaborated, each respective attribute is found encompassed, and realized, in its numerically corresponding principle:

- God was Lord before humans existed: He is Creator of the universe.

- God is the same Lord today: He alone is our God and ever will be.

- God is: He cannot be characterized by a physical form.

- God is our heavenly Father Who compassionately protects us: His care is eternal.

- God is gracious in responding to those who call on Him: He is the only One to Whom our prayers should be directed.

- God is slow to anger: So He sent prophets to remind us of our transgressions.

- God is abundantly kind: So He sent us Moses, above

all the prophets.

- God is truth: And thus His revealed word, the Torah, is perfectly true.

- God's kindness lasts for thousands of generations: And thus will the Torah endure forever.

- God forgives iniquities, or premeditated sins: He must know all of our thoughts and actions.

- God forgives transgressions, or sins of rebellion: He rewards those Who keep His commandments and punishes those who do not.

- God forgives all sins, advertent or inadvertent: He is preparing us to receive a messiah.

- God remits punishment for those who repent: Likewise, He will bring the dead back to life.

The Rambam's thirteen principles represent an expression and extension of God's thirteen attributes into the realm of human activity. They are a translation of God's attributes into a set of affirmations that taken to heart can help us to not "disregard My ways" (Malachi 2:9). Ideally, these principles should inspire us to take the same moral stances and the same ethical actions that God does, and that He asks us to take. No matter that we may interpret one or more of God's attributes metaphorically rather than literally or that we may question Maimonides' bold imposition of a creed comprising particular points with which we may disagree. Regardless, each principle, derived from or consonant as it is with a respective Godly attribute, calls us to engage it—to reflect, consider, wrestle, parse, reconsider, and ultimately decide for ourselves whether and how we might translate it into personal or social behavior. This is one way, it could be said, in which we love God and His ways.

The late British Rabbi Isidore Epstein, esteemed editor and translator of the Soncino Talmud, reflected on our charge to mimic God's attributes in our actions. In *The Faith of Judaism*, in his discussion of the "divine purpose of creation,"[14] Rabbi Epstein affirmed that we are to be as God is and do as God does:

Made in the image of God, man, as we have seen, is possessed of unique attributes that are divine—reason, freedom, creativeness and moral goodness. And these attributes were not bestowed on man in vain, but in order to enable him to participate in the work of God.[15]

This is no simple task, for traditional or liberal Jew. There is no definitive Jewish position on how what we know or believe about God does or should become transmuted into human action. There is not even much consensus. There is only agreement that this must happen, that this is an essential obligation. At a minimum, there is an understanding that intellectual recognition of God's love for us should resonate within our hearts, motivating us to "follow the Lord your God" (I Samuel 12:14)—that is, to "revere the Lord, worship Him, and obey Him" (I Samuel 12:14).

The eleventh-century Spanish philosopher Rabbi Bachya ibn Pakuda wrote at length about the *chovot hal'vavot,* or "duties of the heart," in his famous book of the same name.[16] This great work, influential still today, comprises ten *she'arim* ("gates"), or discourses, together making the case for our obligation to maintain faith in God and to serve Him by fulfilling His commandments. These include what Rabbi Bachya called the gates of unity, recognition, service of God, humility, and repentance, among others. The final gate is named *shaar ahavat Hashem,* the "gate of the love of God."

In the tenth gate, Rabbi Bachya identified three reasons why we should love God. His language is reminiscent of God's attributes as described to Moses. We should love God because we have learned that He is kind and good, because He forgives our sins, and, above all, "for Himself, for His honor, His greatness and exaltedness."[17]

How do we come to love God? Rabbi Bachya's teaching is explicit, though involved. We come to love God through what he described as eight required "dedications," or focused intentions. There are two kinds of dedications of the heart: accepting God's oneness and consecrating our actions to Him. There are two kinds of surrender: to God and to God-fearing people. There are two kinds of introspection: about our obligations to God and about God's patience and forgiveness. Finally, there are two kinds of reflection: on the past, by learning Torah, and on the wondrousness of God's creation.[18]

These dedications thus encompass and engage the fullness of our psychological functions: thinking, feeling, and behaving. Through occupying ourselves with "nothing but the service of God,"[19] we will soon come to experience the love of God. This Rabbi Bachya casts in language almost kabbalistic as "the demonstration of the soul's longing and inherent affinity for the Creator that gives it the capacity to cling to His supernal light."[20]

Thus, loving God and following in His ways are mutually reinforcing. Each thing fortifies the other. The more we contemplate our obligations to God, the more we fall in love with Him. And the more we feel in our hearts this love for God, the more we will ache to emulate Him through our actions in the world and toward others.

A similar sentiment is voiced by a more contemporary authority who, while speaking from a quite different perspective, nonetheless echoes some of Rabbi Bachya's salient points. Philosopher Martin Buber, in *Good and Evil*, discourses on what he has termed "the ways"—a *d'rash* on the first of the psalms.[21] Here, we are told, there are the righteous, there are sinners, and there are the wicked. Each follows a respective way or *derech* (Psalms 1:1, 6), the same root word that is used to tell us, "The way of God is perfect" (II Samuel 22:31). Sinners are those who fall short of this way repeatedly; the wicked oppose it and refuse to act in accord with God, ever. In Buber's words, "The sinner does evil, the wicked man is evil."[22] Neither will survive judgment, and both are doomed (Psalms 1:5–6).

The righteous are different. Such people are "happy" (*ashrei*) (Psalms 1:1), a status that is "to be understood only from a man's intercourse with God."[23] At each stage of life, each location along the way, "they experience the divine contact afresh . . . shown by God in his 'direction,' the Torah."[24] According to Buber, accepting this direction, this elaboration of God's way, is not enough, just as merely accepting God is only the first of Rabbi Bachya's dedications. We must fully engage it. For Rabbi Bachya, this means consecration, surrender, introspection, and reflection, leading us to passionately "cling" to God's light. For Buber, "We must 'delight' in it, we must cling to it with a passion,"[25] in constancy and through study and reflection "day and night" (Psalms 1:2), leading us to a destiny "irradiated"[26] by God.

HOW IS LOVING GOD DIFFERENT?

These descriptions of the experience and consequences of loving God, of engaging the divine, are written in words that heighten their drama and magnificence. They depict the most peak kinds of perceptions and sensations imaginable to us as physical beings, resulting from an earnest devotion to God's way, and they promise a divine reward. Among the types of relationships that we may have with God, surely this is the ultimate.

Another category of divine relationship is captured by the word *emunah*, or faith. In Judaism, faith does not occupy the same centrality to the core of dogma that it does in other religions, including the Western monotheistic traditions. That is, faith is not primary and instrumental to personal salvation, as it is, for example, among many Christian communions or denominations—a soteriological concept (personal salvation), moreover, that does not exist in the same individual and eschatological context in normative Judaism. Nor is faith defined in terms of perfect submission to God and thus explicitly implicated in matters of divine reward and judgment, as in Islam. For Jews, it is our actions, especially involving other beings, that are paramount. Indeed, the word "faith," in variant spellings and endings, appears fewer than a dozen times in the Hebrew Bible (e.g., only once as *emun*, in Deuteronomy 32:20, and there it does not even refer to God).

This does not mean that faith is unimportant in Judaism. Rather, faith is a means to a more significant and profound psychological end. The Rambam's *emunah shleimah*, or "perfect faith," is held up as an ideal characteristic of belief—in the nature of God and His ways—that affirmed in concert with all other faithfully held beliefs renders one a pious Jew. But this alone does not make one an observant Jew, a lover of God. That identity comes to full flower only through translation of these faith-fed beliefs into physical deeds, *mitzvot*—including the familiar acts of *tz'dakah* and *g'milut chasadim* specified in so many places throughout the Torah and Talmud. Only if our faith has succeeded in producing righteous actions can it be said not to have been a worthless badge.

Love of God, in contrast to faith in God, is something more—something more elevated and more intense. Faith may be a component of this love, a necessary condition, but is not sufficient. The nineteenth-century Rabbi Tzadok HaKohen, the Izbitzer Rebbe, defined faith as "based on an unqualified belief in Divine supervision."[27] But believing in such a thing and acting on it, submitting to it, are two different things. To love God, we first must believe that He exists and watches over us. Many of us are at such a place in our beliefs but cannot take the next step.

In his insightful *Faith and Love*, Rabbi A. Alan Steinbach describes the love of God as "complete surrender....the seal of the Divine upon man's finite heart."[28] Whereas love of other humans "makes us one with a kindred spirit; Divine Love makes us one with God."[29] For Rabbi Steinbach, this kind of love is something different in both degree and kind from mere belief or trust in God. In describing this, he uses imagery evocative of Jacob's ladder and the kabbalistic *etz chayyim*, or tree of life: "Love elevates us to a rung higher than faith."[30]

This "rung" is described as a spiritual place filled with the glory of God. In a commentary on the *Sh'ma*, Rabbi Abba described it thus: "One who loves God is crowned with lovingkindness on all sides and does lovingkindness throughout, sparing neither his person nor his money" (*Zohar* 3:267a). This allusion to money, incidentally, is not unique. Rabbi Bachya's *d'rash* on the same verse (Deuteronomy 6:5) asserts, "A sign of the love of God being in you is your renouncing everything superfluous that distracts you from your service to the Creator."[31] In one of the rare approbations of something akin to asceticism to be found in Jewish writings, Rabbi Bachya made clear that he was referring here to one's body, one's soul, and one's money. This, he stated, is what God meant when He commanded us to love Him with "all your might" (Deuteronomy 6:5).

Incidentally, the same interpretation is found in the Mishnah's exploration of this verse (*M. B'rakhot* 9:5), and this understanding is also implicit in the associated *g'mara* (*B'rakhot* 61b). Also, in the Midrash, we find Rabbi Eliezer's comment:

For those whose bodies are more precious to them than their wealth, it says with all your soul. For those whose wealth is more precious than their bodies, it says with all your might. (Sifre Deuteronomy §32)

Loving God thus encompasses more than just having faith in God. It requires all of our heart or emotions, all of our soul or intellectual and rational capacities, and all of our might— our commitment to action. Foremost among such actions is to put our money where our mouth is, so to speak, by supporting those causes that further God's way, His *derech*.

We can now distinguish between having faith in God and loving Him. One is more an internal exercise, the other an externalized act. To love requires something considerably more than to believe or to trust. It requires a total commitment of one's being, a disregard for one's material status relative to the concern one feels for the other, human or divine. True love elicits a willingness to sacrifice, physically and materially, for the object of love. This is the same, or at least should be the same, whether we are speaking of loving God or loving people, other living beings, material things, or ideals. How, then, is loving God different from these more worldly kinds of love?

A better question would be: *Is loving God different from these other kinds of love?* Is it different, for example, from the love we might feel toward, say, our spouse or children? For Judaism, this question is not easily answered.

For one, the love of certain other beings, such as one's neighbor, is inclusive in and inseparable from the love of God. Professor Irving Singer noted that

for the Jews the first commandment was never to be taken in isolation. God was the prime, the most exalted, object of love; but not the only one. The Jews had even assumed that one could not love God properly unless one also loved every aspect of his creation—one's neighbor as oneself, but also nature and the world at large.[32]

In contemplating what it means to love God in contrast to loving, say, my wife, Lea, I have to confess that I find the distinctions too discrete to draw. Sometimes I believe that I have a handle on it: they differ in kind, but not degree. I love both God and Lea with all my heart, all my soul, and all my might, but I grant that somewhere deep inside, these are two different psychological operations. One is not more or better or higher than the other, just…different. At other times, I conclude that this makes no sense to me, and I am compelled to affirm just the opposite: my love of God and love of Lea differ in degree but not in kind. But in such instances, it is not an easy task to decide which love is deeper and more complete. Perhaps the truth is that these two loves differ in no real way at all. Love is love, and, not resisted, it becomes infinite.

Occasionally, one reads a clever maxim pertaining to the love of God, originating from one or another non-Jewish source. One popular affirmation among Christians is that "I am third"—that is, that first comes God, then comes one's family and loved ones, then oneself. I would not dispute the worthiness of putting the needs of others before one's own. That is as much a Jewish value as a Christian one. In fact, like many other so-called Christian virtues, its origins can be found in the Jewish canon. We are commanded not to oppress "the widow, the orphan, the stranger, and the poor" (Zechariah 7:10) and not to loathe or abhor our erstwhile enemy "for he is your kinsman" (Deuteronomy 23:8). A famous *g'mara* even teaches that "Rav Yehudah said in the name of Rav: 'A man is forbidden to eat before he gives food to his beast'" (*B'rakhot* 40a). The survival needs of strangers and enemies and even farm animals are to come become our own personal needs.

The idea of putting anyone or anything, even God, ahead of one's charges, however, is an impossibility for a Jew. Our dearest loved ones must always come first. If there is a choice to be made, for example, between attending worship services or fulfilling a ritual obligation, on the one hand, and tending to a sick or needy spouse or child or parent or stranger, on the other, there is scarcely a choice to be made. Our God is jealous of our love, but remember that we express our love of Him through loving acts to others. Every one of the cultic trappings of Judaism—the Torah, *shabbat*, the *mitzvot*, and all the rest—were created for our sake, for our use and edification and enjoyment, to enhance our spirituality; we were not created for their sake (*M. Sanhedrin* 4:5).

One should not necessarily conclude, however, that we are to love our families first, putting their needs ahead of all others, worldly and cultic, then attend to our religious duties, then see to everyone and everything else, including ourselves.

Who, precisely, constitutes what I have referred to as our "charges" is another provocative issue that threatens any simple distinction between us and them and between duties to humankind and duties to God.

In *Middot HaRayah*, Rabbi Abraham Isaac Kook, former Chief Rabbi of Palestine just before the establishment of the nation of Israel, outlined what he called his "moral principles."[33] These are a collection of discourses, the first of which addresses love, followed by faith, covenant, and numerous other concepts and virtues.

Rav Kook's first discourse begins boldly: "The heart must be filled with love for all."[34] This straightforward precept is then elaborated in a kind of hierarchy:

> *The love of all creation comes first, then comes the love for all mankind, and then follows the love for the Jewish people.... All these loves are to be expressed in practical action, by pursuing the welfare of those we are bidden to love.*[35]

Elsewhere, to ensure that his point is not missed, he reiterates that he is imploring us to "a love for all people and a love for all nations."[36] This is because "the degree of love in the soul of the righteous embraces all creatures, it excludes nothing, and no people or tongue."[37]

So how is loving God different? We can summarize this as follows: Loving God is something more than having faith in God. It is the culmination of faith, the fruition of a commitment of our body, mind, and spirit to embrace God's ways. Loving God, furthermore, is not distinct from loving other beings. Rather, loving others is a principal manifestation of loving God, and, in this, we do not differentiate between Jew and gentile. If anything, we are to attend lovingly to others before attending to ourselves. Taking this a step further, we are to place the immediate needs of others—regarding physical survival, material sustenance, injustices—before we are to worry about addressing immediate concerns in our own lives that are not life-threatening. I believe that these concerns include certain ritual obligations.

We are taught that all of the *mitzvot* may be breached except for those forbidding adultery, idolatry, and murder (*Sanhedrin* 74a). The imperative here is that we "choose life—

if you and your offspring would live" (Deuteronomy 30:19). Fulfillment of a ritual duty or other religious obligation must be forsaken if it threatens our life, other than the *mitzvot* listed, for we are "to live by them, but not die by them" (*Avodah Zarah* 27b). Exactly whose life must be threatened is usually taken to mean that of the Jewish would-be *mitzvah*-doer. But this places a severely individualized straightjacket around the concept of Jewish identity that, in my opinion, is unmerited.

We are one people, *k'lal Yisrael*, for sure. But perhaps that does not go far enough. We have a duty to "all people" and "all nations," of whom we are a very small part. All of us, all of the myriad peoples of God's creation, are together a *"k'lal"* as well. To be good Jews, acting on our faith in God, obedient to His ways, we must love God. We do that first, and foremost, by acting lovingly and ethically toward all of His people. That is our ultimate religious duty to God.

THIS IS THE WHOLE DUTY OF MAN

That we have duties to God implies our allegiance to Him. Such an allegiance, moreover, implies a relationship governed by ethical obligations—a covenant, in essence. God speaks to us of His expectations through His *mitzvot* and through their explication by our sages and rabbis. We speak to Him through prayer and through our actions.

This special relationship between us and God has been described by Rabbi David Hartman as

> a total way of life organized by mitzvah. It is part of living with the knowledge that one has particular obligations and that God is concerned about and responsive to the human situation and to the way human beings live.[38]

In this way, we get to experience "a life lived in the spirit of a constantly reaffirmed covenant."[39]

Such a covenant, involving partners connected through revelation and prayer and deeds, must imply, by necessity, a sense of separation, of distance. While we may strive to become like God, to emulate those of His attributes of which we are capable, in the end we cannot become God. Nor, as long as we exist in bodies here in the physical world, can we permanently dissolve away, absorbed somehow into God's Being, relinquishing forever all traces of our personal identity. Our mystical longing for union with the One competes, unsuccessfully, with this One's own longing for us to be His agents on this plane. For the Jewish person of faith, this presents a paradox. Our closest approach to spiritual union with God must await our deaths, a prospect that Rabbi Joseph B. Soloveitchik famously referred to as "lonely."[40]

But perhaps our expectations betray us. Rabbi Abba Hillel Silver explained, "To 'cling to God,' to 'seek His nearness'—*hitdabkut*—even in their most intensive modes among the Jewish mystics, never involved crossing of the barriers separating mortal man from immortal God."[41] This is a critical distinction and may seem unacceptable and unsatisfying to Jewish hearts and minds informed and shaped by the past couple of decades of pop mysticism emitting from non-Jewish sources. But it is an essential element of our uniquely Jewish covenant with the One "who has created us, sustained us, and brought us to this day," as the familiar words of the *Shehecheyanu* prayer tell us. It is also, from my perspective, immensely satisfying and comforting.

Even in coming near to the majesty of God, the uniqueness of both humans and God is retained. There is no perfect mystical union or dissolving into oneness, as in pagan or non-Western religions. God does not want to consume us and does not require our dissolution. He wants us to "choose life" (Deuteronomy 30:19), "go forth" (Genesis 12:1), and "repair the breaches of the house wheresoever any breach shall be found" (II Kings 12:6). We come close to God through our actions—not via any kind of arcane contemplation—and even in our closest approach, we are still separate. This is good—not bad, as so many would claim—for it means that we are still manifest in the created world of forms and things and thus capable of performing good deeds and acts of charity and justice to further the cause of healing and redemption in the world. These are also causes that God implores us to commit ourselves to—not to disappearing from this world in some subtle vapor or mist, which would leave the rest of God's creation behind in the hands of the wicked.

This discussion should not be misread as a cosmological statement. Ultimately, as the kabbalists tell us, we are all one. We all come from God; we are composed of God-ness. The *Sefer Yetzirah* tells us that we come from "nothingness" (*b'limah*) until, filled with the "breath of the living God" (*ruach*

Elohim chayyim), we become alive.[42] Our separate identities, our individuation, the spaces among us and those between us and God—in a sense, these are illusions. But practically and morally, as far as the focus of our waking conscious intentions—there is great utility in seeing a world of separate things and a metaphysical distance between us and God.

As Jews, we do not resist seeking to become "one" with God—merging into Him until our individuality disappears—because of any fear of committing blasphemy by trying to become a god ourselves. It is not that at all. Rather, we do not seek to become gods, as if such a transformation were even possible, purely out of practicality. It is not our charge, and it would steal us away from our unique mission here in the world. We should rejoice in our mortal nature. There is much work to accomplish here, and our God, our Lord, our King, and our Savior needs us to finish the work that He began.

CHAPTER THREE

HOW DO WE LOVE GOD?

"These are the things that you shall do; speak every man the truth (emet) to his neighbor; execute the judgment (mishpat) of truth and peace (shalom) in your gates."
(Zechariah 8:16)

In Chapter 2, we spoke of "the whole duty of man." This, our tradition tells us, consists of loving God and translating that love into ethical behavior. Our actions and our morality thus matter deeply. They matter for our own spiritual growth and development, for sure. But more important, they matter for this great collective work to which we Jews were consecrated when Moses read aloud the *sefer hab'rit*, the record of the covenant, and we answered, "All that the Lord has spoken we will faithfully do!" (Exodus 24:7).

This is no burden. All of us should innately care enough about our fellow Jews and fellow human beings to want to assist them on their way. We must also recognize that each of us can serve as a beacon, lighting the path for others who seek to know God's desires for us. Our actions are immeasurably valuable to God, for they are His means to touch others with His love for them. How we comport ourselves reflects not only on our own character but also on God's. If we behave kindly toward another, it is as if we are wearing a sign around our necks that is telling the world that our God is kind. If instead we behave selfishly, God forbid, then we are desecrating God's name.

The Midrash elaborates: "The end of man's conduct is that all proclaim his deeds, [saying], 'So-and-so was right-living,' 'So-and-so was God-fearing'" (Ecclesiastes *Rabbah* 12:12). In the plain sense, the meaning of this passage is straightforward: our actions tell the world who we are. But another way to interpret this passage is to read "his" as a reference to God. The non-Jewish world can know Who our God is only through how we represent Him through what we do, the actions we undertake, in relation to their world. All Jews should meditate upon this thought and recognize the great responsibility that God has placed upon our shoulders. While the prophet assures us that "the Lord shall be your light everlasting" (Isaiah 60:19), it falls upon us alone to ensure that His eternal light is never extinguished.

Loving God and fulfilling our obligations to Him thus bring many benefits. The direct impact of our deeds enables fulfillment of whatever good intentions are our aim: hospitality to a stranger, comfort to the sick, kindness to the bereaved, charity to the needy, mercy to the afflicted, justice to the oppressed. The indirect influence of our deeds is several. They reflect our good character and thus bring honor and merit to ourselves and our families. They also do the same for God. More significantly, our righteous actions serve to represent Jewish values to the non-Jewish world as well as the value of Jewish ethical observance to any other Jew who may not yet have chosen to "accept upon himself the yoke of the kingdom of heaven" (M. B'rakhot 2:2).

That God needs us to act as His agents here in the world, completing the work that He began, should be enough to inform us of the vital importance of our lives and of the seriousness of what we have been created to accomplish. This realization should be enough to motivate us to dedicate ourselves to His service. But for so many of us, it is not enough. We seem convinced that in submitting ourselves to God's intentions for us, we will somehow relinquish our autonomy, our freedom of conscience, the stewardship over our lives—all matters that loom large in the consciousness of so many Jews in today's world. No matter that God has assured us, as He did Moses, of "all the treasures in which the rewards of the righteous are stored away" (Exodus Rabbah 45:6) for those of us who simply do good.

What holds us back?

Perhaps one of the barriers is that we really do not know God or, rather, do not know how to know God. Consequently, we labor under false perceptions of what God expects from us and what obeying God will cost us. Nowhere does normative

Judaism inform us that God requires a sacrifice of our freedom or individuality to be good Jews. The Jewish religion and Judaism's God do not require mortification of the flesh, dissolution of the ego, transcendence of the emotions, submission of the will, or suppression of the uniqueness of each human life, as so many other religions do. Yet under the sway of a civilization and a culture in which these other ideologies predominate, many Jews fall victim to their tacit definitions of God and of our duties to Him, erroneously taking their truths to be our own.

Our God is not like that at all. He made us to be free-thinking, endowed with creativity and the strength of will to exert dominion over His creation to further the material, intellectual, moral, and spiritual progress of human beings and human institutions. The nineteenth-century Italian kabbalist Rabbi Israel Benamozegh described us as being in "partnership with God,"[1] created with free will, and thus able to "[exert] influence on the entire universe, both consciously and unconsciously."[2] God has great confidence in us and gave us all the tools that we will need. In fact, Rabbi Benamozegh adds, "the law of God and the law of man are single and identical, for cooperation is possible only if both parties take inspiration from the same thought, if they follow a single rule."[3]

Why would God entrust so much to us? According to Rabbi Benamozegh, the answer is simple: "[We have] the duty of participating in the divine plan: that is, to improve the works of God instead of allowing them to degenerate."[4] A more contemporary voice, Rabbi Neil Gillman, explains that "God and humanity are partners in redemption"[5]—in saving, repairing, and healing the world; in promoting justice and preventing war; and in attending to the public welfare. God needs us, to join with Him in completing a task that is ours alone to complete, not His. "There is," Rabbi Gillman concludes, "no more powerful statement of God's dependence on humanity."[6]

Surely, this is a God Who thinks the world of us, not one who demands austerities or requires ascetic devotions—repressions of our true self for some imagined spiritual end. God wants us to live our lives to their fullest, using all of our precious intellectual, emotional, and physical capacities. After all, He created those capacities for a grand purpose, and like the psalmist, we pray, "May the Lord fulfill His purpose for me" (Psalms 138:8).

THE LETTERS OF GOD'S NAME

To love God, we must come to know Him. But we must come to know Him not according to descriptions of the deity in other religions and not according to the means that other faiths endorse. We cannot afford to let non-Jewish traditions define what for us is a distinctively Jewish relationship. Ours is a personal connection with God that emerges from the uniqueness of our covenant, and it is unlike the relationship that any other people has with God. It is not better or deeper or more important, just different—but nonetheless perfect for us. Moreover, it defines the terms by which we come close to God, by which we accomplish His will for us, and by which we express our gratitude to Him.

Specifically, we know God through our encounters with Him, through our engagement of the divine. These include those encounters that He initiated—the revelation at Sinai, "Thy greatness and Thy strong hand" (*B'rakhot* 32a) that have sustained us throughout our history—and those that we initiate—through studying His revelation to us, worshipping and praising Him for His faithfulness to us, and fulfilling His commandments to us. The beloved Rabbi Levi Yitzchak, the eighteenth-century Berditchever Rebbe, in his *d'rash* on *Parashat Vayyera*, taught that

> anyone who wishes to be worthy and to come to some comprehension of Him has no choice but to come to Him by means of three types of service: study of Torah, prayer, and acts of charity. These are, so to speak, the letters of God's Name.[7]

Rabbi Elliot N. Dorff, contemporary Jewish author, has written at great length on this topic. In his aptly titled *Knowing God*, he details the various ways in which Jews can come to know God, drawing upon his own personal search.[8] We may come to know God through the words of His revelation to us, in the Torah, in *halakhah* and the interpretations of the rabbis, and in the study and public reading of sacred texts. We may come to know God through prayers—spoken, chanted, sung; communal, personal; liturgical, expressive. We may come to know God through our actions and those of God Himself—

by fulfilling our religious duties and by experiencing God's justice and goodness.

Rabbi Dorff is ambiguous about the eventual outcome of this quest to know God. His book is subtitled "Jewish Journeys to the Unknowable." But this is okay, he notes: "Faith is like that: if it is alive and stimulating, it forever raises new questions as it resolves old ones."[9]

So let us summarize what we have discussed in this book up to now. We are directed to love God. This we are to do with "all your heart and with all your soul and with all your might" (Deuteronomy 6:5). We can achieve this through fulfilling our covenant with God, which entails performing specific *mitzvot* involving our minds, hearts, and actions. These obligations, fulfilled, define an observant Jewish life. To understand these obligations, we first must know God, the One to Whom they pertain. To come to know Him, we are implored to attend to the same three things—*torah, avodah, g'milut chasadim*—that elsewhere define loving Him and also define the fullness of a Jewish life lived to its potential.

Superficially, there may seem to be considerable circularity in all of this reasoning. Through "these three things," we may know God. Once we know God, we will inevitably wish to follow His plan for our lives. This we do through "these three things." Ultimately, we will come to love Him, which we express through "these three things." Does this make sense? What comes first? What happens in what order? What does this mean, in practical terms, for our lives?

With a bit of insight, we can come to recognize the essential identity—the oneness—and the simultaneity of all of these ways of engaging the divine. Knowing God, serving or obeying God, loving God—these are different facets of the same underlying relationship whereby we "hold fast to the Lord your God" (Joshua 23:8). They all bespeak the same affectionate bond between the Creator of the universe and "my treasured possession among all the peoples" (Exodus 19:5). They all go hand in hand, as in Moses' words that to "choose life" we do so "by loving the Lord your God, heeding His commands, and holding fast to Him" (Deuteronomy 30:20), and thus, according to the rabbis, "honor will come in the end" (*N'darim* 62a). They all sit upon the same three-legged stool, the same "these three things." Clearly, this is a motif of wide-ranging application and enduring power and salience for Judaism.

Besides the citations of *Pirke Avot* and elsewhere, noted in Chapters 1 and 2, Jewish literature is replete with reference to learning, worship, and righteous behavior as the three divine paths that lead us to our closest encounter with God. For example, the psalms contain these beautiful couplets:

Faithfulness and truth meet; justice and well-being kiss. Truth springs up from the earth; justice looks down from heaven. (Psalms 85:11–12)

Truth is the familiar *emet*; justice is in the form of *tzedek*. The word translated as "faithfulness" is actually *chesed* (kindness), and well-being is how the New Jewish Publication Society (NJPS) translation renders *shalom*. We can deduce from these psalms something akin to a divine syllogism (almost): kindness equals truth; justice equals peace; humans are a source of truth, thus of kindness; God is a source of justice, thus of peace. Kindness, truth, justice, peace—all intertwined in a beautiful *mandala*.

As another example, the Midrash contains a succinct summary of Moses' greatness:

[Y]ou find in the case of Moses that he gave his life to the pursuit of three things and they were called by his name. They are the following: Justice, the Torah, and the Tabernacle. (Numbers Rabbah 12:9)

Here is the same nod to learning, worship, and justice—just using different words and in a different order and applied descriptively to one historical figure rather than prescriptively to the whole of the Jewish people.

The Talmud contains an interesting conversation regarding the 613 *mitzvot* given to Moses (*Makkot* 23b–24a). Among all of the myriad positive and negative commandments, can it be said that there is a smaller group of precepts that encompass the total—a *sine qua non*, an essential bottom line? If so, what are these commandments?

The starting point for this discussion is the Torah verse in which God says to Moses, "You shall keep My laws and My rules, by the pursuit of which man shall live" (Leviticus 18:5). In the Mishnah, Rabbi Shimon interpreted this to mean, "Lo, whoever sits and does no transgression—they give him a reward like that which goes to one who [goes and] does a religious duty" (*M. Makkot* 3:15). This is followed by Rav Chanania ben Akashia, who added, "The Holy One, blessed be he, wanted to give merit to Israel, therefore he gave them abundant Torah and numerous commandments" (*M. Makkot* 3:16).

In the G'mara, Rabbi Simlai noted that of the 613 *mitzvot*, only 611 were actually given through Moses. He proved both by *g'matria* and by reasoning that the first two commandments were heard proclaimed directly from God.

Rav Hamnuna then noted that David reduced these to eleven essential commandments: walking uprightly, working for righteousness, speaking truth, avoiding slander, doing no evil, avoiding reproach of one's neighbor, despising a vile person, honoring those who fear the Lord, honoring an oath even when hurt, lending without interest, and taking no bribes (Psalms 15:1–5). Various rabbis were then given as exemplars of one or another of these ethically virtuous behaviors.

The G'mara records that Isaiah reduced these further to six principles—walking righteously, speaking uprightly, despising gain from oppression, eschewing bribes, stopping one's ears from hearing of blood, and shutting one's eyes to evil (Isaiah 33:15–16)—and that Micah reduced them to three: do justly, love mercy, and walk humbly before God (Micah 6:8).

Isaiah, it is noted, then reduced these to two: "Observe what is right (*mishpat*) and do what is just (*tz'dakah*)" (Isaiah 56:1), variant ways to imply "justice."

Finally, Amos is credited with reducing the commandments to one: "Seek Me, and you will live" (Amos 5:4).

Rav Nachman bar Yitzchak closed the discussion by asking rhetorically whether Amos should not instead have said, "Seek Me by observing the whole Torah and live." The answer: "But it is Havakkuk who came and based them all on one [principle], as it is said, 'But the righteous shall live by his faith' [Habakkuk 2:4]."

From 613 commandments to 611 to eleven to six to three to two to one, it is not hard to discern the same three themes manifested throughout these various lists. One theme, however, predominates: in our relationship with God, certain obligations are eternal, foremost among which are those involving ethical behavior to our fellow human beings. Whether expressed as justice, righteousness, charity, mercy, or kindness, it is through our moral actions toward others that we best fulfill, and represent, the covenant that we affirmed with God. These actions, in turn, tell the world who we are and Who our God is. They are the means by which the world knows our God and by which we recognize Him and each other.

KNOWING GOD AND LOVING GOD

Many years ago, an academic medical colleague wrote to me, telling me of her struggle to come to a place in her life where she could feel a sense of loving connection with God. She asked for my thoughts and suggestions. This matter was a source of grief for her, as she longed to experience that sense of divine love written about by so many mystics throughout history. She was resolute and earnest in her quest, hopeful for some trigger that would open the floodgates of feeling. She was anxious for this to happen, as she looked forward to drawing on such feelings of love in fostering deeper connections with other people. Was there some sort of spiritual practice that I could recommend, she asked, such as a type of meditation?

This letter was a challenge for me. I had never been asked anything like this before and, to be honest, had never given the matter much thought. I responded the best that I could, drawing upon my modest awareness of what I believed was a Jewish perspective on her question. I do not believe that my colleague was Jewish, but I never inquired.

My response was that the straightest, most direct path to what she sought could be found through compassionate acts of service to others. This she was already expert at through her successful medical practice. Rather than trying to engineer a feeling through a spiritual practice of some type and then hoping that the feeling would motivate a desire to behave more lovingly, perhaps one would do best to turn the equation on its head. If we first devote ourselves to doing good without waiting for the requisite emotion or affect to surface, then maybe that feeling of love will eventually emerge anyway, as a sort of grace.

I never did hear back from my colleague, but in the years since, I have not stopped thinking about our brief correspondence. Some Jewish voices would affirm that a cognitive or emotional connection to God ideally precedes our reciprocal actions toward God and/or others. For example, Rabbi Aryeh Kaplan recognized that "the more aware we become of God's love for us, the more open become to loving God."[10] This may be so for many people and is a wonderful thing, but I would respectfully also flip this around: the more we express our love of God—through loving actions toward others—the more we may become aware of His love for us and experience any concomitant good feelings.

Admittedly, this runs somewhat counter to the default new age philosophy that dominates so much of popular consciousness, whereby we are told that our thoughts and feelings are as important as, perhaps more important than, our actions. Moreover, our *kavvanah*, or intentions, are paramount—the wrong intentions will invalidate an otherwise good deed. Likewise, the best of intentions will make up for and excuse an otherwise catastrophic act, even a destructive political decision or social policy. The most important thing to do when a situation requires immediate action, we are told, is first to wrestle with how one feels about it. Only when that is worked out should one then move forward.

There is nothing remotely Jewish about this perspective. When faced with a moral imperative, we are told that "the people who know their God shall be strong, and take action" (Daniel 11.32). There is no reward in emotional deliberation when there is a clear moral act to be taken. There is no time to ensure that our feelings or motivations are fully crystallized or in sync with some ideology or framework when there are lives to be saved or good to be done. The Lubavitcher Rebbe reiterated, "It is primarily our actions and not our intent which G-d judges."[11] The Talmud elaborates: "Rav Yehuda said in Rav's name: 'A man should always occupy himself with Torah and good deeds, though it is not for their own sake, for out of [doing good] with an ulterior motive there comes [doing good] for its own sake'" (*P'sachim* 50b).

In short, the worst of motives for a good deed—monetary reward, political favor, fame, respect, power—do not override the goodness of the action. They do not negate whatever benefit came to the recipient. Such intentions may not bespeak an entirely wholesome or well-adjusted person, but they are not implicitly sinful and do not necessarily signify anything wicked. What is evil, indeed among the worst evil that Judaism can imagine, is "to subvert the cause of the poor, to rob of their rights the needy of My people" (Isaiah 10:2)—to avert one's eyes so that "the poor and the needy seek water, and there is none" (Isaiah 41:17).

One's intentions, while important to the doer in terms of his or her spiritual growth, are not as important as whether or not one performs a positive commandment of the type that will benefit others. The best of intentions surrounding every nuance of a *mitzvah* are not required in order to accomplish it. Likewise, the worst of intentions are of minimal consequence if the thought of a terrible sin cows its thinker into never committing it.

In an odd way, this discussion of intentions and actions reminds me of the furor that followed the comments of then presidential candidate Jimmy Carter nearly four decades ago, when he admitted in an interview that he was guilty of having feelings of "adultery in my heart many times."[12] This presumably had never resulted in actual adulterous behavior, thank God, but from the sniping of political commentators, one would think that he had admitted to a grave sin that made him unfit for office. Apparently, distortions of the Puritan ethos still hold considerable sway in large segments of the (Christian) United States. Apparently, too, negotiating the intersecting paths connecting our duties, motives, intentions, thoughts, and actions requires a complex calculus.

For Judaism, such complexity is not inherently present. This is because we are not nearly as concerned about the doer of a *mitzvah* as about the recipient. What truly matters is that justice is done, charity is given, kindness is shared, hospitality is received. Ours is not a religion focused above all on growing self-actualized, self-realized masters. Our focus is on repairing the world, redeeming the sparks, acting compassionately and swiftly as God's agents in the world in which we live, the world that He created. Our aim is to heal the brokenhearted, comfort the sick, provide for the needy, bring justice to the oppressed, and so on. This is what God demands from us. This is how we love Him. If we benefit besides, psychologically or materially, then all the better, but this is not our main objective. This is not why we do good. In any event, our most sublime personal benefit will not be received until we reach the world to come.

Our goal in life, as Jews, is to be "a holy people unto the Lord thy God" (Deuteronomy 7:6) and thus part of a collective effort seeking *tikkun olam*, or repair of the world. We have a responsibility to God and to the world, implicit in the covenant that our ancestors consecrated at Sinai. As was noted before, we do not define our life's purpose in terms of an individual drama of personal salvation. Personal attainments— even one as significant as the advancement of our soul—are not our primary focus. Rather, we are to occupy ourselves more with our brothers' and sisters' souls, bellies, and freedom than with our own.

Not to worry, though; this does us no disservice or harm. It pays to keep in mind that we *are* our brothers and sisters: "And the Lord said: 'Behold, they are one people'" (Genesis 11:6). What we do for others, we are also doing for ourselves.

There is nothing wrong with seeking enlightenment, spiritual growth, and self-actualization, of course. Our world needs more enlightened and actualized people, whether Jew or gentile. But for Jews, our Godly actions must by necessity precede our ultimate enlightenment. We cannot afford for it to be the other way around, and, by design, it is not.

The Ramchal noted that "the purpose of the creation of the human species is that man should become worthy of attaining true good, namely, being drawn close to Him."[13] So in a sense, actualization and spiritual growth and intimate connection with God do constitute our destiny as Jews. But we cannot fulfill this destiny if it is all that we care about and all that we seek. According to the Ramchal,

> The preparation of the individual is his attainment of perfection through his deeds. . . . The everlasting recompense of the worthy individual is a bond of closeness with Him forever.[14]

This describes a kind of cosmic paradox, but a sweet one. We are destined to know God, but we cannot ever do so by direct efforts to do so. We can know God only by first turning our focus elsewhere, to performing the loving actions toward others that He decrees. In the end, we are promised, this will transform the world, completing His work and returning us home to His presence. For other religions, spirituality and piety are end goals. For Judaism, the only kinds of spirituality and piety that matter are the ones that remind us, "I the Lord am your God: follow My laws and be careful to observe My rules" (Ezekiel 20:19).

There is thus no better way to know God intimately, to know His true nature, than to perform the *mitzvot* regarding lovingkindness that He revealed to Moses. In fact, the Torah tells us that this is how we can become like Him.

In Jeremiah, an inspiring verse describes the depth of God's love for humankind:

> *From afar the Lord appeared unto me. "Yea, I have loved thee with an everlasting love; therefore with affection have I drawn thee.'" (Jeremiah 31:2)*

This is from the original Jewish Publication Society (JPS) translation, and it is quite beautiful. The NJPS revises "therefore with affection have I drawn thee" to read, "Therefore I continue My grace to you." The Koren Tenakh translation changes it to "therefore I have remained true to thee." The original, however, is the best and most literal. The words translated as "love" and "affection" are both variants of the Hebrew word *ahavah*, love, whose root *ahv* "signifies not only emotion but also action."[15] When we act out of love, including *ahavat chesed*, love of kindness, we are reflecting the One who drew us, how we were drawn, and thus exactly who we are.

Knowing God through loving Him and loving God through actions that lead us to know Him define a singularly Jewish map to enlightenment. It is a *dharma*, if you will, quite unlike that of any other religion. Our relationship to the world of manifested things, of material reality, of the physical flesh bears little resemblance to what is taught by other faiths. Judaism does not require mortification and renunciation, as in Christianity, or nonattachment and transcendence, as in Buddhism. This is because, for us, the physical world and humankind are neither inherently wicked nor inherently illusory.

For Jews, God's creation is full of marvelous things that we can use to fashion goodnesses that are now present only in their potential. God has given us the building blocks; it is up to us to do something with them. This arrangement is a fruit of

God's love for us and provides us with a means for expressing our love for Him in return.

In *How to Be a Jew*, Rabbis Byron L. Sherwin and Seymour J. Cohen insightfully explore this issue. They explain, "For the rabbis, love of God was not to be a rare emotion, restricted to a spiritual elite in fleeting moments of rapture, but a perpetual opportunity, an everyday activity."[16] These opportunities are ongoing, ever presenting themselves to us as long as any portion of the world remains unredeemed. Nothing can be more loving than to occupy oneself with this unfinished work. "In this view, loving is doing. Love is not a prelude to action, but action itself."[17] If we love God by accepting this yoke, "and so God will join us" (*Zohar* 1:157a); he will continue to provide us with opportunities to partner with Him.

That there exists an intrinsically Jewish pathway toward enlightenment, whose steps and endpoints are defined in specifically Jewish context, is not an original idea. The Ramchal, for one, treated this issue in depth in *Mesillat Yesharim*, one of the enduring classics of Jewish ethics and piety.[18] This work was an elaboration of the words of the saintly Rav Pinchas ben Yair, who formulated ten steps by which we may come close to God (*Avodah Zarah* 20b).

More recently, Rabbi David A. Cooper, in his wonderful book *God Is a Verb*, restated and expanded this model in terms conducive to an integration of traditional Jewish teaching and modern contemplative practices.[19] Rabbi Cooper, a leading figure in the Jewish Renewal movement, explored at great length what he termed "the path of the *tzaddik*":

> *Learning leads to respect, respect leads to generosity, generosity leads to acts of lovingkindness, acts of lovingkindness lead to moderation in living, moderation in living leads to purity of thought, purity of thought leads to joy, joy leads to selflessness, selflessness leads to awe, awe leads to equanimity, equanimity leads to extraordinary mind-states, and extraordinary mind-states lead to life eternal (God consciousness).*[20]

This represents as carefully crafted a description of the Jewish path to actualization and enlightenment as one can find by a contemporary rabbi. These twelve steps, fulfilled, represent a mix of intellectual, emotional, and behavioral masteries culminating in our invitation into "the inner sanctum of God."[21] Note the several steps that have unmistakably ethical resonance in terms of our relationships with others: respect, generosity, lovingkindness, moderation in living, selflessness. Rabbi Cooper's model reveals the inseparability of the journeys that we take to know God, to love God, to serve Him and others, and to grow in awareness. They are the same journey; they end where they began—in God—and "these three things" represent our signposts.

LOVING GOD THROUGH JEWISH LEARNING

The "letters of God's name" spoken of by the Berditchever Rebbe define three distinct paths by which we may come to know God. *Talmud torah* and *avodah*—Jewish learning and worship—together with ethical and charitable actions: these are the main roads on the map directing us to God. These are the answers to the question "How do we love God?"

This metaphor that I have used, of signposts along a road, is really more than a metaphor, and it is not original. In Jeremiah, God speaks of how He yearns for Ephraim: "I will receive him back in love—declares the Lord" (Jeremiah 31:20). Immediately afterward, as if to tell us specifically how we are to be received in love, we are told, "Erect markers, set up signposts; keep in mind the highway, the road that you traveled. Return, Maiden Israel!" (Jeremiah 31:21).

Just as humans are composed of mind, heart, and body, so do the ways in which we can love God involve the operation of these same three parts of ourselves consecrated to holy service. Each one is its own road, and each has its specific markers.

We may love God through using our mind for study of sacred texts—for thinking, learning, reasoning, and applying our intellect to understand God's desires for us. This is no easy task, as according to the Talmud, "Rabbi Dostai b. Rabbi Yannai preached [as follows]: 'Observe that the ways of God are not like the ways of flesh and blood'" (*Bava Batra* 10a). True Torah learning involves more than consumption and memorization of texts; it requires diligence (*Sanhedrin* 38b), and it requires discernment, which comes from God (Proverbs 2:6).

We may love God through using our heart, and spirit, for worship—through prayers, meditations, and participation in the rhythms and cycles of Jewish life. Requisite instructions and guidance are found throughout the prayer book and liturgy. These devotions of the heart encompass the myriad rites and practices that make up a Jewish home and life lived Jewishly—the customs, observances, and *b'rakhot*, formal or informal, individual or familial or communal, that define what it means to live in Jewish space and Jewish time and to sanctify them. No wonder the sages refer to prayer as a "manifestation of sanctification" (*B'rakhot* 21b).

We may love God through behaving according to the ethical precepts that God gave to us. In this way, we consecrate our bodies, our flesh, to serving God. This duty is so cherished, we are told in the Midrash, that our ancestor Jacob "purchased the birthright in order that he might serve God" (Exodus *Rabbah* 5:7). As Jews, we are charged with performing our uniquely constituted *mitzvot*. This call is unequivocal: "Hear the terms of this covenant, and perform them" (Jeremiah 11:6).

While these are three distinct pathways leading us to God, they are certainly not unconnected. Torah learning and praying with others, while involving our intellect and emotions, respectively, are both actions we undertake using our bodies, and both fulfill commandments to us. Acts of kindness and acts of service, as well as inspiring insights gained through reading the *parashiyyot*, make us feel happy. Learning the truth about God's intent for us leads us to worship Him in our hearts and to care for the physical and material needs of others.

Study of the Torah and the writings of the sages—contained in the Talmud, Midrash, and later works—is especially valued. Of the three pillars of *Pirke Avot*, learning Torah is considered by some authorities to be the first among equals— "it surpasses them all" (*Shabbat* 127a). This is true of Torah learning for its own sake and for instrumental ends.

Concomitantly, neglect of the study of scripture is considered a moral laxity: "Those who forsake the Torah praise the wicked" (Proverbs 28:4). The consequences are personal, as well: "Rabbi Tabi said in the name of Rabbi Yosiah: 'Whoso is faint in the study of the Torah will have no strength to stand in the day of trouble'" (*B'rakhot* 63a).

Reading, studying, and learning from sacred Jewish texts is therefore important because of the benefits to us of the knowledge contained in the words of God, of Moses, of the prophets, and of the rabbis. But *talmud torah* also matters because this is how we ultimately recognize the holiness inherent in God's creation and the role that we have as God's agents in unlocking this holiness.

Renowned talmudic scholar and rabbi Professor Jacob Neusner has discussed this issue at length, emphasizing the remarkable implications for our self-identity as Jews:

> *We are made in God's image. And that part of us which is like God is not corporeal. It is the thing which separates humanity from the beast: the mind, consciousness. When we use our minds, we are acting like God.*[22]

But this is not all. Professor Neusner adds that "studying Torah is not merely imitating God, who does the same, but is a way to the apprehension of God and the attainment of the sacred."[23] This apprehension and this attainment, in turn, are essential for us if we are to fulfill our divinely dictated role as God's agents in the world. Throughout history, Neusner concludes, "Learning reshaped man into the likeness of God and therefore endowed him with God's powers of creation."[24]

The crucial role played by Torah learning in undergirding our efforts to repair the world was recognized almost universally by the sages. Even particular rabbis who are typically cited as endorsing an extremely rationalistic approach to structuring Jewish life and our relationship with God recognized that a clear understanding of Torah was essential for us for more than the obvious reason: that an ignorant people would not be able to live according to Jewish law. Understanding the Torah was also seen as key to inciting greater piety and attainment of spirituality among individual Jews and to motivating virtuous behavior toward others in its various manifestations.

In the immortal *Moreh Nevukhim*, better known as *Guide for the Perplexed*, the Rambam discoursed on the familiar Torah verse that tells us how we are to "love the Lord your God" (Deuteronomy 6:5). Study of the scriptures is requisite for our understanding of this *mitzvah*, he stated, because "this love is only possible when we comprehend the real nature of things, and understand the divine wisdom displayed therein."[25]

But learning Torah just so that we may glorify God in our words or in our heart does not exhaust the merit of study.

Rather, we must study the Torah so that we can understand its clear intent and thus apply ourselves to fulfilling the ethical *mitzvot* contained therein. In affirming this point, Maimonides spoke in a decidedly prophetic voice:

> The reason of a commandment, whether positive or negative, is clear, and its usefulness evident, if it directly lends to remove injustice, or to teach good conduct that furthers the well-being of society, or to impart a truth which ought to be believed either on its own merit or as being indispensable for facilitating the removal of injustice or the teaching of good morals.[26]

Sixteenth-century philosopher Rabbi Yehudah Loew of Prague, known as the Maharal, also endorsed the instrumentality of Torah learning, both for the Torah learner and for the Jewish people. In *Netivot Olam*, the Maharal acknowledged that Torah has much to offer even beyond the wisdom gained by its study. Drawing upon scriptural and talmudic sources, he explained,

> The Torah is likened to a life-giving balm for man. A physician applies the balm on a person externally, and through the balm comes life. Similarly, the Torah is apart from a person but adheres to him—like a balm which remains external but adheres to the person.[27]

A noted contemporary figure, Rabbi Rifat Sonsino, nicely affirms these main points and elaborates. Torah learning is valued for its own sake but also because it points toward a deepening of our journey to know God:

> In Jewish life, talmud torah *rarely exists in a vacuum. Often prayer and other types of spiritual paths accompany it. Study leads to knowledge, knowledge raises the sense of wonder, and this sense of awe is the basic ingredient of prayer, which for some is a prominent gateway to spirituality.*[28]

To summarize, Torah study produces thoughts, which elicit emotions, which in turn inspire actions. Actions, too, drive feelings and force us to rethink our tacit assumptions. Because the study of Torah and the study of its fruits are thus inseparable, perhaps we ought not overextend the poetic distinction among mind, heart, and body. All of these are interdependent parts of a unified human being.

Still, sacred learning is special, because it is the foundation for all that comes after. *Talmud torah* is therefore accorded a place of high honor among the ways in which we can come to know and love God.

A famous *mishnah* says, "But the study of Torah is equal to them all" (*M. Peah* 1:1). This is in reference to "things the benefit of which a person enjoys in this world, while the principal remains for him in the world to come" (*M. Peah* 1:1), such as bringing honor to one's parents, practicing acts of lovingkindness, and making peace.

A reasonable way to interpret this *mishnah* is to recognize that Torah equals the sum of these great *mitzvot* because, taken to heart, it leads to them. More to the point, it *must* lead to them, or it has been in vain. Rabban Gamliel, son of Rabbi Yehudah Hanasi, was even more blunt: "And all learning of Torah which is not joined with labor is destined to be null and cause sin" (*Pirke Avot* 2:2). This is followed shortly after by one of my favorite passages in the Jewish canon. In Rabbi Shapiro's charming translation, it reads, "Hillel used to say: 'More flesh, more worms. . . . More Torah, more Life'" (*Pirke Avot* 2:7).[29]

In other words, truly it can be said of Torah, "She is a tree of life to those who grasp her" (Proverbs 3:18). But this tree must be cared for so that it bears fruit. Otherwise, God forbid, it will die and become fodder for worms. Torah learning must be translated into positive actions; otherwise, even the best of intentions are useless. This is an insight shared by rabbis across the Jewish religious spectrum.

The nineteenth-century Reform Rabbi Moses Mielziner noted that "even the highest knowledge is of no value, as long as it does not influence our moral life."[30] A half century later, Reform Rabbi Abba Hillel Silver echoed this point when he said, "A spiritual concept or an ethical ideal is desirable only to the extent that it is serviceable to man and society."[31] Rabbi Ismar Schorsch, former chancellor of Jewish Theological Seminary, affirmed, "Salvation in Judaism is about losing ourselves in the welfare of the whole and making a difference in the lives of others."[32]

The great twentieth-century British talmudic scholar Rabbi Abraham Cohen differentiated between "study of the torah"

and "the practice of torah."[33] The latter was the "basic purpose" of the former, namely, "to provide the Jewish people
with a body of teaching which should be more than a creed,
but also a guide of life in every phase."[34] Professor Cohen noted
that *talmud torah* is typically criticized on grounds that it has
"entangled the Jew in the bonds of legalism so that he was
bound hand and foot, and lost all sense of freedom and spirituality."[35] This view he attributed to "outsiders" and "receives
not the slightest corroboration,"[36] he asserted, in the canon
itself. Sadly, I suspect that many Jews, outsiders not by birth
but perhaps by lack of Jewish learning, may profess the same
erroneous view.

LOVING GOD THROUGH JEWISH WORSHIP

Jewish learning is a path to loving God because, through
talmud torah, we get to know God and we get to know what
God expects of us. Fulfilling our destiny as Jews, through informed actions in this world, spreads holiness and makes a
fitting "dwelling-place for the Mighty One of Jacob" (*Z'vachim*
54b). In this way, engaging our mind and our intellect serves
to tighten our bond to God.

Engaging our heart and our emotions also serves to
strengthen our connection with God. More perhaps than learning and even good deeds, this is what we are most likely to
think of when we imagine what it means to love God.

Concepts such as *avodah, t'fillah, emunah, kavvanah, chasidut,
hitlahavut, devekut*—worship, prayer, faith, intention, devotion,
ecstasy, union—these all describe emotion-driven or emotion-
laden practices or states related to our adoring the Source of
our being. They involve mainly the life of the spirit rather than
solely the life of the mind. They are felt, experienced. They
describe our communion with God. While words may be invoked or actions undertaken, the path of the heart is distinct,
beyond words and actions.

Ironically, it is through worship and prayer that we may
be able to access wisdom and understanding far deeper than
any attainable through study. Our senses heightened, including our subtle intuitions and perceptions and our attunements
to spirit, we may find reality and truth revealing itself to us in
ways that we could never hope for by even the most earnest
attention to sacred texts.

The great *tzaddik* Rabbi Abraham Joshua Heschel once said, "To pray is to take notice of the wonder, to regain a sense of the mystery that animates all beings, the divine margin in all attainments."[37] Rabbi Heschel's life was a testament to how this wonder, this recognition of the "divine margin," could drive a life devoted to furthering social justice and goodwill among all people. Equal parts Jewish mystic and radical political activist, he worked to respiritualize contemporary Judaism, urging reconsideration of ancient Jewish traditions such as *shabbat* while marching for civil rights at Selma.

Prayer is not a solitary act, divorced from the wider context of Jewish worship and Jewish life. It takes many forms and is our lifeline to the One Who makes clear the unclear in our world. A different voice, Rabbi Joseph B. Soloveitchik, favored a drier, more functional definition: "Prayer is an awareness of man finding himself in the presence of and addressing himself to his Maker, and to pray has one connotation only: to stand before God."[38]

Nevertheless, it would be wrong to see prayer as purely directional—something originating in us and aimed at God. Jewish prayer is as much about God's encounter with us as it is about our encounter with Him. This was a point emphasized by Rabbi Heschel in his aptly titled *God in Search of Man*.[39]

Several years ago, in a scholarly work prepared for a social science conference on the study of religion, I discussed the multiformity of prayer both among and within respective religions.[40] Jewish prayer, especially, is notable for its implicit diversity—in its functions and forms and its reflection of the myriad temporal cycles of Jewish life. Always, regardless of the themes invoked, prayer is about our relationship with God and how we characterize ourselves in the moment in relation to Him.

Across Jewish traditions and throughout our sacred writings, prayer is described and defined in many ways. In the psalms, in the Torah, in Rashi, and in our sages from the Ramchal to more contemporary rabbis, various themes emerge: prayer as sacrifice, prayer as a way to connect with God's ubiquitous presence, prayer as an expression of gratitude, prayer as a way to access God's will for us, prayer as an opportunity given by God to approach Him, prayer as a way to explore the symbolism of spiritual spaces hidden deep within our psyches.[41]

What forms does all this praying take?

In an earlier scholarly article that I wrote with my colleague Professor Robert Joseph Taylor, distinguished sociologist at the University of Michigan, we summarized the significant variations in the meaning, role, and norms of praying just among observant Jews.[42] For example, regular synagogue attendance, such as for daily *minyan* or *shabbat* services, may occur principally or solely to enable the communal recitation of certain prayers—the *Bar'khu, Amidah, Aleinu, Kaddish*. In private, other prayers are said at prescribed times daily (the *Sh'ma, Birkhat Hamazon*), weekly (the *b'rakhah* for the *shabbat* candles), monthly (at *rosh chodesh*), yearly (*Kol Nidre*), or as specific circumstances arise (*Yizkor, Mi Shebeirakh, Shehecheyanu*).[43]

Still other prayers are prayed, alone or collectively, in public or private, according to codified liturgies or spontaneously and informally. Cantor Macy Nulman's excellent resource, *The Encyclopedia of Jewish Prayer*, exceeds 400 pages and includes reference to thousands of individual Jewish prayers and blessings.[44] Truly, we are a prayerful people, with a prayer (or several) for any occasion. The Talmud even states that each of us is "bound to say one hundred blessings daily" (*M'nakhot* 43b), a tradition that originated with David as a way to memorialize the deceased (Numbers *Rabbah* 18:21).

Among the many forms and purposes of prayer is to pray in order to request something from God. A notable example is praying for healing, as for a loved one. The idea that prayers for healing may be therapeutically efficacious, in some regards, is a controversial and contentious issue right now in academic medicine. Despite many negative results, numerous studies have purported to demonstrate, through randomized, double-blind experimental clinical trials, the apparently salutogenic results of distant prayers directed to God on behalf of individuals who are unaware that they are being prayed for or studied.[45] These positive findings have emerged regardless of the religion of the people praying or the people receiving prayer.

Not only have these studies aroused controversy among some scientists and physicians, but their provocative findings have angered and bewildered people of great faith across the spectrum of Christian belief.[46] These results strike a chord, it seems, challenging conventional notions of who their deity is, how and why He responds to the petitions and pleas of the faithful, how and why He seems to ignore the pleas of others, what constitutes a legitimate prayer, what categories of people are eligible for blessing, and what categories of people are not.

Interestingly, these studies have aroused almost no such dissent or discomfort among religious Jews.

For one thing, Jewish history is an unmistakable testimony to the faithfulness of God—to His willingness to respond to prayers sent up from the most desperate of straits. Compared to the exodus and Sinai and the rebuilt Temple and our survival of pogroms and holocausts, the restoring of one from a physical malady seems like a drop in the bucket for our God.

Furthermore, what is usually termed petitionary or supplicatory prayer (*bakkashah*) makes up a far smaller proportion of Jewish prayer, I suspect, than in other religions. This is not to dispute its centrality in Jewish worship, a subject of much rabbinic discussion.[47] Among Jews, however, prayer is about so much more—even prayers prayed for purposes of healing.

When we approach God for the healing of a loved one, it is hard to consider our encounter one of mere petition for a human-defined outcome. The *Mi Shebeirakh*, for example, typically said for the sick, is actually an invocation of a communal blessing. It has many places, traditionally, in the Jewish liturgy and in Jewish customs.[48] Asking God to bless the ill is just one of the uses for this prayer. The words of the *Mi Shebeirakh* ask God for compassion and for strengthening of the soul as well as the body, for all people and all humankind. Throughout our history, it has been said in far more contexts and settings than for healing: at the occasion of an *aliyah* or a fast, upon childbirth or conversion, on anniversaries or birthdays, at sacred times during the year, for the protection of loved ones or the defenders of freedom.

Significantly, then, our most notable prayer for healing is no more just about directing God to fix a broken body than the *Kaddish* is just about lamenting the dead. Both prayers are about praising God, celebrating His gifts to us, and humbly thanking Him for a continuance of wholeness and peace for all beings.

In Judaism, prayer often takes forms other than individual recitation of fixed liturgical formulae. There are singing or chanting of *z'mirot* and *piyyutim*, contemporary or traditional songs and poems of inspiration, and reciting of original homiletical compositions based upon specific scriptures or rabbinic commentaries. In addition, there are the numerous motions of the body—standing, bowing, swaying, stretching on tiptoes, covering the eyes—that enliven and enrich the *Sh'ma*, the *K'dushah*, the *Aleinu*, and miscellaneous *b'rakhot*. The body may also be involved in other ways during prayer, such as the wrapping of the arm and head with *t'fillin*.

It is thus customary for us to worship God with "all my bones" (Psalms 35:10). The Midrash elaborates that David meant what he said, quite literally: "I shall praise Thee with all the parts of my body" (*Midrash T'hillim* 35:2). This included his head, hair, neck, eyes, mouth, lips, beard, tongue, face, throat, heart, breast, back and front, right and left hands, nose, ears, nails, inmost parts, loins, male organ, knees, and right and left feet—all bodily parts used in one instance or another for some worshipful act. For David, as for all Jews, prayer is not a formality, something to be taken lightly. Rather, it requires our full presence and our full being, and it infiltrates the entirety of Jewish worship.

Prayer and worship, accordingly, are not meant to reinforce the separation that exists between us and God but are instead about the experience of God and His *Sh'khinah*, or Divine Presence. The inspiring words of Brother Lawrence, a seventeenth-century French Carmelite, who offered Christian instruction on "practicing the presence of God,"[49] thus would have made sense to communities of Jews of his day and in the present day as well.

This is not to suggest that among our rabbis there is, or ever was, any kind of consensus on how far to take this—how much effort to place on seeking "divine" experiences rather than seeking to function normally in linear, waking consciousness. The importance or value of experiencing a deeper, more intimate knowledge of God than one could expect through normative Jewish practice—this merits our most heartfelt quest, our most steadfast avoidance, or our most dispassionate indifference, depending upon who is consulted. Arcane gnosis acquired through esoteric rites; mystical attainments such as visions of Ezekiel's *merkavah,* or chariot; and other even more fantastic outcomes have been described at one time or another by apostles of a more mystically engaged Judaism.

Jewish history, among both Torah-observant and liberal Jews and especially over the past couple of hundred years, has been underlined by tension and acrimony between rationalists and mystics. While kabbalistic movements and texts have been present since the twelfth century or earlier and their concepts have been in circulation perhaps for millennia,[50] the main ideas of esoteric Judaism did not attain wide currency until the emergence of Chasidism in eastern Europe in the eighteenth century. Its founder, Rabbi Israel ben Eliezer, known as the Baal Shem Tov, was instrumental in translating key kabbalistic teachings, such as regarding the importance of *kavvanah* for Jewish practice, into a practical system that appealed to common folks alienated from talmudic discourse. His work was expanded by those who followed, especially by Rabbi Schneur Zalman, the Baal HaTanya, founder of Chabad, the Lubavitch branch of Chasidism.

Practically an identifying mark of contemporary Chasids is their espousal of joy as a hallmark of Jewish observance. Their embrace of joyousness and happiness as instrumental for *devekut*—as both pathways to and fruits of mystical union with God—bespeaks a valuation of emotions over intellect, heart over mind. Or, more accurately perhaps, they view these respective pairs as being on equal footing rather than downplaying or disregarding the importance of human feeling, of the heart, in Jewish worship and Jewish life.

Initially, this perspective did not enamor Chasids to the rabbinic leadership of the Jewish religion, led by the rabbis of the great Lithuanian and Belarusian *y'shivot,* or rabbinic academies. These included famous institutions such as the Kovno Kollel and Volozhin Yeshivah, schools where, incidentally, my great-grandfather, Rabbi Yehudah Leib Levin, received his training and *s'michah,* or rabbinic ordination, from the respective Rosh Yeshivot, the esteemed Rabbi Yitzchak Elchanan Spektor, and Rabbi Naftali Tzvi Yehuda Berlin (known as the Netziv).[51]

The favoring of prayer and Jewish experience over and above *talmud torah* was considered heterodox at best and an abrogation of the covenant, immoral, and a threat to Jewish survival at worst. The rabbis opposed this movement, often vigorously and stridently—thus their label as *mitnagdim*, or "those who opposed." Upon the emergence sometime later of the *haskalah* movement, or Jewish enlightenment, and a century later upon the arrival of the first German Reformists, tempers cooled and animosities waned in response to what might have been seen as a larger mutual threat.

The descendants of these two groups, the modern-day Chabadniks and Yeshivish Jews, constitute *charedi* or traditional Judaism, known pejoratively in some quarters as "ultra-Orthodox." Together with the modern or centrist Orthodox, based in North America at Yeshiva University and the Orthodox Union, these constitute the major communities of Orthodox Jews in the world today. There is still little consensus among them as to the relative value of reason or emotion in bringing us closer to God.

The past few decades have also seen the emergence of several streams of neo-mysticism within the Jewish religion. The Jewish Renewal movement is an outgrowth of the life, work, and teachings of Rabbi Zalman Schachter-Shalomi, a former Lubavitch Jew educated at the Reform movement's Hebrew Union College and at one time on the faculty of Temple University. Renewal is equal parts Reconstructionist-derived liturgy, *chavurah*-style worship, and an ethos informed by insights from a variety of culturally progressive influences: the human potential and psychedelic movements, transpersonal psychology, feminism, the ecology movement, and circumscribed interfaith encounters.

Jewish Renewal is sometimes disparaged as "new age Judaism" or "hippie Judaism." But this is no more accurate a description than the criticisms of Chasidic Judaism as being anti-intellectual. In both instances, it seems, there is a perceived need to disapprove of forms of religious expression that favor a more balanced and holistic perspective on Jewish spirituality and an openness to heart-centered modes of worship. This is counterproductive, according to Reb Zalman, as "acts of faith are not made on an empty heart."[52]

Renewal is open and welcoming to the gamut of Jewish tradition and, notwithstanding its left-of-center informality, probably fosters more devoted and traditional observance than the other liberal movements in Judaism. It is an able repository for the wisdom of the Jewish mystics. Moreover, in the willingness of its leaders, adherents, and even liturgies to engage the issues of the day—social justice, the environment, civil rights, interreligious dialogue, world peace—it is far less otherworldly in its outlook than is Chasidism.

A lasting and influential outgrowth of Renewal has been the widespread rebirth of interest in meditative practices among Jews. Earlier in our history the province mainly of eccentric kabbalists, Jewish meditation has received spirited endorsement within Renewal *chavurot*. Undoubtedly, this development is an outgrowth of previous experiences among members, a lot of whom are *baalei t'shuvah*, or returners to the fold, at least in a non-Orthodox sense, whose Jewish-mystical formation was influenced by involvement in Eastern religious movements such as Yoga or Zen. Significantly, however, the most authoritative and popular modern texts on Jewish meditation were composed by the late Rabbi Aryeh Kaplan, a beloved and revered paragon of Orthodoxy.[53]

Thus even in their (seeming) heterodoxy, their embrace of modes of experience-seeking that more rationally minded rabbis would reject, followers of Renewal are unmistakably Jewish and in line with Jewish tradition. They are oriented to the here and now, fully in their bodies, embracing the world. Unlike the monastics and dervishes and renunciates of other faiths, Jewish mystics and experientialists of all schools—Chasids and neo-mystics alike—reject ascetic tendencies. They embrace the physical life, including human sexuality in its fullness as expressed in loving monogamous relationships, rather than seeking to deny it or transcend it. These movements are about feeling our connections with God, with great joyousness, not through suppressing the ego and our natural human needs and desires.

By contrast, a well-publicized group of modern-day syncretists, known vernacularly as JUBUs, combine elements of Judaism and Buddhism.[54] In beliefs and practices, the prototypical JUBU is mostly BU and very little JU. JUBUs typically are ethnic Jews, raised observantly or more often secularly, who have traveled abroad, figuratively and often literally, settling into religious lifestyles centered on Buddhist practice according to various traditions, notably Tibetan Buddhism. A smaller cadre of JUBUs, influenced by Buddhism and Hinduism, have incorporated certain Eastern beliefs and practices into their principally Jewish observance. There is a strong JUBU influence within Renewal, but Reb Zalman was always careful about not going "too far out....too far afield,"[55] crossing boundaries that, by necessity, encircle Jewish tradition.

Beyond the Chasids and Renewal and JUBUs on the Jewish-mystical spectrum are various quasi-kabbalistic groups that have flourished in recent years among the disaffected and susceptible. These organizations, built around charismatic teachers, exist at the fringes of Judaism, barely, and appeal to people without much Jewish learning. Some of the most avid followers are wealthy popular culture figures—actors, rock singers—and many are not Jewish. To them, "the kabbalah" is something that one can "do," divorced from any kind of normative Jewish context. Replete with amulets, incantations, zodiacal musings, made-up Hebrew names, and the like, this does not even merit the label of heterodox Judaism. One is reminded of Rabbi Kaplan's admonition that throughout Jewish history, "People who could not reach the spiritual heights of the prophets took the easy way of idolatry and occultism instead."[56]

Of course, most Jews are not mystics or ecstatics or esotericists of any stripe; nor do Chasidism and Renewal comprise more than a small proportion of Jewry. Without devoting one's entire way of life to a Judaism built around mysticism, the daily life of both traditional and liberal Jews engaged in the practice of normative Judaism consists of all sorts of opportunities for heartfelt expression, sharing of meaning-laden and feeling-rich moments with others, and experiencing the gamut of affects and emotions. These opportunities come, most of all, through our loving interactions with and on behalf of other people.

For Jews, prayer and worship do not stand alone. They are to fortify us for something larger. A *b'rakhah*, or blessing, is not considered completed until the action that was consecrated is undertaken.[57] Failure to follow through is considered a *hafsaka*, an unjustified break or interruption, and negates the prayer, even if said with great *kavvanah*.

In that regard, what can be said of Jewish learning can be said too of Jewish worship. Both are legitimate paths leading to God. They are ways for us to know God and ways for us to love God. But their highest service to us is in prodding us to perform ethical acts within the context of the larger communities in which our lives and worship are embedded. As with *torah talmud*, sometimes it is a time not for prayer but for action.

In *Parashat B'shallach*, Moses cries out to God in response to the people's first round of complaints after escaping from Egypt. The Torah records, "Then the Lord said to Moses, 'Why do you cry out to Me? Tell the Israelites to go forward'" (Exodus 14:15). In his learned commentary, Rabbi Yaakov ben Asher, known as the Baal HaTurim, explained what God meant by this:

> For there is a time to shorten [prayer] and a time to lengthen [prayer]. But now is not a time for prayer at all. Rather, "Speak to the Children of Israel and let them journey forth."[58]

This is something that Rabbi Heschel surely would have understood.

Prayerful intent and worshipful feelings, even the most heartfelt and *kavvanah*-laden, without proper follow-up are null. They are mere words or sentiments, emitted from us but reaching nowhere beyond our lips. Bottled up inside and not shared or externalized into action, they are our heart's destruction rather than a means to our community's redemption and flourishing.

LOVING GOD THROUGH ETHICAL BEHAVIOR

By now, it should be understood that I believe our highest duty as Jews—to God, to each other, to all humans—encompasses translating our moral duties and responsibilities as outlined in the Torah into ethical behavior. This transformation of revealed words on a page into human actions is a sacred kind of magic that uniquely defines the Jewish role in the world. Nothing can better exemplify the words of Rabbi Emil Fackenheim, who bluntly stated that "Judaism believes in the co-workership of God and man."[59] God inspired the words; they inspire us to act.

For us to fulfill God's desires for us, individually and as a people, and for His world, we need to take on the great "work of righteousness (*hatz'dakah*) [which] shall be peace (*shalom*)" (Isaiah 32:17). Reading about *tz'dakah*, studying it, and learning about it do not produce *shalom*. Feeling good feelings, enraptured in the love of Torah or of God, also does not produce *shalom*. But if drawing upon God's instructions to us and on the sentiments they arouse within our hearts can awaken us to be His emissaries in the world, then learning and worship can rightly occupy their place as two of the pillars upon which the world stands.

The idea that Jewish observance is more about action than belief is often cited as a truism so self-evident that it requires no further explanation. While this idea as generally expressed is probably overstated—Judaism is not formally creedal, but still, there are ideas and concepts that we all affirm—the consensus on what it means to live a Jewish life, ideally, is indeed constructed around a negotiation of norms of praxis rather than of strict conformance to a code of theoretical beliefs. Christians speak of practical theology, bringing theological insight to bear on issues in daily life, and Roman Catholics use the term "moral theology" to describe the application of theological principles to human conduct. All Jewish theology, I believe, is practical and moral theology.

Rabbis and scholars across the branches of Judaism and throughout history have emphasized the idea that while intellect and spirituality certainly do matter to us, why they matter, above all, is in motivating behavior that is consistent with the commandments that define our covenant with God. Moreover, to best describe what it means to love God, we must appreciate the centrality of ethical behavior as its foundation. If we check the first two boxes, growing Jewishly in mind and heart but insufficiently to motivate us to externalize this growth through ethical actions in the world in which we live, then our Jewish learning and worship are in vain. We have failed to truly love God.

For many years, I have accumulated a file of quotations from rabbis and Jewish scholars affirming this very point. Here is a selection of these.

From Rabbi Elie Munk, leader of the French Orthodox community during World War II, in his great Torah commentary

Kol HaTorah: Judaism instructs us in "the imperative of duty and moral conduct" as a means to obey the command to "love Hashem,"[60] and the Jewish soul is thus satisfied "only through concrete acts aimed at creating the Kingdom of God on earth."[61]

These words echo the author of the fifteenth-century German ethical treatise *Orchot Tzaddikim*, who declared, in the section entitled *"Shaar Haahavah"* (the Gate of Love), that the love of God "endures only for one who undertakes the performance of all the mitzvos," especially those regarding righteous action.[62] Going back even further, we can see this viewpoint in the midrashic work *Tanna Debe Eliyyahu*, in its *d'rash* on Deuteronomy 6:5: "Hence you are to be loving in the give-and-take of everyday life—in your going about in the marketplace and in your dealing with men."[63]

We also find this perspective among more contemporary voices, such as Rabbi Schorsch, who noted in his Conservative Torah commentary *Canon Without Closure* that for Jews "the remedy for the human condition is *mitzvot*, not messianism, deeds and not faith."[64] He went on to explain, "Individual survival and salvation are not Judaism's highest values; its deep sense of community and peoplehood moderates our overriding concern with self."[65] Accordingly, Rabbi Naftali Rothenberg tells us, when we do wrong to another person, "it is done less from hatred than from self-absorption and ignorance of the other's existence."[66]

A recent Torah commentary from Reform Rabbi Seymour Rossel notes that, in Judaism, the love of God is not defined principally as a longing or deep caring for God as much as it is about us "acting as God commanded us to act."[67] Contemporary scholars interpret this action in a fairly uniform way; that is, to "'walk in God's ways' is to respond with compassion to the suffering of others,"[68] "to intimately cling to God [is] through the observance of His law,"[69] and to love your neighbor as yourself (Leviticus 19:18) is "the most important commandment of the Torah."[70]

Professor Lawrence H. Schiffman of Yeshiva University sums this all up most succinctly: "Love of God calls on humans to live an ethical life....Love of God is expressed by observance of God's law."[71] With this in mind, it follows that "apostasy is described as the violation of the trust of love [of God]."[72]

If we are truly to love God, then, our actions are essential—not just any accumulated wisdom about how we should relate to Him or just our good intentions toward others. But what specifically should these actions be? We are to make manifest our love of God through behaving ethically in all our dealings, but are there core principles or concepts that guide us to the kinds of behavior that matter most of all?

Throughout the Torah and the writings of the rabbis, several words appear over and over to signify the kinds of behaviors that God intends for us to pursue. The most commonly used words are variations of *tz'dakah* and *chesed*. Each appears many dozens of times throughout the Torah and the Talmud, translated variously, depending upon the context.

Tz'dakah, or its variants, such as *tzedek*, is usually rendered as justice, as in "Justice, justice shall you pursue, that you may thrive and occupy the land that the Lord your God is giving you" (Deuteronomy 16:20). Note the implied contractual nature of this obligation—an "if, then" relationship. If we are just in all of our dealings, then we will thrive. Alternatively, if we wish to receive God's blessing, then we must act justly.

Sometimes *tz'dakah*, in its various forms, is translated as "righteousness," as in God's call for Israel to repent, spoken through the prophetic words of Ezekiel who explained that "they would save themselves alone by their righteousness" (Ezekiel 14:20). Again, use of *tz'dakah* here implies mutual obligations: deliverance is promised, but only as a consequence of our behavior.

The Midrash poignantly describes the impact of righteousness and righteous people on our world. Rav Pinchas said, "You find that when the righteous are born nobody feels any difference, but when they die everybody feels it" (Ecclesiastes *Rabbah* 7:4). The examples given included Miriam, Aaron, Moses, and Joshua. One also recalls the astonishing public memorial service for Bl. Mother Teresa, when heads of state from nearly half the nations of the earth silently filed past her coffin, one at a time, to pay homage to the saintly Catholic nun.

Whether justice or righteousness, these usages of *tz'dakah* are not all that different. Justice and righteousness could be thought of as different moral tenses of *tz'dakah*. The two concepts are often used in tandem, somewhat interchangeably, often with another Hebrew word signifying justice substituting for *tz'dakah*, such as variations of *mishpat* or *din*, which sometimes have a more legal connotation, as in the word "judgment." Thus, not only does *tz'dakah* have more than one connotation, but for one of these, justice, other semiequivalent words may used as well.

The Midrash spends considerable time discussing the meaning of passages that jointly invoke justice and righteousness, such as "Righteousness and justice (*tzedek umishpat*) are the base of Your throne; steadfast love and faithfulness stand before You" (Psalms 89:15). Rav Levi explained that this is as if God were telling us, "And if you will respect both righteousness and justice I will immediately redeem you with a complete redemption" (Deuteronomy *Rabbah* 5:7). The rabbis noted the double-sided nature of this promise: "God said: 'Since the punishment for [wresting] judgment is so severe, take [great] heed'" (Deuteronomy *Rabbah* 5:1).

As with *tz'dakah*, the word *chesed* takes on different but morally equivalent meanings, depending upon the context. It means kindness, as in "my kindness shall not depart from you" (Isaiah 54:10). Often, it is implicit that this kindness is modified by or infused with love; thus, use of the word "lovingkindness" in many instances. The close connection of kind acts and loving acts, whatever language is used, is recognized widely.

It is this meaning of *chesed* from which derive the important concepts of *g'milut chasidim*, usually translated as "acts of lovingkindness," and *ahavat chesed*, "the love of kindness." The latter was the topic of much moral instruction by the Chofetz Chaim,[73] one of our greatest teachers. The former, of course, is one of "these three things" upon which the world stands. According to Rabbi S. R. Hirsch, it is "the very first trait of godliness."[74]

Chesed is also sometimes translated as "mercy," as when Abraham's servant first encountered the great generosity of Rebekah: "Blessed be the Lord God of my master Abraham, who has not left destitute my master of his mercy and his truth" (Genesis 24:27). This meaning is found especially throughout kabbalistic discourse on the nature of God's name. The word for "God," *Elohim*, designates His attribute of justice, whereas the word for God's name, the unpronounceable tetragrammaton, signifies His attribute of mercy. These two attributes are represented among the holy *s'firot*, or spheres, occupying the *etz chayyim*, or tree of life, a symbolic representation of the sacred concepts and energies that enliven and operate within a human being. Justice here is represented by yet another word, *g'vurah*, which also implies judgment, power, and control. Mercy is denoted by *chesed*, which is said to be "produced by the union of Wisdom & Understanding."[75]

Just as *tz'dakah* means more than justice and justice has other Hebrew equivalents, so too for *chesed* and mercy. The word that is usually translated as "mercy" is *rachamim*. This is found in the Torah, in Daniel's words, "To the Lord our God belong mercy and forgiveness" (Daniel 9:9). It is also found in talmudic (*B'rakhot* 32a) and kabbalistic (*Zohar* 2:19b) discussions of God's "attribute(s) of mercy" in the form of "*middot rachamim*" or "*middot harachamim*." Finally, *chesed* is sometimes also translated as "faithfulness," "goodness," or "love."

In whatever word form and by whatever translation, the concept of mercy is of profound moral significance for Judaism and for the life and spiritual destiny of individual Jews. Eschewing mercy is our surest way to cast off God's veil of protection and speed our path to hell, as the Midrash bluntly warns: "Be careful not to withhold mercy, for whosoever withholds mercy is analogous to transgressors and throws off the yoke of heaven" (*Sifre* Deuteronomy §117).

All of these words and concepts point to significant duties by which we are beholden to each other. The rabbis taught that if one has "occupied thyself with [the study of] the Torah as well as with acts of benevolence (*g'milut chasadim*)," then one will be rescued; not so for one who is occupied with "Torah alone" (*Avodah Zarah* 17b). Worse, according to the Yerushalmi, "And said Rabbi Yochanan, 'It would have been better for a person who learns without concern for practice if his placenta smothered him [at birth] and he never entered the world'" (*Y. B'rakhot* 1:2). Worse still, according to Rav Huna, "He who only occupies himself with the study of the Torah is as if he had no God" (*Avodah Zarah* 17b).

This is affirmed by the Tosefta. Rabbi Yehoshua ben Korcha said that "anyone who loses sight [of the importance of giving] charity [is viewed] as if he worshipped idolatry" (*T. Peah*

4:20). Accordingly, the rabbis declared, "Charity and righteous deeds outweigh all other commandments" (*T. Peah* 4:19).

This theme is prominent elsewhere throughout the Torah and rabbinic writings. Through the prophet Hosea, God tells us, "I desire goodness (*chesed*), not sacrifice" (Hosea 6:6). Likewise, "To do what is right and just (*tz'dakah umishpat*) is more desired by the Lord than sacrifice" (Proverbs 21:3). On this basis, the rabbis concluded that goodness and mercy, righteousness and justice, matter more to God than any sacrifice. Their exemplar was Daniel, who gave alms to the poor. Rabban Yochanan ben Zakkai referred to him as "Daniel, that greatly beloved man, that he was engaged in acts of loving-kindness [all his days]" (*Avot d'Rabbi Natan* 4).

Another great *chesed* is hospitality, or *hakhnasat orchim*. It is so important that the Chofetz Chaim devotes two chapters to it in his *Sefer Ahavat Chesed*. How important? According to the Talmud, "Rabbi Yochanan and Resh Lakish both explain: 'At the time when the Temple stood, the altar used to make atonement for a person; now a person's table makes atonement for him'" (*Chagigah* 27a), that is, by way of the food served to poor guests.

These *mitzvot*, above all others, are so powerful that they were believed to substitute for prescribed rites in the atonement of sins. Since the rabbis were writing at a time in which the Temple no longer existed and the priesthood had no formal cultic role, as in the present day, their subtext was clear: through kindness, we Jews attain redemption.

Thus, even among the ethical *mitzvot*, there is a hierarchy. Charity and justice—two ways to translate *tz'dakah*—great as they are, do not quite measure up to kindness and mercy. According to Rabbi Eleazar, while charity and justice are greater than sacrifice, as we have noted, "*g'milut chasadim* is greater than charity" (*Sukkah* 49b). Why? "Rabbi Eleazar further stated, 'The reward of charity depends entirely upon the extent of the kindness in it'" (*Sukkah* 49b), that is, "the grace, gentleness, and sympathy that accompany the act of charity."[76]

Further, within the category of *chesed*, there are degrees of kindness. In *Sha'are Orah*, the thirteenth-century kabbalist Rabbi Yosef ben Avraham Gikatilla defined several kinds of *chesed*, differentiated on the basis of their contamination with judgment (*din*) in any way. There is *chesed tachton*, or the "lower" lovingkindness, representative of the best efforts of most people. Next are *chesed Avraham* and *chesed David*, whereby great mercy is intertwined with and tempered by judgment; thus, the mercy comes and goes. Finally, there is *chesed elyon*, the "highest" lovingkindness. This is pure *chesed* and is said to emanate directly from heaven.[77]

Among the great kindnesses that merit special mention are three: visiting the sick (*bikkur cholim*); duties to the bereaved or deceased, including attending funerals (*levayat hamet*); and relieving the suffering of animals (*tzaar baalei chayyim*). These are viewed as especially meritorious because of the relative powerlessness of the people or beings that require our attention.

Volumes have been written on the topic of these *mitzvot*, so they need not be dissected here. The seriousness of our charge not to neglect these obligations, however, should be highlighted. Causing pain or suffering to come to a vulnerable person, disrespect to be shown to the deceased, or needless harm to be exercised on an animal all have been equated with the most awful of transgressions. Likewise, our failure to prevent such misdeeds or failure to attempt to rectify them once they have occurred are also grave misdeeds.

The Talmud says, "Rav Akiva went forth and lectured: 'He who does not visit the sick is like a shedder of blood'" (*N'darim* 40a). This is because with each visit to a sick person, according to Rabbi Acha bar Chaninah, "He who visits an invalid takes away a sixtieth of his pain" (*N'darim* 39b). Whether or not this is literally true, if our presence can in any way bring comfort to a suffering friend or loved one, then we are obliged to visit, even if the cost is some measure of inconvenience or discomfort to us.

Our duties to the deceased include establishing a *chevra kaddisha*, or burial society, in every Jewish community, providing a proper burial, and maintaining the dignity of gravesites. These are among the most meritorious of all *mitzvot* because the recipient cannot say thank you or pay reimbursement.[78] Included among these obligations is our responsibility to care for the bereaved who are left behind. God reserves His harshest imprecations for those who violate the command "You shall not ill-treat any widow" (Exodus 22:21): "If you do mistreat them, I will heed their outcry as soon as they cry out to Me, and My anger shall blaze forth and I will put you to the sword" (Exodus 22:22–23).

Similarly, we are to be exceedingly kind to our animal companions. Those animals who do work for us must even be allowed to rest, as we do, on *shabbat*. It is no accident that the *mitzvah* to "cease from labor" (Exodus 23:12) during *shabbat* is given specifically "in order that your ox and your ass may rest, and that your bondman and the stranger may be refreshed" (Exodus 23:12). Much as animals are dependent upon us, so too are we dependent upon them. This is true with respect to their labor, as in the case of beasts of burden or farm animals, and their service, as in the case of seeing-eye dogs. But we also rely on animals for their companionship and emotional support. We are to treat them with the same regard that we give to other members of our family or household.

Of special note are the kindnesses and other obligations that we owe to strangers. Rabbi Silver has described as a measure of the greatness of Judaism our belief that all humans are created equal. He stated, "One law of basic social justice was established for the native born, proselyte, and alien free man."[79] This is repeated throughout the Torah for emphasis, nearly word for word (Exodus 12:49; Leviticus 24:22; Numbers 15:16). The reason, according to Rabbi Silver, is because "God is the God of all men; all are equal in their claim upon His compassionate love. All men, regardless of race or creed, are entitled to respect, fair dealing, and charity."[80]

Lovingkindness is thus owed by us to all beings, not just Jews. The reason is obvious but often forgotten or ignored. In *A History of the Jews*, British historian Paul Johnson made plain this fundamental tenet of Jewish belief:

> As God owns all and everyone, he is an injured party in all offences against fellow men. A sin against God is serious but a sin against a fellow man is more serious since it is against God too.[81]

This adds some additional context to the enduringly tragic circumstances of our troubled relations with so many of the people and nations of the world.

"LOVING" OR "GOD": WHAT MATTERS MOST?

Some of the best Jews are not religious—neither strictly Torah-observant nor formally involved in the practice of Judaism as sanctioned by one of its non-Orthodox branches. How can one who does not accept normative Jewish beliefs or participate in institutional Jewish religion be considered a good Jew?

Some of the greatest champions of social justice, especially in the last century, have been Jews who, while not drawn to practice our religion in a formal sense, nonetheless devoted their themselves to *tz'dakah* and *chesed*. Examples include Supreme Court Justice Louis B. Brandeis, nursing pioneer Lillian Wald, Professor Albert Einstein, labor leader Walter Reuther, and Theodor Herzl, father of modern Zionism. Their lives are models for us of morally grounded ethical behavior in pursuit of the most valued ends endorsed by Jewish sacred teachings. This ought to be true even for those of us whose beliefs may not occupy the same place on the political spectrum.

Modern-day Jews who manage to live their lives like these great role models may not qualify as religious Jews, as defined by practice of the Jewish religion, but they would still be considered very, very good Jews. Through their actions, they are manifesting a love of God, whether or not they believe in His existence. It could be argued that such people are indeed "religious," in the unique sense that Judaism defines the term—as obedience to the commandments—because they are being obedient to the commandments that matter most of all, the horizontal or ethical *mitzvot*.

But even so—granting that atheism, agnosticism, or other kinds of religious doubt preclude categorizing one as a religious person in Judaism—being unanimously adjudged "religious" is not the *sine qua non* of Jewish identity. That would be matrilineal descent (*Y'vamot* 45b; *Kiddushin* 68b), except within the North American Reform movement, where, controversially, patrilineal descent is now recognized.[02] Nor does unwavering compliance with religious dogma in tandem with unsurpassed piety in religious devotion define the *sine qua non* of Jewish *mensch*-hood. That would be commitment to pursuing the ethical *mitzvot*.

This is not meant as a blanket endorsement of everything on the social and political agenda of secular Jews. There may be a danger, among those who lack a formal Jewish education or familiarity with Jewish history and sacred writings, of falling prey to nonce political fashions driven by non-Jewish beliefs.

For example, a unique and misapprehended feature of Judaism's commitment to ethical behavior is our nonembrace of pacifism. We have rejected an unwavering adherence to this ideology, with reason, at all stages of our history. No doubt, this has preserved us as a people.

To save one's life, the Talmud is clear: "If a man comes to kill you, rise early and kill him first" (*B'rakhot* 58a). Moreover, we are not to stand by idly if we are able to separate combatants or to prevent use of force against innocent parties. This means that we are obliged to use deadly force to stop murderers: "Whosoever would shed the blood of a man, to save that man, shall his blood be shed" (*Sanhedrin* 72a). While nonviolence and negotiation are preferred in all other situations, because "no vessel can retain blessing so effectively as peace" (Numbers *Rabbah* 11:7), the ideology of "turn the other cheek" has only a small place in the moral vocabulary of Judaism. "Great is peace" (Leviticus *Rabbah* 9:9), the rabbis tell us. But absolute pacifism in the face of monsters such as Hitler? Never.

A more relevant concept for Judaism is *tikkun olam*. This refers to the ultimate purpose of Jewish existence: to take part in the restoration, and thus completion, of the world. Repairing the broken, healing the sick, connecting the disconnected, making whole the shattered, resacralizing the profane—all of these actions are about restoring to their innate holiness the pieces of God's creation that, for one reason or another, became separated from their true identity.

Rabbi Dorff has insightfully described *tikkun olam* in a way that links together the various domains of Jewish ethical action discussed earlier. "In many ways," he noted, "*chesed* denotes the personal, individual aspects of *tikkun olam*, while *tzedek* and *mishpat* denote its social elements."[83] In response to the criticism that *tikkun olam* was being "used by those who want to abandon traditional Judaism and remake Judaism into a religion of social action,"[84] Rabbi Dorff responded, correctly, that *tikkun olam* stands for obligations that "are core values of the Jewish tradition."[85] Commitment to justice and mercy and kindness, through individual acts or through organized social action, *is* traditional Judaism.

Historically, much of what constitutes social action or pursuit of social justice within Judaism has originated on the political left. Secular Jewish activists, since early in the twentieth century, have gravitated to socialism and to progressive political causes. Traditional Jewish values supportive of justice and human rights and a pervasive identification with the underdog were especially influential from the 1920s through the 1960s, leading to Jewish involvement and leadership in the labor, civil rights, and antiwar movements.

Recognition of this social history has occasionally led to a stereotyping of Jewish liberalism and activism as a product of Jews allowing their tacit political assumptions to trump their (ostensibly) religious values. While this undoubtedly holds true for particular individuals—the caricature of the limousine liberal comes to mind—I believe that this general criticism is unfair and greatly misplaced.

For one thing, who would assert that classical liberalism is ideologically inconsistent with Jewish ethical teachings? Liberty, charity, and universal human rights are all values that our tradition holds dear. "A righteous man is concerned with the cause of the wretched," a proverb begins. "A wicked man cannot understand such concern" (Proverbs 29:7).

Second, many secular Jews may not have enough familiarity with normative Jewish values to know whether or when they are being trumped. So many Jews are ignorant of the basics of Judaism, even within our finest synagogues. But if the worst that can be said of them is that they gravitate to well-intentioned social causes, this hardly merits our condemnation. Another proverb states, "To punish also the righteous is not good, nor to strike the noble for their uprightness" (Proverbs 17:26).

Most important, secular Jews are not the only Jewish liberals, nor are they its mainstays. Practicing Jews across the spectrum of Jewish observance have served as articulate voices for progressive political causes.

A notable example is Rabbi Michael Lerner, editor of the magazine *Tikkun*, who received training at the Jewish Theological Seminary under Rabbi Heschel and is a prominent spokesperson for progressive social change. Rabbi Lerner has been vocal in his criticisms of both the antireligious sentiments of the Jewish secular left[86] and the anti-Semitic sentiments of non-Jewish socialists.[87] His rabbinate and life's work show that one can be both observantly Jewish and Jewishly liberal. Indeed, the latter may best be nourished by the former.

At the same time, well-known Jewish opinion leaders have arisen in conservative political circles, equally inspired and motivated by a commitment to *tz'dakah* and *chesed* informed by Jewish observance. Examples include Michael Medved, Don Feder, Mona Charen, Ben Shapiro, Dennis Prager, Caroline Glick, Yuval Levin, and the editors of *Commentary* magazine. Just as the Jewish left is populated by both secular and religious Jews, so too can one find secular, liberal, and traditionally observant Jews among Jewish centrists and conservatives.

Two of the most intelligent and thought-provoking books that I have read on the place of Jewish values in American politics are by religious Jews at opposite ends of the political spectrum. Rabbi Arthur Waskow, a founding fellow of the far-left Institute for Policy Studies and a Reconstructionist Jew, in *These Holy Sparks*,[88] and Elliott Abrams, an attorney, former political appointee of both Bush administrations, and Conservative Jew, in *Faith or Fear*,[89] both addressed the complex interplay of faith, politics, Jewish observance, and the threat of cooptation by forces that do not have the best interests of religious Jews, of whatever political persuasion, in mind. It might be awfully hard to fathom if one has read neither book, but the authors were in concurrence on key points.

Foremost was their recognition of the dilemmas encountered by Jews whose destiny as a people is not being served by the political ideologies to which they adhere and the political allies with which they are aligned. Making common cause with our otherwise natural political allies, depending upon one's political perspective, is not risk-free for Jews whose activism is motivated by religious principles. Grave dangers inhere for Jews in permitting the increasingly anti-Zionist secular left to define the political agenda of Jewish progressives (Rabbi Waskow's concern) and in enabling the Christian right to impose its moral and religious agenda on Jewish conservatives (Mr. Abrams's concern). Both ostensible allies seek our conversion, figuratively or literally, and thus our obliteration.

Clearly, Jewish observance can motivate and inspire thoughtful engagement of political discourse across the spectrum of Jewish religiousness and across the political spectrum. There are secular or liberal Jews who are Jewish liberals and Torah-observant Jews who are Jewish conservatives. At the same time, there are liberal Jews who are Jewish conservatives—Professor Neusner, for example—and traditionally observant Jews who are politically radical—Rabbi Heschel was a representative example. The commonality is a sincere commitment to mimic our God, Who acts "with kindness, justice, and equity (*chesed mishpat utz'dakah*) in the world; for in these I delight" (Jeremiah 9:23).

Reasonable Jews can disagree about what constitutes acceptable ritual observance or responsible political positions about pressing social issues of the day. Reasonable Jews can also disagree about the existence and nature of God. But we cannot afford to disagree about the stated fact that our tradition calls for us, unequivocally, to draw on our ancient font of moral instruction to ameliorate the suffering and injustices in this world. The respective political praxis toward which we gravitate may vary among us, but the ends that we seek—we presume, at least—are God's as well.

Among the worst sins for a Jew is apathy. In the Talmud, Rabbi Yehoshua ben Korcha, reflecting on *Parashat Sh'mot*, suggested that "all the meritorious deeds performed by Moses our teacher did not stand him in good stead when he displayed apathy [*shenat*; literally "sleep"] towards circumcision, as it is written, and the Lord met him, and sought to kill him" (*N'darim* 31b). By ignoring God's call to "take diligent heed to do the commandment and the law" (Joshua 22:5), we are guilty not just of a personal transgression but also of hastening a great loss to the Jewish community and to the world. One good deed, the Mishnah tells us, leads to an even greater deed (*M. Sotah* 9:15). The *tz'dakah* or *chesed* that we neglect or avoid is lost forever, along with whatever additional good that it might have inspired.

God requires our devotion, but not empty devotion devoid of sincerity. For a Jew, that means devotion translated into acts of justice, charity, kindness, and mercy. I believe that God would much rather that we occupy ourselves with doing good yet entertain questions about His existence and His qualities than that we affirm His majesty in word or thought or feeling only. That would be spirituality in a vacuum, not true Jewish spirituality. The latter requires us to be bold actors in the physical world of material things. Whether on a global scale or locally, as in the popular saying "Think globally, act locally," we are commanded first to "sing of mercy and justice (*chesed-umishpat*)" and only then "unto Thee, O Lord, will I sing praises" (Psalms 101:1). It is by way of exercising mercy and justice that we go about praising God.

CHAPTER FOUR

HOW DOES LOVING GOD AFFECT OUR LIVES?

"A person can only love the Blessed Holy One to the extent that he is mindful of Him. The degree of love is in proportion to that of this mindfulness."[1]

We Jews have many ways of expressing our love of God, as we have seen. Through a commitment to studying God's expectations for us as revealed in sacred writings, through heartfelt prayer and devotion that draw us intimately into His presence, and especially through ethical behavior that seeks to relieve suffering and promote *tikkun olam*, we manifest our covenantal charge "O you who love the Lord, hate evil!" (Psalms 97:10).

The word for evil in this verse is *"ra,"* the same word as in *yetzer hara*, the evil inclination. Along with the *yetzer hatov*, the good inclination, these are the two forces that do battle within our psyche. According to the Ramchal, each of us is able to draw close to God only to the extent to which we are able to overcome our *yetzer hara* by "consciously deciding to subjugate himself to his Creator, and fulfill God's commands."[2] This is how we become holy.

For the Ramchal, the attainment of holiness occurs in two stages:

It begins with worship and it ends with reward; it begins with effort and ends with a gift. The meaning of this is that one begins by sanctifying himself and ends up by being sanctified.[3]

The initial effort on our part, through "the pursuit of true knowledge and diligent reflection [of transcendent matters] with regard to the sanctification of deeds,"[4] leads to what he called *tahor*, or purity. Eventually, this effort is returned in kind by God, and we achieve a state of *k'dushah*, or holiness. This is characterized by one "who cleaves to his God constantly and whose soul walks about [immersed] in thought regarding those matters that are [of a] transcendent [nature] in his love for his Creator."[5]

Making the effort to love God, by whichever of the means discussed throughout this book, thus clearly has consequences. Fulfilling God's commandments has consequences that are collective and communal, external to ourselves, as is obvious when considering *mitzvot* such as *g'milut chasadim* and *tz'dakah*. For example, because we love God, we are to consider the plight of the stranger and "shall love him as yourself, for you were strangers in the land of Egypt" (Leviticus 19:34). A collective consequence of loving God is that we see the inherent oneness linking all of God's creations.

But there are also personal consequences to loving God. While we are instructed to focus on the former consequences rather than on the latter, the gifts that we receive may be considerable. Moreover, the benefits to each of us of engaging our mind, our heart, and our body in service to God can be highly functional. The psychological effects of loving God ideally strengthen us in our pursuit of *tz'dakah* and *chesed*, providing us with the inner resources to overcome obstacles both external and internal. These include the resistance we face from our *yetzer hara* and from a world that perhaps does not value studiousness, piety, and morality as much as we do.

Therefore, we should not fall prey to the false belief that it is wrong to seek self-betterment or actualization, as if these were "lower" and more selfish life goals than seeking to do justice and mercy. While our ultimate aim, as Jews, should be to help others, we do not reject or repress any benefits that may accrue to ourselves as a result of our fulfilling our covenantal obligations. Such a response exemplifies a sort of asceticism and self-denial that may be representative of other religions but is not at all characteristic of Judaism. God wants us to experience the greatest well-being imaginable, for as the psalmist reminds us, "Happy (*ashrei*) are all those who take refuge in Him" (Psalms 2:12).

Happiness is a concept mentioned frequently in the Torah, especially in the psalms, whose very first word is *ashrei* (Psalms 1:1). These verses, in turn, are referenced scores of times throughout the Talmud and Midrash. Significantly, happiness is said to result from each of the three pillars of *Pirke Avot*: from acts of learning, worship, and kindness or justice.

Happiness is promised to those "whose way is blameless, who follow the teaching of the Lord" (Psalms 119:1), to "the man who makes the Lord his trust" (Psalms 40:5), to "those who observe His decrees, who turn to Him wholeheartedly" (Psalms 119:2), and to "he who is thoughtful of the wretched [*dal*; literally "poor" or "weak"]" (Psalms 41:2). In short, "Happy are the righteous!" (*Yoma* 87a), a gift so valuable that "not only do they acquire merit, but they bestow merit upon their children and children's children to the end of all generations" (*Yoma* 87a).

The theme of happiness is so important that it is enshrined in a special prayer, entitled *Ashrei*, recited daily, on *shabbat*, and at special times throughout the liturgical year.[6] This familiar hymn is based on the 145th Psalm, one of several psalms arranged as an alphabetical acrostic, such as Psalms 25, 34, 37, 111, 112, and 119. Each verse begins with a respective letter of the Hebrew alphabet, arrayed in order from *aleph* to *tav* (excluding *nun*), the mnemonic design serving to enhance memory of the prayer.

In *Ashrei*, as contained in both traditional and liberal prayer books,[7] God is referred to almost always as Lord, the form of His name that denotes His attribute of mercy. The Lord is to be praised, and we are to be happy, because He is wondrous, abundant, gracious, compassionate, merciful, tender, and "good to all." Each of these traits describes a warm, emotionally inviting, personal God. Our natural response, accordingly, is joyousness because "He fulfills the desire of those who revere Him . . . and preserves all who love Him."[8] Furthermore, according to the Midrash on this psalm, "In the time-to-come Israel will never cease signing, but will ceaselessly sing praises and blessings" (*Midrash T'hillim* 145:1).

This concern with our happiness hardly bespeaks a religion whose God demands harsh austerities in return for nothing but an uncertain reprieve from eternal damnation. Quite the opposite. The Yerushalmi teaches that we are to enjoy and appreciate the world that God has gifted to us: "Rav Chizkiah [and] Rav Kohen in the name of Rav: 'In the future a man is going to have to give an account of himself for everything that his eye saw and he did not eat'" (*Y. Kiddushin* 4:12).

But while we are assured that God wishes for us to be happy and sated, happiness does not always come easily. The best way to obtain satisfaction in this life, both sages and contemporary rabbis tell us, is to turn our attention elsewhere. This runs counter to the ideology of pop psychology, which urges us to attend to all of our own needs first and to enshrine the maximizing of our happiness as our ultimate life goal. Judaism has different advice.

The Ramchal is especially insightful when it comes to the complicated relationship between our worldly duties and concomitant rewards, including the emotional ones. In *Mesillat Yesharim*, he taught that

> *the main purpose of man's existence in this world is solely to do mitzvos, to serve the Eternal, and to overcome tribulations. The pleasures of this world are only meant to aid and assist him and to give him contentment and peace of mind, thereby allowing him to turn his heart toward that service that is his responsibility.[9]*

The brilliant Conservative Rabbi David J. Wolpe would concur. His advice is lucid and is key to understanding how Jews ought to frame the concept of happiness. Rabbi Wolpe concluded,

> *A relationship to God can be satisfying and at times will make one happy, but it is not that dreamed-of road to perfect contentment....Judaism's counsel is clear: Lay the maddening chimera of constant happiness to one side and seek instead to emulate that highest prophetic ideal—to do justice, to love mercy, and to walk humbly with God.[10]*

In the preface to one of his many popular books, Rabbi Joseph Telushkin reflected on the "purpose of Jewish existence." His words are so elegant that I incorporated them into our Passover *seder* for many years. Our purpose, he stated,

> *is not to eat Jewish foods, or tell Jewish jokes, or use Yiddish words. It is to fight evil and to reduce suffering in the world. It is a source of deep pain to me to recognize how few people know this.[11]*

For Jews, there is no implicit choice between celebrating *yiddishikeit* and living a holy life, between religious observance and concern for social justice, between doing *mitzvot* and loving God. Our culture and our covenant, our religion and our social consciousness, our obedience to God and our devotion to Him—these go hand in hand. Jewish life should be full of richness and satisfaction, replete with experiences that bring enjoyment and satisfaction to ourselves, our families, our congregations, and our communities. Whether this results from our shared tribal folkways, our worship experiences, the good that we do, or our relationship with God, we should accept and embrace the joyousness that comes from being Jewish.

It is only when we artificially separate our covenantal obligations from our personal relationship with God, putting one or another upon a pedestal and elevating it above all else, that we can run into trouble. Throughout the Torah, especially in Deuteronomy, God makes clear that the surest way to love Him and the surest way to receive His blessings in our life is by keeping His commandments (Deuteronomy 11:13, 19:9, 30:16). My thoughts on the why and how of this charge have already been offered. God also makes clear that the way in which we keep His commandments is to "love the Lord your God with all your heart and with all your soul and with all your might" (Deuteronomy 6:5).

It may appear that God is relying upon circular logic: through the *mitzvot*, we love God, and loving God is how we do *mitzvot*. This seems confusing, but it makes great sense. God is telling us that the emotional dimension of a relationship with Him—the proximity to His holy presence sought by so many people—is best nourished by the performance of acts that indicate our willingness to serve as His proxy in the great work of spreading holiness in this world.

Rabbi Bradley Shavit Artson, longtime dean of the rabbinic school at American Jewish University, discussed this issue with great insight in his *d'rash* on *Parashat Vaetchannan*. In his Torah commentary,[12] he exhibits a gift for clarifying the seemingly opaque. Rabbi Artson identified a problem as old as the Jewish religion: the presence of "many Jews who purport to love God [but] do not observe the *mitzvot*, and many Jews zealous in their performance of *mitzvot* [who] seemed not to grasp the implications of loving God."[13] The former fall prey to

a kind of self-worship, as if God is obligated to love each of us solely on our own terms. Mitzvot *then may be performed because of their beauty, emotional power, or wisdom, with no sense at all that we perform* mitzvot *to please the Cre-*

ator of the Universe, or to honor the sacred and command-
ing voice resonating throughout the mundane deeds of Jew-
ish living.[14]

The latter fall prey to performing *mitzvot* solely as

a form of self-righteousness, in which piety in themselves
and others is measured by external punctiliousness. Mitzvot
become a kind of cosmic scoreboard, in which the one who
makes the most hoops, wins.[15]

According to Rabbi Artson, "Both of these approaches present the danger of becoming forms of idolatry: One idolizes warm feelings and individual autonomy; the other idolizes sterile practice and unthinking obedience."[16] True Judaism, by contrast, "insists on the observance of *mitzvot* as a method of cultivating a love of God and of responding to Divine command."[17]

Loving God thus entails something akin to a positive feedback loop: the more we love God—through the actions entailed in "these three things"—the more we will want to fulfill His commandments to us in order that we help to accomplish His will for the world; and the more we are able to observe His commandments, the more we will cement our bond with God. Through experiencing the love that flows between us and God, we tap into a never-ending supply of strength and goodness that nourishes us and girds us to do battle with the forces of injustice and unkindness. This love originates in God, but it also comes from us, because our actions can stimulate the flow of more love.

A loving relationship with God is in many ways a radically illogical idea. That we can be intimately connected with an existential presence is not something that can be validated through observation or proven by any other means. It finds expression and manifestation in our lives in unique ways that vary among individual Jews. Loving God leaves its traces in who we are and in how our core of self finds expression— through our beliefs, emotions, behaviors, attitudes, values, thoughts, motivations, and perspectives on life. These in turn may affect, directly or indirectly, the quality of our own life as well as the quality of all lives.

In short, loving God has consequences for us, not just collectively but also individually. No, our main objective in life is not to focus solely on the benefits that might come to us, psychologically, spiritually, or otherwise. We ought not to dwell on these and lose touch with why the world needs a Jewish presence. But these personal consequences are nonetheless invaluable, not just in their own right but because they reinforce our love of the One Who "girded me with might" (Psalms 18:33) for the covenantal duties that we agreed to on Sinai.

OUR RELATIONSHIP WITH GOD

To understand the consequences of a relationship with God, we first must understand the nature of such a relationship. The most telling portrayal of the intrinsic relationship between humans and God is found in its earliest description. In the first *parashah* in the Torah, the Creator makes clear the intimacy and identity that He shares with each of us: "And God said, 'Let us make man in our image, after our likeness'" (Genesis 1:26). The Midrash interpreted that to mean that from now on, none of us are to be created "without the Divine Spirit (*Sh'khinah*)" (Genesis Rabbah 8:9).

Throughout sacred Jewish writings, the *Sh'khinah* is identified with God in the form that He takes when He is present with us. *Sh'khinah* is the word used to describe that manifestation of God that enlivens us as individuals. It is also the word used for the presence of God that stands with us as a people. The Talmud speaks of this Divine Presence being with us specifically when we fulfill our covenantal charge to labor in the cause of justice, mercy, and holiness. The *Sh'khinah* is there with us when we learn Torah, pray together, judge righteously, and make peace (*B'rakhot* 6a)—when we pursue each of the three pillars spoken of in *Pirke Avot*.

If we eschew these commands, then the *Sh'khinah* may hide itself. This can result from personal laxity. We are told, for example, that "the Divine Presence rests [upon] man neither through gloom, nor through sloth, nor through frivolity, nor through levity, nor through talk, nor through idle chatter, save through a matter of joy" (*Shabbat* 30b).

Collective failures can also lead to an obscuring of the Divine Presence. The transgression, though, must be serious. Religious sins are not enough, for, as we are told, "even when they are unclean, the Divine Presence is among them" (*Yoma*

56b). It takes wickedness against fellow humans to arouse God's ire enough to hide Himself from us:

> *Rabbi Yochanan said: "The Divine Presence tarried for Israel in the wilderness six months in the hope that they would repent. When [it saw that] they did not repent, it said, 'Let their soul expire.'"* (Rosh Hashanah 31a)

The conclusion is inescapable. Since we were created in God's image with His *Sh'khinah* indwelling, since the *Sh'khinah* is God's life-giving presence within us, and since God and the rabbis outline for us the specific actions to take to merit this presence, then it must be that we were created to serve as God's representatives. We were fashioned by God as vessels for His presence so that we might conduct ourselves as His proxies in the world that He created. When we are remiss in our duties, as individuals and as a people, we temporarily lose that connection to God, that identity with God that defines us and our special mission.

This God-given identity and mission essentially give us life. Because of the great plans that God had for us, we were created. As Jews, our very existence depends upon, and has always depended upon, our understanding of Who created us, why we were created, and just what it is that we are to be doing here. When we do not fulfill what we were put here to do, it is as if our soul has expired.

In turn, God's existence in the world is dependent upon our recognition of who we are in relation to the One Who made us. Like the light of the lamps burning in the *ohel moed*, or Tent of Meeting, the fulfillment of our prescribed obligations as Jews on behalf of others "is a testimony to mankind that the Divine Presence rests in Israel" (*M'nakhot* 86b). The Creator of the universe has made Himself vulnerable, in a sense, by relying upon us to make this world "fit for a Temple for the Divine Presence" (Numbers *Rabbah* 7:8). If we do our part, God will do His, as in His promise that "I will abide among the children of Israel, and I will never forsake My people Israel" (I Kings 6:13).

In Judaism, entering into a personal relationship with God is not about undergoing a profound spiritual transformation that changes us from how we were created into something new. That would imply that God made us incomplete and inherently unlike Himself. As we have seen, such a belief is inconsistent with Jewish teaching on the relationship between humans and God. This perspective is found instead in pagan mystery cults and in Christianity, in which humans require a metaphoric second birth to save them from spiritual oblivion or death. Through rituals of regeneration[18] or through the vicarious atonement of a sacrificed god-man, humans are redeemed from a state of ignorance or evil, from enslavement, from a broken relationship with their creator[19] and are reborn as new creatures.

For Jews, experiencing a personal relationship with God does not require that we search outside of ourselves for an arcane rite of initiation or for a human or divine mediator. We already possess such a relationship, through the *Sh'khinah*, the part of God that He left within us when He gave us life. In this context, the word denoting God's presence specifically implies proximity. According to Rabbi Simon Glustrom, use of the term *Sh'khinah* "is always associated with God's nearness either to the people of Israel or the individual Jew."[20]

If God is ever-near, then we do not have far to go to enter into the closest possible relationship with Him. Experiencing such a relationship and the joyous feelings that come from knowing that "nearness to God is good" (Psalms 73:28) is more about restoring, reaffirming, renewing—recognizing the presence of something and Someone that was always there and behaving accordingly.

For those of us who may have drifted away from this recognition, there is always the opportunity to return. This is the essence of repentance in Judaism, the word for which is *t'shuvah*, which literally means "returning." The Midrash says, "What God is there like this, who loves those that love Him and draws the distant ones as close to Himself as those that are near Him, if they come in honor of His name?" (Numbers *Rabbah* 8:4). It is not God that makes Himself distant from us; it is we that make ourselves distant from Him. If we honor God's name—that is, if we honor our covenantal duties—then God will remove the veil from His *Sh'khinah*, and its light will burn brightly within our hearts.

For each one of us, the key to a personal relationship with God—activating it, maintaining it, restoring it—is in being true to the Divine Presence that animates us as individuals and as a people. That presence of the "great and awesome God, who stays faithful to His covenant with those who love Him and keep His commandments" (Nehemiah 1:5) defines for us our identity and our mission. It tells us who we are and why we are here. But what are its functional consequences? How does it affect our lives?

To be in a relationship with God—to love God and to experience His love in return—exerts far-reaching effects on the life of any Jew who confesses, "Surely You are our Father" (Isaiah 63:16). The system of mutual promises and obligations that define this relationship serves to reflect and shape our character, to define our spirituality, and to determine our destiny. We are who we are, and who we will be, only because we love God and He loves us.

First, who we are in relation to our Creator imparts to us a specific identity and self-image as a people uniquely chosen by God. He depends on us to "own" our innate Jewishness and all that it entails. After all, there are sparks to redeem, as the mystics would say, and it is our job to do so. The world depends on us, although it may not be fully aware that it does.

Second, the unique nature of our love affair with God gives birth to our unique spirituality. The Jewish spiritual path is unlike any other. It was created just for us, and it comprises a style of life, a worldview, a religious practice, and an eschatology that cannot be equated with those of other religions. Our encounter with God is ours alone. Being Jewish and doing Judaism are distinct from being and doing any other faith. So too are the rewards of a Jewish life, psychologically and spiritually.

Third, by being mindful of who we are and how we are to be, we can better fulfill what we are here to do. In so doing, we may benefit ourselves as well as others, since we are a part of the whole. As agents of justice and mercy and healing, we may partake in these blessings too. As we are laborers for the redemption of the world, our redemption is inextricably tied into, and depends upon, the work that we are able to accomplish. We have to live in the world that we help to create, and it is in our interest to abide by the plan that God entrusted to us.

JEWISH IDENTITY AND SELF-IMAGE

We love God most of all because He loves us. When we love God, accomplishing the tasks that He set before us, we fulfill our part of the covenant that our ancestors affirmed with Him. Loving God should be a natural inclination for us, as God has left traces of Himself in each of us. We are made of God, more or less—not just because He fashioned us from the earth that He created, but because a piece of His *Sh'khinah* is breathed into every one of us.

God made us and sanctified us. His breath became our spirit. His presence elevates our soul. If we cannot love God, then we are rejecting our very essence as human beings and as Jews. If we hate ourselves, then we are despising God.

For too many Jews, self-hatred and self-denial are a way of life, passed down through families like any other hereditary trait. We have allowed distorted images of our covenant and our heritage, of our special relationship with God, and of our collective mission in the world to color our understanding of what it means to be a "people that dwells apart" (Numbers 23:9). We have allowed our affluence and comfort, our seamless socialization into the generic Western culture, and our ability to pass as other than who we are to destroy our memories of when we whispered to God, "My beloved is mine and I am His" (Song of Songs 2:16). We have allowed the lie that assimilation equals safety to assuage our fear that celebration of our Jewish identity is a threat to our survival.

Our self-images are not our own. They have been drawn by our lack of Jewish education, our covetousness and envy of all things not Jewish, and our fear of being discovered and labeled as "other." So we adopt false identities. After a time, we may even become so acclimated to these facades that we forget that they are lies. Despite our best efforts, we can never completely obliterate our Jewishness because Jews are who God made us to be when He instilled us with the Divine Presence.

We may run from who we are, and eventually we may believe that we have escaped. But we cannot escape the spiritual void that remains. For a Jewish *n'shamah*, "there is none like the Lord our God" (Exodus 8:6). Nothing can take His place. But that is not to say that few of us try. It is no surprise, for example, that so many of the adherents of Eastern religions, mystical orders and metaphysical brotherhoods, and new age groups of one sort or another are fallen-away Jews.

But I am not speaking here principally of religious conversion or dabbling in unusual syncretisms. While I would not endorse the abandonment of the Jewish religion for some other faith, frankly there are much worse apostasies than seeking spiritual solace in another tradition when one's religion of birth is no more familiar than a stranger's shirt. The "strange gods" (Deuteronomy 32:16) with which we rouse God to jealousy do not have to be religious, strictly speaking. They may be idols of money, status, social acceptance, mass conformity, indifference, selfishness, greed—the secular gods that our culture tells us demand our worship.

Our history is one of pogroms and holocausts, of organized anti-Semitism of the left and right, of quiet discrimination and whispered quotas. For every Hitler or Stalin, Pharaoh or Nebuchadnezzar, there are hundreds of Professor A. Lawrence Lowell, the Harvard president who in the 1920s proposed restrictions on the number of Jews allowed to attend his university. In the face of such threats—of life and limb and of social exclusion—it may be that shame, embarrassment, and ultimately abandonment of Judaism seem to some a reasoned response.

Jewish assimilation, especially in the United States, accelerated in the couple of decades immediately following World War II. What may have begun as an attempt to escape identification with a people who nearly had been exterminated from the earth soon turned into an offering of "strange fire before the Lord" (Leviticus 10:1). The good life promised by a sanitized, deracinated postwar American existence apparently was more seductive than "the crown of glory" (Proverbs 4:9) bestowed upon us when we seek to acquire wisdom. Like Nadab and Abihu, sons of Aaron, the High Priest himself, Jews found that the seductive flame of assimilation could be as all-consuming as the fires of any *shoah*, or holocaust.

Hiding or pretending to be something other than Jewish is never an effective disguise. The Nazis murdered those Jews who fervently denied their Jewish heritage just as thoroughly as those who preserved their dignity—perhaps more thoroughly, as the surviving descendants of those who wore their

Jewishness proudly until the end were less likely, we can assume, to be lost to Judaism.

Many who have abandoned their Jewish identity would argue that they have done so in the name of survival, but survival of what? What good is our survival if the only thing that survives is our flesh? If we do not carry our Jewish identity with us into the world and into the future, then what is the point of our existence? Our identity as Jews defines our mission as Jews and dictates our core values. Without our covenant to fulfill, who are we? Without our charge to redeem the world through *torah*, *avodah*, and *g'milut chasadim* to make it a place of truth, peace, and justice, what purpose do we serve? Why should we even be here?

When we try to escape from our Jewishness, we only exacerbate the problems that we presume to be avoiding. Many constituencies in the world indeed despise Jews and wish to destroy us, as has always been the case. But if we disown ourselves, then, in Rabbi Fackenheim's famous words, we "give Hitler posthumous victories."[21] This was such an important point to be made that Rabbi Fackenheim referred to it as our 614th commandment, a designation that he meant to be taken literally. In the aftermath of the Holocaust, he believed, instead of surrendering our Jewish identity and our attachment to the agenda set for us by God, we should remain committed and hopeful. In the terrible events that transpired in Europe, one might also see "a manifestation of God's will that his chosen people survive."[22]

By rejecting Judaism and the Jewish God in order to shed identification with the otherness that has so vexed us for the entirety of our peoplehood, we end up costing ourselves far more than we gain. There is no small irony in this, according to Rabbi Yosef Dov Ber Soloveitchik, the nineteenth-century rabbi known as the Bait HaLevi of Brisk and at one time Rosh Yeshivah at Volozhin: "Whenever the Jews try to assimilate, Hashem renews this separation by filling the hearts of [others] with hatred."[23]

We were selected by God for a reason, namely, to prepare for the day when we will declare, "Elijah is here!" (I Kings 18:11), the one who comes "to make peace in the world" (*M.*

Eduyyot 8:7). This is a monumental task, one that we alone agreed to "of all the peoples on earth" (Deuteronomy 7:6).

The final chapter of the Book of Joshua records a wonderful conversation between the Jewish people and their leader. Joshua had just synopsized the entirety of Jewish history, emphasizing God's sovereignty, much as Moses did in Deuteronomy but in a more abbreviated fashion. He presented a stark choice to the people: the God of our forefathers or the idols of the heathens. Joshua made clear what his own choice was, with the famous declaration that "I and my household will serve the Lord" (Joshua 24:15).

The people responded that they too "will serve the Lord, for He is our God" (Joshua 24:18). Joshua was skeptical, and the following words were exchanged:

Joshua, however, said to the people, "You will not be able to serve the Lord, for He is a holy God. He is a jealous God; He will not forgive your transgressions and your sins. If you forsake the Lord and serve alien gods, He will turn and deal harshly with you and make an end of you, after having been gracious to you." But the people replied to Joshua, "No, we will serve the Lord!" Thereupon Joshua said to the people, "You are witnesses against yourselves that you have by your own act chosen to serve the Lord." "Yes, we are!" they responded. "Then put away the alien gods that you have among you and direct your hearts to the Lord, the God of Israel." And the people declared to Joshua, "We will serve none but the Lord our God, and we will obey none but Him." (Joshua 24:19–24)

In this way, we once again reiterated our devotion to God, our commitment "to love the Lord your God and to walk in all His ways" (Joshua 22:5), which are "mercy, justice, and righteousness" (Jeremiah 9:23). The world thus depends upon us to own our Jewishness. Our religious values are essential to the survival of the world that God created. Without the moral cornerstones that God entrusted to us, the world would stand on a foundation of quicksand.

This tremendous responsibility—to God and to humankind—is the true meaning of the often misinterpreted phrase "chosen people." God was looking for a people to take on this burden, this obligation, and we agreed. We chose God. The familiar words of Rabbi Tarfon remind us that this covenant has never expired. Although the time is short, the work is difficult, and its beneficiaries may be indifferent, "it is not your duty to finish the work, but you are not at liberty to neglect it" (*Pirke Avot* 2:15–16). If any one of us denies our identity as a people who chose this mighty work, it is as if we are consenting to God's heartbreaking lament, "I have abandoned My house, I have deserted My possession, I have given over My dearly beloved into the hands of her enemies" (Jeremiah 12:7).

If we abandon our Jewishness, God forbid, then we are guaranteeing our obliteration as a people. We are blaspheming against our God, assaulting Him in a terrible and personal way.

The work may indeed be hard and, as history teaches, dangerous to our physical being. But it is not without its rewards. If we take only the long view, we will miss the delight that accompanies laboring in the service of God. We need not focus just on a distant glory in the world to come or on a far-distant messianic age in which the trees that we have planted will finally bear fruit. There are glory and fruit to be found and experienced in every moment of a Jewish life.

The commentary on Rabbi Tarfon's words mitigate their apparent severity. We have chosen a formidable task, no less than the backbreaking labor imposed upon us by Pharaoh. But unlike our days of servitude in Egypt, we are surrounded by blessings that are ours for the taking. To those who might complain or give up, the advice is simple: "If he should grow impatient, he is told: 'Wretch! Why dost thou grow impatient? Every day take thy reward, a golden denar!'" (*Avot d'Rabbi Natan* 27).

For the life lived Jewishly, embracing God and our covenantal charge, there are buckets of golden *denarim* at every corner. Not literally, of course, but in other important ways—psychologically, spiritually. Saying, "Yes, we are!" to who God made us to be connects us to the true Source of who we are. It also connects us to an eternal wellspring of love.

This loving relationship that lasts forever is captured beautifully in Rabbi Rami M. Shapiro's poetic rendering of the *Ahavat Olam* prayer that precedes the *Sh'ma* in the evening service:

We are loved by an unending love. We are embraced by arms that find us even when we are hidden from ourselves. We are touched by fingers that soothe us even when we are too proud for soothing. We are counseled by voices that guide us even when we are too embittered to hear. We are loved by an unending love. We are supported by hands that uplift us even in the midst of a fall.[24]

These words have found their way into liturgies of healing and renewal used in Reform, Conservative, and Reconstructionist congregations. Tellingly, they are followed in the traditional prayer by the phrase "Blessed art Thou, Lord who loves His people Israel."[25] In the *Ahavah Rabbah*, the version of this prayer used in the morning service, the closing line becomes "Blessed art Thou, Lord who chooses His people Israel with love."[26] The rabbis actually debated these two wordings, concluding that both were appropriate in their own ways (*B'rakhot* 11b). God loves us and God chose us with love.

Our God is more to us than God, Lord, King, and Savior. According to the Midrash, our relationship has many facets, like a beautiful jewel:

He is my God and I am His [chosen] nation. . . . He is as a father to me, and I am as a son to Him. . . . He is a shepherd to me . . . I am to Him as a flock. . . . He is to me as a keeper . . . I am His vineyard. . . . He fights for me against those that challenge me, and I fight for Him against those that provoke Him. (Song of Songs Rabbah 2:45)

Jewish canon is unanimous about God's love for the Jewish people. Because of His *Sh'khinah* dwelling within us, giving us life, His love for us comes as easily as His love of Himself. Likewise, our love, devotion, and respect for God should come as easily to us as self-respect.

Our liturgies and sacred texts are filled with wonderfully positive self-images of Jewishness. In most regards, we take after our Father. He is "mighty and valiant" (Psalms 24:8); we are encouraged, as Moses encouraged Joshua, to be "strong and resolute" (Deuteronomy 31:23). He is "true and faithful" (Jeremiah 42:5); we are to be, like Hezekiah, "good, upright, and faithful" (II Chronicles 31:20). He is "compassionate and gracious, slow to anger, abounding in steadfast love" (Psalms

103:8); we are to "pursueth after righteousness and loving kindness" (*Kiddushin* 40a). We do not need to accept the negative self-images and stereotypes placed upon us by others. We know who God says that we are.

Acknowledging the true Self within each of us, the Divine Presence that binds us forever to God, cementing our choice of the Lord to be our God, is the only way in which we Jews will ever attain a measure of self-worth or self-esteem. We will never find it in systems of belief—or nonbelief—that deny the truths that inspired the writers of our sacred texts. We will never find it in pursuit of transient pleasures that debase the ideals of our noble ancestors who lived by, and often died on account of, their affirmation of our tradition's moral code.

A life that incorporates a mix of religious piety, ethical observance, and Jewish customs is, for Jews, the pot of gold at the end of the rainbow. By proudly embracing such a life and its concomitant identity, we can access the merit of an ancient and unbroken covenant with a God Who "satisfies the longing soul, and fills the hungry soul with goodness" (Psalms 107:9). Our Jewishness, fully engaged and uncompromisingly embraced, is our best remedy for inherited indifference and our best hedge against falling into despair.

REPENTANCE AND SPIRITUALITY

A Jewish life, lived passionately and fully, is the best kind of a life for Jews. But for many reasons, some of us become separated from the great traditions that define such a life. Detached from the moorings of the Jewish religion and perhaps from Jewish culture, we find ourselves adrift in the transient secular wasteland that threatens to devour everything that wanders into it. The profane mindlessness of consumerism, materialism, popular culture, the mass media, and the fashionable causes of the day pitched to us by flacks, barkers, and opinion leaders are no substitute for a meaningful connection with the God Who "will grant you the desires of your heart" (Psalms 37:4).

We all know this implicitly. But without a grounding in the teachings of our religion, the obligations that we owe God and are owed by Him, and the Jewish way of life, it may be hard to know where to begin to reverse our course. So many Jews today, unexposed to the beauty and majesty of Judaism or repelled by distorted versions of Judaism experienced as children, go searching elsewhere to fill the void in their *n'shamah*.

Earlier I stated that, for Jews, attaining a personal relationship with God does not require the kind of rebirth spoken of in other religious traditions. It simply requires that one affirm or reaffirm a willingness to "first accept upon himself the yoke of the kingdom of heaven and then take upon himself the yoke of the commandments" (*M. B'rakhot* 2:2). It is all about our actions: no matter where we are on our life's journey, no matter where we have been, we can always choose in any given moment to return to the covenantal path laid down by God, the "path of life" (Psalms 16:11) that has guided our ancestors for thousands of years.

In one sense, this returning does constitute a spiritual rebirth. To return to the Jewish path, to make *t'shuvah*, represents a uniquely Jewish "born-again" experience. It does not entail petitioning God to enter into one's heart and make one a new being, as in other religions. The *Sh'khinah* is already within us. It also does not entail confession in quite the same context as is found in other religions. Confession is certainly a vital part of the redemptive process in Judaism. But like so many other features of redemption, confession is largely a communal rite, as in the *Vidui* prayer repeated by the congregation at Yom Kippur. For Jews, what *t'shuvah* entails is simply this: to set a new intention and to go forward.

The Rambam outlined the actions required of anyone seeking to return to God.[27] The first step "consists in this, that the sinner abandon his sin, remove it from his thoughts, and resolve in his heart never to repeat it." The second step requires "that he regret the past." The final step is "that he calls Him who knows all secrets to witness that he will never return to this sin again." Of course, if one is guilty of a misdeed against another person, forgiveness must be sought and restitution made (*Yoma* 87a). But in the higher sense of *t'shuvah*—return to Judaism following estrangement, a misdeed against God, if you will—our religion does not require our public exposure. The formula is simple: "Only repentance and good deeds" (*Yoma* 87a).

But is *t'shuvah*, returning, really possible for a person who, perhaps because of familial indifference, was never truly connected to Judaism? How is it possible to return to something that one has never experienced?

The great contemporary *tzaddik* Rabbi Adin Steinsaltz eloquently addressed this issue in *The Thirteen Petalled Rose*. His words were hopeful: "In spite of the vast range of ways in which a Jew can alienate himself from his past and express himself in foreign cultural forms, he nevertheless retains a metaphysically, almost genetically, imprinted image of his Jewishness."[28] Because God's Divine Presence already dwells within each Jewish *n'shamah*, our reawakening is always possible.

Rabbi Steinsaltz also underscored the distinctively Jewish belief that *t'shuvah*, like so many other aspects of Jewish religious observance and commitment, is more about what we do than about how we feel. Returning to God—restoring our relationship with our Creator or establishing a meaningful relationship with Him for the first time—may feel wonderful in so many ways, but "Jewish thought pays little attention to inner tranquility and peace of mind."[29] For those who return, who choose to be a part of the people who say, "I love the Lord" (Psalms 116:1), "the essence of repentance is bound up more with turning than with response."[30]

The value for us in *t'shuvah*, in discovering or rediscovering how to love God, is not so much in how it makes us feel but in what it motivates us to do. As Rabbi Steinsaltz explained,

> *Repentance does not bring a sense of serenity or of completion, but stimulates a reaching out in further effort. Indeed, the power and the potential of repentance lie in increased incentive and enhanced capacity to follow the path even farther.*[31]

Just as the injustices and mercilessness that characterize our world inspire Jews to act, not just to pray for divine intercession and wait, so too when a person "senses the wrongness, evil, and emptiness in his life, it is not enough that he yearn for God or try to change his way of life."[32] What is required of us, according to Rabbi Steinsaltz, is *tikkun*, the same word contained in the phrase *tikkun olam*, repairing or perfecting the world, the ultimate mission of the Jewish people.

This is no coincidence. The two *tikkunim* are not all that separate. Again, Rabbi Steinsaltz:

Repentance is not just a psychological phenomenon, a storm within a human teacup, but is a process that can effect real change in the world, in all the worlds. Every human action elicits certain inevitable results that extend beyond their immediate context.[33]

When we are restored to our ancient faith, we further a process that brings restoration to our world. The *baal t'shuvah* movement that has emerged over the past three decades, whereby younger secular or nonobservant Jews adopt an Orthodox lifestyle, is actually part of a much larger movement that spans the fullness of the Jewish religious spectrum. The growth of Chabad and of *charedi* Judaism in the United States and Israel may be its most visible aspects. But Jewish seekers are repopulating all of the main branches of Judaism, which are themselves showing signs of "returning," at an institutional level.

For Reform Jews, for example, replacement of the old *Union Prayer Book* with *Shaarei T'fillah* in the late 1970s signaled that Judaism's most liberal branch was moving beyond the Classical Reform accommodations that had sustained the movement for the previous century. Since then, more traditional forms of Jewish liturgy, worship styles, and personal observance have come to characterize Reform Judaism. *Kipot* and *tallitot* worn during synagogue services, *bar* and *bat mitzvot* with chanted *parashiyyot*, Talmud classes, indications of renewed *shabbat* and *kashrut* observance, partly or fully restored traditional prayers in the *siddur*, services in which congregants speak or chant almost as much Hebrew as the rabbi and cantor—these are among the most obvious changes from the Reform Judaism that I recall from childhood to the Reform Judaism of today.

The commitment to ethical monotheism, to social justice, to personal autonomy in navigating through *halakhah*, to belief that contemporary rabbinic *responsa* may draw upon an ongoing revelation not locked in place at the time of the rabbinic sages—these remain. But the Reform movement as a whole has "returned" to a realization that, regardless of one's interpretation of Jewish law, Jewish observance is an irreplaceable resource for personal spirituality, communal solidarity, and religious continuity and survival. A small wing of resistance still protests these changes, but its numbers have dwindled to insignificance.

Liberal Jews have come to recognize, along with more traditional Jews, that experiencing the joy of greater Jewish spirituality advances the important work that we are appointed to complete as much as this work benefits and feeds our spirituality. One of the most beloved Jewish treatises on attaining spirituality is the Ramchal's *Mesillat Yesharim*. This great text, as interpreted by Rabbi David A. Cooper, was cited in Chapter 3 in the context of providing a road map to self-actualization.

The Ramchal's specific intention was to guide us along a path leading to spirituality. This path is like a ladder, with one step taking us to a next higher step. The ladder metaphor originates in a teaching by Rav Pinchas ben Yair (*Avodah Zarah* 20b). Each rung on the ladder represents a particular virtue that we must cultivate to become a holy people and thus fulfill our duty in the world. For most of these respective virtues, the Ramchal detailed its value to us, its constituent features, how we go about acquiring it, and how to avoid the stumbling blocks that undermine it.

In the Ramchal's formulation, these virtues are vigilance, alacrity, cleanliness, abstinence, purity, piety, humility, fear of sin, and holiness.[14] Climbing this ladder is how we attain and experience Jewish spirituality. It is how we get to a place where the love of God and God's love for us merge into one love. This concept, spirituality, implies for Jews both an outcome and a process. To attain spirituality is to commit oneself to the process by which one's spirit is nourished and becomes awakened to the fact that even here in this broken world, "The love of God lasts for all time" (Psalms 52:3).

It is no accident that this great handbook of spirituality is entitled with a phrase usually translated as "Path of the Just." Not the path of the studious or the path of the pious, although these are certainly meritorious paths, but the path of the just. This suggests a noble and universal purpose for our spiritual growth. When we seek to "hold fast to the Lord your God" (Joshua 23:8), we must always keep in mind that our attainment of spirituality is a means to an even greater end.

Martin Buber articulated this most profoundly in *Ten Rungs*, his discourse on a different series of steps, this one distilled from various Chasidic teachings. His words could serve as a subtitle or précis for the present book. The true *tzaddik*, according to Buber, knows that "the love of God is unreal, unless it is crowned with love for one's fellow men."[35] By this, he referred not simply to feelings of love toward others but specifically to acts of service seeking to ameliorate evil and to promote good.

Warm personal feelings, a peaceful heart, and moments of transcendent bliss are magnificent gifts, should we be fortunate enough to receive them. But they are not why Jews should choose to follow a path toward spirituality. We do not strive to love God because of how doing so may make us feel. In such a case, our feelings can become a distraction. A famous Buddhist anecdote describes this humorously, in a somewhat different context:

> A student went to his meditation teacher and said, "My meditation is horrible! I feel so distracted, or my legs ache, or I'm constantly falling asleep! It's just horrible!"
>
> "It will pass," the teacher said matter-of-factly.
>
> A week later, the student came back to his teacher. "My meditation is wonderful! I feel so aware, so peaceful, so alive! It's just wonderful!"
>
> "It will pass," the teacher replied matter-of-factly.[36]

Many sincere Jewish seekers find a sense of loving connectedness—to God, to other people, to all sentient beings—that is undetectable in the formal liturgies, worship modes, and congregational life of institutional Judaism. Why should it be otherwise? It is absent almost everywhere else in our culture. At the same time, we are also told, ubiquitously, that these feelings of love and union are what define spirituality. So disaffected Jews, just like the disaffected of other great religions, march off in search of philosophies that promise "true" spirituality.

Just as we have allowed non-Jewish beliefs and values to shape our self-identity and our understanding of why we are here, we have permitted alien ideologies to shape our conceptions of Jewish spirituality. This is no better exemplified than in the cliché "I'm not religious, but I'm spiritual," which has become practically a *mantra* for the nonobservant of every major religion, including legions of Jews.

Professor Huston Smith, the esteemed religious scholar, astutely narrated how "religion," a word with a precise and sympathetic meaning, has been cast aside in favor of the amorphous and mostly meaningless "spirituality." In his aptly named book *Why Religion Matters*, he noted:

> *Uncontaminated,* religion *is a noble word; deriving as it does from the Latin* religio, *to rebind, the word targets what religion is essentially about. But because it challenges the prevailing worldview, it has lost some of its respectability. Mention the word in public and its sins are what jump first to mind. . . . Enter the word* spirituality *to name (without specification) what is good about religion. Being no more than a human attribute, spirituality is not institutionalized, and this exempts it from the problems that inevitably attend institutions. . . .*
>
> *It is a bad sign when* spiritual, *an adjective, gets turned into a noun,* spirituality, *for this has a dog chasing its own tail. Grammatically,* spirit *is the noun in question, and* spiritual *its adjective.* Spirituality *is a neologism that has come into existence because* spirit *has no referent in science's world, and without grounding there, we are left unsure as to what the word denotes.*[37]

I agree wholeheartedly with Professor Smith, up until his last point. The word "spirituality," while indeed misapplied, abused, and trivialized, is not a neologism, although its current usage is clearly neologistic. The word does have a traditional meaning, and it is one worth reclaiming, especially for Judaism. I discussed this at some length (although not in a Jewish context) in the introduction to a previous book. My publisher had insisted, to my horror, that I change every instance of "religion" or "faith" to "spirituality," including in the book's title. I refused. The compromise that we reached, under protest on both sides, was that they include the word in the subtitle of my book and I was allowed to provide my take on this issue, which is excerpted here:

> *Historically, "religion" has denoted three things: particular churches or organized religious institutions (e.g., the Christian religion); a scholarly field of study; and the domain of life that deals with things of the spirit and matters of "ultimate concern." To talk of practicing religion or being religious refers to behaviors, attitudes, beliefs, experiences, and so on, that involve this domain of life. This is so whether one takes part in organized activities of an estab-*

lished religious institution or one has an inner life of the spirit apart from organized religions.

"Spirituality," as the term traditionally has been used, refers to a state of being that is acquired through religious devotion, piety, and observance. Attaining spirituality— union or connection with God or the divine—is an ultimate goal of religion, and is a state not everyone reaches. According to this usage, spirituality is a subset of a larger phenomenon, religion, and by definition is sought through religious participation. Religious scholars, historians, clergy and mystics of all faiths, and laypeople have always used the term in this way, almost without exception.[38]

In this context, spirituality connotes, as was mentioned earlier, both an outcome and a process. Through earnest observance of a faith tradition, we hope to elevate our souls to a point at which someday we might be able to stand before God, figuratively or in the world to come, and be judged to have attained spiritual maturity, in full flower, as our tradition defines it. At the same time, the word "spirituality" also refers to the unique elements defining the path of religious maturation within respective traditions. Thus, we can speak of Jewish spirituality, Buddhist spirituality, Roman Catholic spirituality, and the like. For Judaism, engaging "these three things" of *Pirke Avot* and translating our good intentions regarding *torah*, *avodah*, and *g'milut chasadim* into concrete deeds essentially define the Jewish spiritual path and its idealized endpoint.

As we are all aware, the past quarter century has seen new age authors, holistic healers, and media figures, many of them hostile to institutional religion, misappropriate the word "spirituality." They have transmuted it into a catchall encompassing religious practices such as meditation and certain types of prayer along with secular transcendent states such as feeling at one with nature. These are wonderful things, to be sure, not meriting disparagement. But as I noted, "Such efforts to avoid the perceived stigma of 'religion' shift all of its favored aspects to the old term, 'spirituality.'"[39] This new usage can be found in reference to every major religion, including Judaism. It is nowhere more in evidence than in the burgeoning and, sadly, often shallow popular literature on *kabbalah*.

Spirituality, for Jews who are unfamiliar with Judaism as for the nonobservant of other faiths, thus effectively has been divorced from religion. This does no one any favors. Two generations of Jews have been mistaught that being "spiritual," in its neologistic sense, is the primary objective of being Jewish, that it can be obtained outside of the Jewish religion—although, oddly, it can best be found through the formal beliefs and rituals of other religions—and that it has everything to do with how we feel but nothing much to do with our obligations to God or to anyone else.

This is a *faux*-Judaism and a *faux*-spirituality. Excised from its context in great works of moral instruction—*Mesillat Yesharim, Netivot Olam, Sefer Ahavat Chesed, S'fat Emet, Middot HaRayah, Sefer HaMiddot,* and *Shaarei T'shuvah* being just a few—Jewish spirituality risks conversion into the worst kind of counterfeit. I have read many recent books and articles on the topic of spirituality, which will go unnamed here in the interest of avoiding *lashon hara*, and they resemble something as crass as what one might find in the writing of a self-help guru in a glossy magazine. Spirituality here is mostly about "me" and my "needs" and "growth" with rarely a reference to seeking to become a person who is better equipped to meet the needs of others.

Growth is important for Jewish spirituality, but it is a different sort of growth than what is spoken of here. According to Rabbi Shmuel Shmayeh, the Ostrovitzer Rebbe,

> *a person must serve Hashem by constantly increasing his actions in the service of Hashem, as though [H]e has not amended anything. Therefore, Hashem will absolve the sins of Israel as long as they are constantly increasing their actions.*[40]

We are duty-bound to grow in spirituality, in our connectedness to God. This we can best accomplish through our actions—through *torah* and *t'fillah*, through *tz'dakah* and *chesed*, through fulfilling the *mitzvot* that direct us to "rescue the wretched and the needy; save them from the hand of the wicked" (Psalms 82:4). True Jewish spirituality can be attained only through faithfulness to the Jewish moral tradition. The teachings that it encompasses were ideally crafted by God for our Jewish *n'shamot*. The most profound teaching of all is that our own spirituality is unattainable without first addressing the spiritual and material needs of our brothers and sisters.

RENEWAL AND REDEMPTION

Dedicating oneself to follow the Jewish spiritual path requires a commitment of our intellect, our heart, and our body. It entails our setting an intention that through learning, piety, and ethical acts we will work for the betterment of humankind. In so doing, we better ourselves.

For Jews, seeking to become spiritual is highly labor-intensive. It is not a passive pursuit that involves sitting in a lotus posture waiting for a superconscious revelation. There are lessons to master, compassion to be roused, and specific actions to be undertaken in relation to other living beings and human institutions. Jewish spirituality cannot be pursued in isolation, nor can it be attained outside of an encounter with other Jews who also seek to repair the world. All of us together are needed to complete the work that we have been assigned. This is our inalienable moral charge.

The rabbis agreed, as revealed in their exegesis of the psalm that states, "Out of Zion, the perfection of beauty" (Psalms 50:2). They interpreted this verse as referring to the origins of goodness and perfection in the world. In their minds, the psalmist "means from Zion was the beauty of the world perfected" (*Yoma* 54b).

This gigantic task has not been completed. It is like a massive building project. We have the plans in hand, and many of the structures have been erected. But there are many more yet to construct. We know what the finished product will look like, as we have had a glimpse of its majesty. It is the responsibility of Jews to ensure that the blueprints are followed and that the project progresses in a timely manner until completion.

We must not allow the burden of the task to overwhelm us. It must not cause a diminution of the good in our life. Our spirituality, our *t'shuvah*, or returning, is not about renunciation but about embracing, taking on. We do not accomplish our goals by miserably relinquishing pieces of our happiness. Our God does not vengefully wish that we see penitence as sacrifice and emptiness; rather, we are to see it as a turn to renewal and fullness. Jews know that starving and putting on hair shirts do nothing to make the wrong right. Our suffering alleviates the suffering of no one.

We are to take the moral and material resources that we have been blessed with and consecrate them for a higher good. This we should do willingly, with our full effort, and with great delight. Rabbi Abba Hillel Silver observed,

Judaism's aim was not to make men morosely penitent but joyfully active in moral enterprise. It did not seek to curb the impulses and desires of the human heart but to direct them toward the "wholeness" and harmony of living.[41]

As with so many other aspects of Jewish life and Jewish religious observance, the purpose of Jewish spirituality is to further the causes of *tz'dakah* and *chesed*, justice and mercy. Our *t'shuvah*, as individual Jews and as a people, has value only to the extent to which it creates vibrant and energized souls, committed to lives filled with *g'milut chasadim*. We cannot very well spread lovingkindness if we are filled with anger, hate, depression, or sadness.

The intersections among our God-given duties, the ultimate objectives of our existence, our personal journeys of returning and of Jewish growth, and our pursuit of wholeness are complex and perhaps confusing. The focus of our life should be about striving to do good, not about improving our own well-being. This wholeness and harmony of body and mind and emotions should come from knowing that we have served God in the manner in which He implored us to. Yet without this peace of heart, we may be unable to accomplish all the good that we were put here to do.

It is not easy to reconcile these themes. Moreover, it is not easy to be perfectly selfless beings, putting the needs of all others before our own and caring not about our own welfare. Yet this is not what Judaism asks of us. We are not called to an ascetic ideal or to an ideal requiring any kind of absolute perfection, even moral. We are called, rather, to a steadfastness of intention, to a promise to God that we will never forget our obligations and that we will labor in remembrance that "righteousness and justice are the base of Your throne" (Psalms 89:15). Rav Nachman interpreted this verse to mean, "God said: 'My children, seeing that justice is so beloved before Me, be mindful of it'" (Deuteronomy *Rabbah* 5:3).

The word for "mindful" here is *z'hirin*, which is very close to the word for "remembrance," *zikharon*. They differ by only one letter, the respective second consonants, *heh* and *khaf*, which sound similar. For Jews, mindfulness implies remembrance and thus a temporal connection, a relationship with time. There is no sense of the kind of timelessness and distancing from physical existence characteristic of the mystical ideals promulgated by other religions that speak of mindfulness, such as in a meditative context. We are to recall many things: our Creator, the reasons that He created us, the purpose for which He created us, the covenantal obligations to which we agreed, and the ways in which we are to fulfill these obligations.

Our mindfulness, our remembrance, of the reason that there are Jews in the world is our *mantra*. Our success in taking this to heart, in making efforts to relieve suffering and correct injustices, is our *samādhi*, our touchstone. *T'shuvah*, for Jews, is a lifelong, ongoing process; it never ends. We are always returning to God, coming ever closer to Him through our intentions and actions. When we choose to join with the masses of other Jews who are also on this path of returning, we become a part of an enormous, collective natural experiment in repentance and redemption that is the pursuit of Jewish spirituality.

Thankfully, God listens. If we are sincere in our efforts to be His partners in *tikkun olam*, then He honors His promise to be our active partner as well. Rav Yehudah stated "that through man's penitence the Almighty Himself, as it were, rectifies on high the wrong committed, and thus the world is put right again" (*Zohar* 3:122a).

These themes of penitence, spirituality, morality, and ethical virtue were taken up by Rabbi Abraham Isaac Kook in his inspiring book *Orot Hat'shuvah* (The Lights of Penitence). The inseparability of personal and societal renewal, for Jews, derives from God's having entrusted His universal moral code for safekeeping in the hands of "His holy people" (Deuteronomy 28:9). When we succeed in advancing, personally, in our journey of returning, we contribute to our collective returning and thus to the repair of the world. When we fail, we all fail—we fail ourselves, our fellow Jews, and the beings that depend upon us, whether they know this or not.

Rabbi Kook explained,

> The soul of the people of Israel expresses itself in the striving for absolute justice, which, to be effectuated, must in-

clude the realization of all moral virtues. It is for this rea-
son that any moral misdeed committed by an individual
Jews weakens his link with the soul of the people. The basic
step in penitence is to attach oneself again to the soul of the
people.[42]

For Rabbi Kook, *t'shuvah* is not just about righting past wrongs. It is about raising us from the dead, figuratively speaking; it is about restoring light to darkness. Separated from a consciousness of what we are here for, it is as if we are not really alive. "Penitence is the renewal of life,"[43] he stated. Once back alive, we are obliged to step back onto the sacred path directing our coreligionists to our mutual destination. Without this step, there is no repentance. Again, Rabbi Kook: "The focus of penitence must always be directed toward improving the future."[44]

The world benefits from our renewal. According to Rabbi Kook, this happens both because of the actions we take, of course, and because of the positive character traits that are grown and reinforced in penitent and renewed Jewish individuals. Our spiritual renewal elevates us above the fray without removing us from the world and "thereby raises the world and life itself"[45] with us. The more we dedicate ourselves to our renewal, the more we "will find in it the source of heroism and the most basic content for a life of practicality and idealism."[46]

The result of a Jewish people so renewed and restored, so emboldened, so motivated and inspired to follow Abraham and "go forth" (Genesis 12:1), will be a world transformed. On this point, Rabbi Kook was especially eloquent:

When the desire for absolute justice, as envisioned theoreti-
cally in its spiritual form, grows stronger in the human
soul because one has been ennobled by good character and
good deeds, and by full penitence inspired by love, then this
desire will break out from the ethereal realm and thrust
itself to the ground below, and proclaim with force its mis-
sion to establish justice on earth.[47]

The ultimate consequence of our return and our renewal is no less than the redemption of the entire world. Like lost sheep that have strayed and returned (Psalms 119:176), we restore not just ourselves but the entire flock to wholeness.

When each of us "recognizes that he is not an isolated phenomenon, that he is not an essence that exists independently.... This perception is the basis of morality, even societal morality."[48]

The concept of redemption has been touched upon throughout this book. Unlike its meaning in other religions, notably Christianity, redemption in Judaism is a communal experience. Moreover, it is not sin, strictly speaking, from which we are redeemed; rather, we are redeemed from ignorance, falsehood, impiety, strife, mercilessness, and injustice. These are the exact negations of learning, truth, devotion, peace, mercy, and justice—the sum of both versions of "these three things" contained in *Pirke Avot*. We are redeemed, specifically, from our collective failure to redeem the world by way of the moral imperatives conveyed to us through our sacred writings.

Also unlike other traditions, for us redemption is not a one-time event. It is ongoing and never-ceasing. It brings with it not a reminder of judgment but a gateway to perpetual renewal. Rabbi Eleazar said,

> Redemption is likened to sustenance, and the reverse. As redemption is double, so is sustenance double; and as the latter must be earned every day, so does redemption occur every day. (*Genesis* Rabbah 97:3)

The word "redemption" is usually rendered as *g'ulah*. In several instances in the Hebrew Bible, variants of the word *p'dut* are used. For example, the psalmist tells us that "with the Lord is steadfast love and great power to redeem (*p'dut*)" (Psalms 130:7). The only such appearance in the Torah is in *Parashat Mishpatim*, in the form of *pidyon*, spelled defectively (Exodus 21:30). While the word is rendered as "redemption" in most translations, the meaning here is more akin to ransom.

This is the same word used in the phrase *pidyon haben*, referring to the ceremony in which Jews redeem their first-born sons. Instead of consecrating them to Temple service, as in the past, the celebration today is a reminder that all of us belong to God. Instead of giving up a child, a fee is paid as "ransom," which is then usually donated toward a noteworthy cause, such as the child's education. This ritual is generally not celebrated by Reform Jews but still exists in the other branches of Judaism.

The close connection between redemption and ransom is directly relevant to a discussion of repentance and renewal. When we pay a ransom, we are giving something up to get something back. A precious possession is returned to us, one that we once held but not tightly enough. We trade something of value, of equal worth, in compensation for our possession, which is then returned.

When Jews seek the redemption of humankind, we are seeking to recover for the world a realization of its innate holiness. Through millennia of ignorance, falsehood, impiety, strife, mercilessness, and injustice, the world has forgotten its Source, has forgotten what the Jewish people have never forgotten: that "the Lord is God from of old, Creator of the earth from end to end" (Isaiah 40:28). The world's transgressions have become a patina of soot, obscuring the light of holiness that shone at its creation.

What serves as our ransom, what we give up so that the world's light may once again shine brightly, is our best effort, consecrated to the divine service. The Lubavitcher Rebbe described how we should prepare to bring redemption to the world: "By learning about G-d and spirituality so that we may live according to His will."[49] We must be unrelenting in our pursuit of these ends. God tells us to "busy [ourselves] with the Torah, [because] the other nations do not busy themselves with the Torah" (M'gillah 15b). "We must do anything we can," the Rebbe said, "to direct even one ray of light into the darkness."[50] Our learning and our spirituality are imperative if our brothers and sisters are to be rescued.

Any truly Jewish discussion of the benefits of loving God cannot honestly separate out the transient personal gains—in mood, morale, sense of purpose, and well-being—from the more lasting transformation that we seek in society. The important work of growing as Jews, growing as a people who seeks "only to do justice and to love mercy" (Micah 6:8) and to love the Source of justice and mercy, is all directed toward a higher end. Because we need our whole self for the important work of restoring wholeness and holiness to all humankind, our personal well-being indeed matters. But dissected from its utility as sustenance for bodies and minds obliged to do good, our continued vitality of flesh and spirit is like "the great abundance of the wicked" (Psalms 37:16).

That our actions are paramount, that spiritual growth left unconsecrated to good deeds is fruitless, and that the world depends upon each of us are constant themes repeated throughout Jewish sacred writings and the moral teachings of our rabbis. At times, the words of our prophets and sages seem practically relentless. To one raised in Jewish observance or at least in an ethically Jewish home, these expectations of us are probably so ingrained as to be tacit. Whether anyone among us follows through to the best of our capabilities is another matter. Almost all of us probably do not.

Redemption of our culture and of the world depends upon personal renewal. We Jews are accountable to God for the state of the world in which we live. Its continued brokenness is testimony that we have not completed our assignment, that our fulfillment of our covenantal charge remains a work in progress. A more important question than how a personal relationship with God will benefit us is whether the benefits to us of such a relationship can be passed along to others. Our real gain is not in the healing or repair of a mental, emotional, or fleshly wound but in the lasting renewal of our self-identity, our connection to God, and our relationship with humankind. When we are restored, we can join with other restored Jews who await our assistance.

Rav Abbahu provides an insightful *d'rash* on the psalmists' words (Psalms 34:15). The Talmud records,

> *Of peacemaking it is said: "Seek peace and pursue it"; and Rav Abbahu said: "We learn 'pursuing' from 'pursuing.'"*
> (Kiddushin 40a)

This sage's words reveal a greater depth of understanding than is found in the writing of many contemporary psychologists and theologians.

By loving God, we learn about loving God. By loving God in our actions, we may come to love God in our heart. By striving to pursue those acts that define loving God, we can hope to experience the fullness of a personal relationship with God. The emotional dimension of such a relationship—the inner recognition of God's presence in us through His *Sh'khinah*—may not come as easily to some of us as to others. It may always remain impalpable. But there is no other way in which we can hope to experience this Divine Presence than to "depart from evil, and do good; seek peace, and pursue it" (Psalms 34:15). There is no other way.

CHAPTER FIVE

HOW DOES LOVING GOD AFFECT OUR WORLD?

"Rabbi Eleazar on concluding his prayer used to say the following: 'May it be Thy will, O Lord our God, to cause to dwell in our lot love and brotherhood and peace and friendship, and mayest Thou make our borders rich in disciples and prosper our latter end with good prospect and hope, and set our portion in Paradise, and confirm us with a good companion and a good impulse in Thy world.'" (B'rakhot 16b)

Chapter 4 emphasized how loving God is expressed in ways that shape the Jewish character—our identity, our spirituality, our purpose in life. Our relationship with God, how we respond to His call to "follow the Lord your God" (I Samuel 12:14), defines who we are and what we do. Our loving response to God's love for us gives our life meaning and purpose. Whether or not we choose to follow through, to externalize our personal feelings of connection and union with the Source of our being, has implications beyond our individual lives.

When Jews expand the scope of their love for God beyond God to include other humans and other living beings, the world is changed. This is an essential part of our calling as Jews, our covenant with the One who made us Jews. For this, we are to be grateful; to wit, in the second of the fifteen *Birkhot Hashachar* (morning blessings), we thank God for making us Jewish.[1] We thank God for making us a part of a people that gets to know Him and love Him in a unique and promised way, distinctively from all other peoples.

But this special gift carries special obligations. Martin Buber acknowledged this when he concluded bluntly that "the love of God is unreal unless it is crowned with love for one's fellow man."[2] Jews are called upon to excel in manifesting this kind of limitless love. Ideally, we succeed.

This seems, on the surface, to describe an especially merciful, just, and perhaps even altruistic people. Some of this characterization may be so, we should hope; some is no doubt overstated. But this defining feature of the Jewish *mythos* is also strikingly audacious. That specific moral demands inhere in our tribal identity runs counter to the stridently individualistic tone of the past two centuries of Western social and political philosophy. Unfettered autonomy and absolute liberty are bywords of the post-Enlightenment ethos that permeates and drives our *laissez-faire* popular culture, our lax mores, and our innate lack of connection and obligation to other beings. Judaism rejects this vision unequivocally.

Rabbi Jonathan Sacks, former Chief Rabbi of the United Hebrew Congregations of the British Commonwealth, articulated the Jewish response to the peculiar contemporary belief that all of us "enter the world with a clean slate on which we can draw any self-portrait we wish."[3] In his thoughtful and reflective book *A Letter in the Scroll*, Rabbi Sacks asserted, "Against this whole complex of ideas, Jewish life is a sustained countervoice. To be a Jew is to know that this cannot be the full story of who I am."[4]

When God made us Jews, he made us "part of a long line of people who traveled toward a certain destination and whose journey remains unfinished, dependent on [us] to take it further."[5] Throughout history, according to Rabbi Sacks, this has been our "most basic conviction"[6] as Jews, and though the outcome of our journey lies beyond our sight, it is "of immense consequence for mankind."[7] Our ancestors knew this, but too many of us have forgotten. Other things creep into our perspective, obscuring our view of the destination that God laid out for us.

The Western pursuit of personal freedom has become an obsession, with hedonism and pleasure drawing us away to a focus on nonessential enticements that destroy our souls. These addictions are fueled by the incessant messages of innumerable pitchmen imploring us to buy their snake oil, their failed ideologies, their material and intellectual products. If only we turn ourselves over to these lies, we will be perfectly happy and healthy and free, ever relieved of the burden to maneuver our way through the myriad ethical decisions that confront us on a daily basis. Our fragile emotions will no longer be injured by images of injustice and mercilessness because we will be too busy to notice.

Vain pursuits are thus functional in a sense. They excuse us from attending to the sacred charge that God set before us. The Jewish way of life, after all, is laborious and, as history teaches, full of risk. In every epoch of Jewish history, Jews have lost their property, liberty, and life because they strove to carve out a special niche in the world from where we could labor for the redemption of humankind.

But we must resist these vanities. They are not for us. God demands of us, "Thou shalt not follow a multitude to do evil" (Exodus 23:2). Should our persistent indulgence in the world's temptations inure us to disregarding God's voice in our heart, then we will find ourselves permanently decoupled from God. We will then become a people "set apart" (Psalms 4:4) in a way that God never intended. The psalmist explains: "But those who in their crookedness act corruptly, let the Lord make them go the way of evildoers" (Psalms 125:5).

If we insist on being like everyone else, then God will oblige us. We will become one with the multitudes. The loss to the world would be incalculable. These very multitudes spoken of by God depend upon our remaining a people set apart in order that the Torah-constructed values of truth, peace, and justice have an abode in the world. When we ignore our covenantal responsibilities, we thus endanger both ourselves and the rest of the world into which we are so eager to disappear. This irony is apparently lost on the purveyors of temptations that lure us away. Sadly, the irony is also lost on so many Jews.

Our relationship with God has consequences far beyond our own Jewish lives. This was recognized by the rabbis, who affirmed what Professor Neusner called our "mythic present tense."[8] This he described as a faith among the rabbinic redactors and compilers of the oral Torah that the realities they described were eternal, continuous from Moses at Sinai through the present day: one people, one covenant, one epoch.

Their task as they saw it, according to Professor Neusner, was to translate scriptural imperative into worldly laws that would govern how "life should be lived, society should be organized, God should be served"[9] in an era of post-Temple Judaism. Their objective: "They legislate so as to form a perfect society, a people made in the model of the Torah."[10] The ultimate result they sought: "It is through the concrete achievement of the teachings of the Torah, here and now, that the rabbis intended to bring redemption."[11]

We should never underestimate the power that we are capable of marshaling, with God's support, when all Jews together set a common intention. God promises that our collective efforts at learning, prayer, and good deeds—a familiar triplet—will bear fruit and will have the most profound effects on the world. Rabbi Natan explained,

> *The Holy One, blessed be He, says: "If a man occupies himself with the study of the Torah and with works of charity and prays with the congregation, I account it to him as if he had redeemed Me and My children from among the nations of the world." (B'rakhot 8a)*

The word for "redeemed" here is a variation on *pidyon*, which, as was described in Chapter 4, refers to ransom. When we devote ourselves to "these three things" in concert with other Jews, our communal effort effectively gets the world out of captivity and restores it to freedom. Without such effort, we are to presume, the world will remain in bondage.

The freedom that we are capable of obtaining for ourselves and for all humankind is far more precious and lasting than the ersatz freedom beckoning to us if only we loosen God's grip on our soul. The latter "freedom" may deliver a life that for a season is replete with material rewards that delight and impress, intense feelings of pleasure and satisfaction, and praise and approbation for shallow thoughts that ape the basest sentiments sanctioned by the culture in which we live. But soon enough, the culture that defines freedom in such a manner will become a victim of its own dissolute character and will not survive. If we have allowed ourselves to disperse into this abyss, then neither will we survive.

The world depends upon Jews acting in conformity with Jewish ethical teachings. Our moral obligations constitute our sacred trust. Only if we remain true to our God-given mission can we guarantee a safe place for us and our descendants and for all people. If we are resolute, then "Israel shall sprout and blossom, and the face of the world shall be covered with fruit" (Isaiah 27:6).

OUR BROTHER'S KEEPER

The Torah's most famous meditation on our obligations to others and the consequences of our eschewing these obligations is found in the story of Cain and Abel in *Parashat B'reshit*. Cain is overwhelmed by envy of his brother and by resentment toward God, Who favors Abel over Cain and Who reproves Cain for his sinfulness and the miserliness of his offerings. So Cain kills Abel.

> *Cain [spoke] to his brother Abel . . . and when they were in the field, Cain set upon his brother Abel and killed him. The Lord said to Cain, "Where is your brother Abel?" And he said, "I do not know. Am I my brother's keeper?" (Genesis 4:8–9)*

God did not respond to Cain's question directly. But His displeasure was apparent in what He did say. Cain would now be "more cursed than the ground" (Genesis 4:11), a more severe curse even than that received by Adam when he disobeyed God (Genesis 3:17). Worse, God informed Cain, "You shall become a ceaseless wanderer on earth" (Genesis 4:12).

The notion that we are our brother's keeper has been a source of great contention for much of human history. Many of the divisions, philosophical and political, that separate people can be traced to responses to this idea first given widespread airing in the sad story of Cain and Abel. I suspect that a lot of the controversy sparked by the concept of being our brother's keeper originates in misunderstandings of the word "keeper." It seems to imply, to some people, a role akin to that of a sovereign or ruler. Depending upon whether one sees oneself as a potential keeper or brother, this relationship might be considered idyllic or nightmarish.

The word translated here as "keeper" is *hashomer*, based on the same root word as in the phrase *"shomrei shabbat"* in the *yism'chu* prayer. Being a keeper of *shabbat*, in this context, does not imply the concept of keeping as in, say, a zookeeper— a superintendent, one who oversees, rules, or directs or controls the affairs of another being. This would make no sense with respect to *shabbat*. Accordingly, there is nothing inherent in the word *shomer* akin to lording over another person. Rather, it implies being a guardian or protector. It means being one who maintains, who keeps alive, literally. Just as we are to maintain, to be a guardian, a preserver of *shabbat*, we are obliged to preserve our brother's life. To be our brother's keeper means to be a guarantor of his life, well-being, and continued prospering.

Rabbi J. H. Hertz, a predecessor of Rabbi Sacks as British Chief Rabbi, touched on the life-or-death implications of Cain's snide response to God. From the tone of his complaint, one can tell, "Cain's answer is both false and insolent. Only a murderer altogether renounces the obligations of brotherhood."[12]

In *Etz Hayim*, the Conservative *chumash*, or annotated Torah, both the *p'shat* (literal) and *d'rash* (homiletical) commentaries elucidate this point. The purpose of the story of Cain and Abel is "to teach that man is indeed his brother's keeper and that all homicide is fratricide."[13] Thus,

> *For Judaism, the answer to Cain's question "Am I my brother's keeper?" is an unequivocal yes! Survivors of the* Sho-ah *painfully remember not only the cruelty of the Nazis but the cold indifference of their neighbors who looked on and did nothing; or they recall the exceptional courage of the righteous gentiles who sought to help them.*[14]

The Reform *chumash* also underscores the ultimate implications of Cain's words, both for his time and for today:

> *There, the human choice was essentially between life and death; now, in the post-Eden world, God offers us a new choice, the choice between good and evil. Cain chooses murder, the ultimate evil. And having granted humanity moral freedom, God, in a sense, shares in its transgressions. But though we may ask where God was at the hour of violence, God's failure to answer does not reduce our responsibility.*[15]

Rabbi S. R. Hirsch's interpretation of Cain's remarks is especially insightful. Although written down a century before the liberal commentaries just cited, his cogent understanding of Cain's audacity is in accord with these contemporary perspectives on the moral implications of our duties to others. Cain thinks that his disinterested, whining reply "is a perfectly legitimate excuse,"[16] but it serves only to "reflect the abject depravity"[17] of his actions.

> *It is not his business to look after his brother; he already has his hands full attending to his own affairs. In addition to reflecting a most cold-blooded egotism, the foregoing also affords us stern warning that the loveless principle, "Every man for himself" is not far distant from that malevolent hatred which impels a man to murder even the one closest to him if he feels that the latter stands in the way of his self-fulfillment.*[18]

Cain is thus a paradigm of the postmodern, independent person, liberated from any obligations to anyone or anything aside from his or her own nonce desires. Like so many men and women today, raised outside of a faith tradition that holds up a gold standard of personal behavior grounded in ethical responsibilities to others, Cain believed that he was the center of his universe, answerable to no one. From there, it was a small step to exterminate a nuisance whose continued existence threatened his self-esteem and impeded his own selfish pursuits. And from there, it was an even smaller step to dare lie about it—to God, no less.

Cain sounds like so many of the public figures who loom large in our culture. Our politicians, our entertainment celebrities, our media personalities, our purveyors of self-help nostrums for body, mind, and spirit. We are bombarded constantly with messages imploring us to obsess over ourselves: our inner growth, our achievement, our fitness and beauty, our investments, our cultivation of lavish lifestyles that we cannot even afford. We should worry first about number one, we should be our own best friend, we should remember that love of self is the greatest love of all.

This all sounds so benign. It is a bit self-centered, to be sure, and obnoxious perhaps, but is there really any comparison to Cain?

Yes, there is. Think of the news stories we see on a regular basis of people who are too busy to help the victim of a rape that they witness because they are on their cell phones; mothers who dispose of their newborn babies in a garbage dumpster because they have a party to attend; parents who attempt to murder their child's schoolmate because the girls are competing for the same slot on the cheerleading squad.

Or, on a larger scale, think of the politicians whose legislation prevents poor families from seeking to improve the education of their children while they send their own children to elite private schools; corporate criminals who loot their companies' pension funds, thus destroying the lives of thousands of families, in order that they may live like barons on huge estates; clergy and elected officials who speak out against personal and societal immorality while being guilty of the worst crimes of sexual predation against women and minors.

The story of Cain is the story of many of the most prominent people in our culture. It may also be the story of our neighbors and friends. There is more of Cain in us than we may be comfortable admitting. Cain is everyman. Cain is also a complete sociopath. But Cain is something else as well: our ancestor.

After God banished Cain to wander the earth, he married and fathered Enoch. From there, the line of descent goes through Irad, Mehiyael, Methusael, Lamech, and Naamah (Genesis 4:17–22). The Torah then records that Adam and Eve had a new son, Seth, to replace the murdered Abel. From Seth, a parallel line of descent follows: Enosh, Kenan, Mahalalel, Jared, Enoch, Methuselah, Lamech, Noah (Genesis 5:1–31). From Noah's descendents, ultimately, came Abraham, Moses, and the Jewish people.

Much ink has been spilled commenting on the striking similarities, even identity in places, of these two genealogical lines. It is usually concluded that these represent two versions of the same line of descent. It has been suggested that inclusion of the second line "was probably due to the understandable disinclination to have all humans appear to be descended from a murderer."[19] But this point may be moot. The Midrash records that "Rav Abba bar Kahana said: 'Naamah was Noah's wife'" (Genesis *Rabbah* 23:3). Moreover, she was a promoter of idolatry (*l'avodat kokhavim*; literally "worship of stars") (Genesis *Rabbah* 23:3). So in one way or the other, we all are related to Cain, and we all bear the birthright of his curse.

This is good news for us. Just as our great patriarchs who followed Cain were able to rise above whatever hereditary burden resulted from Cain's seed or blood, so too can we. As we struggle with our *yetzer hara*, we have the same resource that our ancestors had, once Moses received the Torah. God's message to us is that He has given us a blueprint to overcome our Cain-ness. The teachings of the Torah provide us with a means both to order our worldly affairs and to refine our character in ways that are consistent with the highest moral principles. God said, succinctly, "You shall observe My laws" (Leviticus 19:19). But if we eschew this advice, if we become "one whose inside is not like his outside" (*Yoma* 72b), then we are not true heirs to the Torah, to the redemption won by Abraham and Moses; rather, we are heirs of Cain.

The best way to manifest the kinds of traits that denote a person of character, but in one's heart and in one's deliberate actions in the world, is to cultivate the most elevated and ennobling of these traits, namely love. God tells us, "Love your fellow as yourself: I am the Lord" (Leviticus 19:18). Commenting upon this verse, the Yerushalmi records, "Rav Akiva says, 'This is the great general rule of the Torah'" (*Y. N'darim* 9:4). As a precursor of sorts to the golden rule, this idea is at the center of the moral traditions of most of the great religions of the world, as C. S. Lewis famously described.[20]

The love that we are to feel for God and for each other provides a model for the construction of our social and political institutions. The means that we undertake to love God through fostering learning, service of the heart, and justice and mercy—values that exist to guide us in our construction of the ideal world that God has entrusted us to build.

Rabbi Sacks has reflected on the significance of the Jewish covenant with God and our relationship with our Creator in informing our unique role in the world:

> *Of all the great religions, Judaism has the strongest conception of freedom and dignity of the individual, beginning with the principle that the human person as such is the one bearer of the image of God. That idea led Israel from its earliest days to search for institutions that would create stable associations combining independence with interdependence. The model it found was the covenant—the morally binding pact between two parties that respects the freedom and dignity of each while bringing them together in creative partnership.*[21]

This implied world is one characterized by the sorts of obligations one might expect to be incumbent upon a people who confesses, "The mercy of God endureth continually" (Psalms 52:3) and "I trust in the mercy of God for ever and ever" (Psalms 52:10). Devotion to social responsibility, social action, social justice—these are touchstones of a life lived consistently in accord with the explicit charge of our covenant to pursue mercy and justice.

Rabbi Elliott N. Dorff has outlined some of the features of an envisioned ideal world, one shaped by the principles of *tikkun olam*.[22] In such a world, people will speak and behave respectfully toward each other, will come to the assistance of the poor, will work to ensure greater prosperity for those without, will labor to free the world from disease and suffering, will seek to promote both procedural and substantive justice, and will strive to bring about a cessation of war.

As Jews, we are keepers and standard bearers of a moral tradition that imposes upon us specific duties to our respective families, congregations, communities, and nations, and to the world. For us, love of God and love of other beings—indeed, love of all beings—are inseparable and require from us the same commitments of mind and heart and body. The intertwining of our personal code of morality and our ethical responsibilities in the larger spheres in which we live and labor is quite apparent in so many of the great works of the *musar* tradition of Jewish ethics and moral instruction.

One of the earliest of these texts is *Shaarei T'shuvah* (The Gates of Repentance), authored by the saintly Rabbi Yonah ben Avraham of Gerona. It is telling to observe how many of the spiritual exercises, practices, and principles espoused by Rabbi Yonah are founded on, and focus on, our responsibilities to other people. Alongside condemnation of moral failures such as evil thoughts, cursing, bearing a grudge, profanity, and covetousness is a much lengthier list of "exhortations involving the closing of one's hand and the abstention from action."[23] These include admonition and rebuke of those who strike one's neighbor, place a stumbling block before others, steal, oppress a debtor, judge corruptly, rob the poor, or cause the populace to sin. Also condemned are those who fail to lend to the poor, to pay a hired worker in a timely fashion, to come to the rescue of one's neighbor and the neighbor's property, or to establish community welfare groups. Our sins are those of both commission and omission.

Judaism asserts that we bear a collective responsibility to ensure the kind of world that God wishes for there to be. It will not evolve into an enlightened utopia by default. Nor will it exist because God inserts Himself directly into history and wills it instantly into being in response to our plea, like a magic genie, irrespective of our actions.

In *The Dignity of Difference*, Rabbi Sacks concluded, "There is nothing inevitable about the survival of civilizations."[24] Rather, only through our taking control of our destiny by taking responsibility for our future can we steer our world to a favorable destination. According to Rabbi Sacks, this will entail a heavy dose of contribution, compassion, creativity, cooperation, conservation, and conciliation. There is no guarantee that we will be successful, but proceeding in any other way guarantees our failure. Rabbi Sacks thus rightly called the religious ideals that inspire this agenda "a covenant of hope."[25]

The religious basis for human rights endures as a gold standard for social behavior that is lacking in human-made ideologies based on moral relativism, in fundamentalist perversions of religion that destroy the moral autonomy of individual believers, and in political revolutions founded on assertions of power that supersede the humanity of individuals in favor of the imagined destiny of a "master race" or "new man." Secularism, theocracy, and totalitarianism are failed religion-substitutes that militate against free exercise of our conscience in service to a noble ideal. They respectively pervert, eradicate, or collectivize the liberties that we require to operate effectively as God's agents in the world. These ideologies are based on ever-shifting sands (secularism), on dogmatic assertions that snuff out dissent (theocracy), and on denial of the intrinsic worth of every human being (totalitarianism). Compared to Judaism, which has managed to sustain a wandering and despised people for thousands of years, enabling them to bestow upon the world their intellect, creativity, and moral acuity, these ideologies are miserable failures.

Our ability to be present with others, to empathize with them, and to respond to their needs requires our identity as individual moral actors. We must be able to identify with our fellow humans, respecting their inalienable natural rights as our own. Seeing and judging others as unique individuals created in God's image, as are we, are the basis for the good deeds that we do. All people deserve our compassion, our assistance, and our fellowship, from our neighbors to the most alienated outsiders, "for you know the feelings of the stranger, having yourselves been strangers" (Exodus 23:9).

PERSONAL AND CULTURAL RENEWAL

Our continued evolvement into a people that is loving, merciful, and just is contingent upon our devotion to "make confession to the Lord, God of your fathers, and do His will" (Ezra 10:11). Accomplishing our assigned tasks in the world serves both to heal and repair the world, as in the concept of *tikkun olam*, and to elevate and repair ourselves. This is a different kind of *tikkun*, known as *tikkun halev*, or repair of the heart.

Our personal growth and renewal, as individuals and as a people, and our work for the repair and renewal of the world, as individuals and as a people, are connected in an uneasy and symbiotic relationship. I have already expressed my belief that the former is not absolutely requisite for the latter. At the same time, I have also expressed my belief that the latter is the best way in which we can ensure the former. What does this mean for us as individual Jews seeking peace of heart for ourselves and peace for the world?

That our self-actualization is not a requirement for us to act mercifully and justly toward others should be evident. But this is not in any way meant to disparage the pursuit of inner growth. Consecrated to making us the best Jews that we can become, the refinement of our character is a noble aim, one that all of us should endeavor toward.

My point is not that Jews should disregard personal growth in favor of selfless service to others. Rather, for Jews, no program or set of spiritual exercises exists that promises to remake us into the divine image in isolation from our relationships with other people. Our self-actualization is not required to precede our efforts at *tikkun olam* because it *cannot* precede it. There is no ideal in Judaism, nor any *mitzvah* or ethical guideline, any esoteric practice or prophetic enjoinder, any rabbinic *responsum*, now or at any time in our history, that suggests that all of us or any of us can become "the holy people, the redeemed of the Lord" (Isaiah 62:12) outside of obeying what God requires of us: "only to do justly, and to love mercy, and to walk humbly with thy God" (Micah 6:8).

A prevailing feature of the human potential and new age movements and of associated programs of self-help is belief that each of us can become like God, even become gods ourselves. These philosophies have proven mighty attractive to many people of Jewish origin, filling a void left empty through detachment from Jewish religious traditions. The recent predilection to borrow from Jewish mysticism, incorporating selected kabbalistic concepts, has served these philosophies well, creating even stronger attraction for disaffected Jews unfamiliar with the context of these teachings. Our brothers and sisters are thus falling under the sway of systems of belief and practice pieced together like a Frankenstein's monster, with just enough presumably Jewish content to appear convincing and perhaps assuage one's guilt.

In one sense, we actually are encouraged to become like God. But this has nothing to do with attainment of a heightened state of consciousness, with practicing a special form of meditation, or with exhibiting magisterial gifts of the spirit. These may be pleasant enough pursuits, even fulfilling and enlightening for those attracted to this mode of spiritual expression. Jewish texts acknowledge and approve of these ways of experiencing the spiritual realm, although in a strictly contextualized fashion quite unlike their place in non-Jewish systems.

For Jews, in no way does meditation, for example, make us into anything substantially different from what we were when we began: Jews in a covenantal relationship with God that requires us to perform specific actions. We may have more peace of mind perhaps, and that is a good thing. But we will have moved not one step closer to effecting tz'dakah and chesed until we stand up, walk out into the physical world, and "break the power of the wicked and evil man" (Psalms 10:15).

The Talmud tells us precisely how we are to emulate God:

Rabbi Chama b. Rabbi Chanina further said: "What means the text: 'Ye shall walk after the Lord your God?' [Deuteronomy 13:5]. Is it, then, possible for a human being to walk after the sh'khinah; for has it not been said: 'For the Lord thy God is a devouring fire?' [Deuteronomy 4:24]. But [the meaning is] to walk after the attributes of the Holy One, blessed be He. As He clothes the naked, for it is written: 'And the Lord God made for Adam and for his wife coats of skin, and clothed them' [Genesis 3:21], so do thou also clothe the naked. The Holy One, blessed be He, visited the sick, for it is written: 'And the Lord appeared unto him by the oaks of Mamre' [Genesis 18:1], so do thou also visit the sick. The Holy One, blessed be He, comforted mourners, for it is written: 'And it came to pass after the death of Abraham, that God blessed Isaac his son' [Genesis 25:11], so do thou also comfort mourners. The Holy one, blessed be He, buried the dead, for it is written: 'And He buried him in the valley' [Deuteronomy 34:6], so do thou also bury the dead." (Sotah 14a)

To be like God, to walk in His shoes, does not imply that we should or could possibly become identified with His spiritual presence, as if some sort of spiritual practice, repeated diligently for years, could transform us into the "cloud of the Lord" (Exodus 40:38) that hovered above the *mishkan*, or Tabernacle. That is not what it means for us to become like God. The greatest spiritual heights that any Jew can ever hope to attain in this worldly existence is simply to become someone who takes after God in his or her behavior: clothing the naked, visiting the sick, comforting mourners, burying the dead. Through performance of *g'milut chasadim*, we become as god-like as is humanly possible.

At all times, we must be cognizant of our duties to others. Just as every time that we "complain and moan" we are assured that "He hears my voice" (Psalms 55:18), God requires us always to be responsive to the pleas and cries of the less fortunate and those in need. This is no easy task. It is simple to long for some idealized state of "oneness" with God or to imagine that we are like God, with all of His knowledge and all of His power. But how many of us long for His responsibilities and His burdens? Since we do not possess His wisdom or His omniscience and omnipotence, it is well and good that we can come no closer to becoming God than to mimic His actions the best that we can as often as we can remember to do so.

The lure of a promised, and impossible, mystical union with God is not the only enticement distracting us from our real obligations. Fallen-away Jews, moreover, are not the only victims of spiritual falsehoods. Disregard for the needs of others can befall otherwise socially conscious Jews who are devoted to the social agenda for our religion just as easily as the unaffiliated, wandering, or spiritually lost.

Some of the most self-centered people I have ever met, I am sorry to say, have been Jews who are deeply committed to one or another social causes. So wrapped up in institution building, fund-raising, political lobbying, cajoling, and the prideful certainty of their own moral rectitude, they lose sight of the real needs of people right in front of them. So busy trying to remake the world in their own image of what is right, they "turn aside the needy in the gate" (Amos 5:12). No matter that their efforts may be sincere or of real benefit, Jews cannot afford to lose sight of the human face of suffering. We should never be so busy with grand causes that we forget about the beggar at our door.

In my limited experience, these folks have been the exception, thank God. But their existence among us warns that it is imperative that we not let our concern for people blot out our compassion for individual persons.

As always, *Pirke Avot* contains a jewel of great wisdom on this topic. We are told, "Shammai says: 'Make of thy Torah study a fixed practice; say little and do much; and receive all men with a cheerful countenance'" (*Pirke Avot* 1:15). The commentary on this passage is a source of great advice. Rabbi Shammai's first point means that "what a man learns, let him practice himself and then teach others that they may practice it"; his second point means that "the righteous say little and do much, but the wicked say much and do not do even a little" (*Avot d'Rabbi Natan* 13). His third point is self-explanatory.

Rabbi Shimon ben Zemah Duran, fourteenth- and fifteenth-century Spanish talmudic scholar, known as the Rashbaz, taught that Rabbi Shammai was urging us to pursue "three human attainments . . . wisdom, strength, riches,"[26] respectively. Learning Torah is a path of wisdom; valuing action over words is a path to riches, material and spiritual; and kindness to others is an indicator of strength and mastery. The Rashbaz explained that pursuit of these attainments—yet another list of "three things" encompassing intellect, action, and heart—helps us to subdue our *yetzer hara* and thus makes us "mighty."[27]

Our journey to the world envisioned by our efforts at *tikkun olam* and the personal journey of each of us seeking *tikkun halev* are thus the same journey. For the questing Jew, peace of heart and peace on earth cannot be distinguished in theory or differentiated in practice. What we do to achieve the one is what we do to accomplish the other. It is not that one leads to the other, in whichever direction. For us, they are one and the same.

In his appropriately titled book *God Is a Verb*, Rabbi David A. Cooper has eloquently described the Jewish-mystical perspective on the interconnection of personal and social renewal. *Tikkun olam* and *tikkun halev* or, in Rabbi Cooper's words, *tikkun hanefesh*, repair of the soul, are much alike. Each is about redeeming sparks, unveiling holiness, bringing itself closer to its Source, whether referring to the world as a whole or to each of our souls.[28]

> *Although initially the ideas of mending the soul and mending the world seem different, in reality they cannot be separated; we cannot raise sparks in ourselves without raising those in the world, and vice versa. Even more important, according to Kabbalah, the process of expanding awareness in ourselves and the world is the fundamental reason for our existence. In fact, when we make no effort to raise our own consciousness and that of the world, we abdicate our humanness.*[29]

There is one way in which these two *tikkunim* do not necessarily go hand in hand. While the actions we undertake in pursuit of both ends may be the same, there is no guarantee that any of us will live to see the work completed. We may strive diligently to repair the world, and we may meet with many successes, but because of the persistence of suffering, there will always remain a gnawing unease in our hearts.

Jews are notorious empaths, restless and dissatisfied, identifying with the downtrodden and oppressed because we were once downtrodden and oppressed. We are complainers—and with good reason. When the world is beset with wickedness and suffering, "Don't worry, be happy," is an obnoxious *man-*

tra that should have no appeal for any Jewish heart. Granted, God wants us to be happy, and, God willing, all of us should attain happiness but not at the price of closing our eyes to the problems in the world that demand our "worry" and attention.

The Midrash describes the danger to all of us when any Jew decides that his or her own *tikkun hanefesh* or *tikkun halev* takes precedence over *tikkun olam*. Rabbi Tanchuma warned that the person who is guilty of

> *secluding himself in the corner of his home and declaring, "What concern are the problems of the community to me?...Why should I listen to them? I will do well (without them)," he helps to destroy the world.* (Midrash Tanchuma *Exodus 6, §2*)

The harmony and balance that we seek in ourselves would thus be more productively sought in the "the problems of the community." In this way, at least we stand a chance of bettering our communities and ourselves rather than ultimately destroying both. Rabbi Wayne Dosick, spiritual guide of a Jewish Renewal congregation in San Diego, identified the real priority of Jewish existence, describing it as lucidly as I have seen anywhere:

> *In partnership with God, the Jewish mission is to take this magnificent and grand universe that God has created and to work to combat the ills and the evils that beset our world; to work to move the world, step by step, closer to transformation and perfection.*[30]

This is the only transformation and perfection worthy of our fullest effort to pursue. If we turn our attention solely to ourselves, we risk removing ourselves from the umbrella of a moral tradition that exists to guide and protect us from competing belief systems posing as truth. Worse, we are likely to mistake the pursuit of absolute freedom as a path to self-transformation and self-improvement. We are then doubly off track. Our ultimate goal is inconsistent with what God expects from us, and our means of getting there will never work anyway.

Many of us seek such freedom, especially the freedom to opt out of the laborious challenges that confront each Jew committed to our ethical mandate. To some of us, this seems like bondage. But however we do or do not choose to accept the reality and authority of Jewish law, however each branch of Judaism interprets the authority of *halakhah*, no Jew is free to ignore the imperatives imposed upon us by the ethical *mitzvot*. To engage them intellectually and then to act on them to the best of our abilities constitute the most basic *sine qua non* of Jewish observance. God forbid that anybody self-identifying as Jewish should choose liberation from such "bondage."

The freedom held up as ideal in our culture represents a double-edged sword. It has guaranteed an environment in which individual Jews have sufficient political liberty to say, "Let us decide for ourselves what is just; let us know among ourselves what is good" (Job 34:4). In other words, we are free to choose a God Who empowers us to take moral actions in pursuit of His will for us. But this freedom also presents temptations that lead us to remake ourselves in the self-absorbed, self-indulgent, corporate-consumerist image that defines what is just and what is good. We need to remember that "for those who choose another god, their sorrows shall be multiplied" (Psalms 16:4). This freedom gives not life but death.

A relationship with our God, through pursuit of acts of lovingkindness and justice that express our love for Him, alone gives us real freedom. Our appropriate response to the false freedoms dangled before us by the world is to use the resoluteness that God implanted in us for courageous acts.

Rabbi Yose offered an inspiring *d'rash* on the familiar words of the *Sh'ma*. He explained that "you shall love the Lord your God" (Deuteronomy 6:5) means that "man should bind himself to Him with very strong love, and that all service performed by man to God should be with love, since there is no service like the love of the Holy One, blessed be He" (*Zohar* 3:267a). Rabbi Abba added that "one who loves God is crowned with lovingkindness on all sides and does lovingkindness throughout, sparing neither his person nor his money" (*Zohar* 3:267a).

Love of God, through service to humankind, requires sacrifice and may demand costs, financial or personal. But it is a great privilege to be able to give of ourselves to help create the world in which God wants us to live. We should not enter into our covenant of mutual love with God expecting only the sort of blessings that the world would acknowledge as such. We love God by following His advice, in essence. If Jewish history is any indication, this is not necessarily the quickest or most direct path to physical, emotional, or financial well-being. The obstacles may be many, but we cannot let them overwhelm us.

Our renewal and our ultimate redemption require that we pursue the renewal and redemption of the world. This requires selflessness, devotion, long-suffering, integrity, courage, and nonattachment to personal gain. These virtues do not make us perfect altruists, strictly speaking, as we are promised our reward in the world to come.[31] But if we have acted righteously and with the correct motives, then no matter our personal status, we can confess, along with a lonely, naked, and decrepit Rabbi Shimon ben Yochai, "Happy is my portion that thou seest me thus, for otherwise I would not be what I am" (*Zohar* 1:11b).

MORALITY AND SOCIAL CHANGE

If we are to address the pressing issues of the day successfully, then this effort will require our virtue and morality. Bettering the lot of our fellow human beings involves working for positive changes in the social, economic, and political spheres as well as working to meet the immediate needs of the individuals who cross our path on a daily basis. Our work is as much about caring for those in need, especially in our own communities, as it is about global transformation. Our focus is on the micro, meso, and macro levels of human life. We seek redemption of individual souls, of social institutions, and of the whole world.

Our Jewish values tell us what our destination is. We seek a world governed by principles that reflect the best and most refined human characteristics. The rabbis have delineated these ideal traits throughout the centuries.

In *Sefer HaMiddot* (The Book of Attributes), Rebbe Nachman of Breslov enumerated over a hundred positive and negative character traits that were intended as guidance for Jews seeking to attain greater spirituality and to improve and perfect the world.[32] Through love, hospitality, respect, humbleness, charity, and the redeeming of captives, for example, as well as through avoiding theft, fraud, slander, envy, and bribery, we can elevate society while representing the best of the unchanging, eternal, and divinely appointed principles that we choose to live by. It is worth noting how many of these attributes reference our social behavior or actions taken in the public arena.

Among the most prominent statements of social morality for our time is one found in the writings of Rabbi Abraham Isaac Kook. In *Middot HaRayah*, he described how we "can be a source of light to the world . . . committed to a vocation of world perfection."[33] This requires a commitment to promote love, faith, freedom, fear (or awe) of God, honor, tolerance, humility, modesty, righteousness, development of our will, reproof of those who go astray, and improvement of the world. In so doing, we remain faithful to our covenant, linking our lives with God and working to redeem the sparks. Concomitantly, we are to rise above anger and to discourage pride and timidity. These are especially evil traits that we must purge completely from our hearts.[34]

Positive, constructive change is not possible where there is no moral code positing ideals and setting boundaries. Otherwise, every potential moral actor would be headed off in a different direction, the work of repair mortally complicated by scores of conflicting visions based on uninformed predispositions, presumptions, lusts, fetishes, and quests for power. Nothing constructive would ever get done; only greater devolution would result.

A shared moral vision, holding up a gold standard of values and behavior, is a prerequisite for planned social change. But there have been many such visions in the twentieth century alone that, carried to fruition, resulted in hell on earth rather than its visionary's promised utopia. Clearly, not just any morality will do.

Rabbi Kook acknowledged the existence and nobility of nonreligious systems of human morality that countenanced the striving for justice as an ultimate value. But, he added, such a moral foundation is insufficient to support the structure of our society. Attempting to do so "on the basis of natural morality alone, without the special revelation of morality the Torah provides, seemed to [Rabbi Kook] 'like a child's building, for it builds the outer shell of life before it knows how to build life itself.'"[35]

Various competing religious moralities are anxious to fill this gap, but they are not all the same. More to the point, they are not ours. John Winthrop's famous shining "citty [*sic*] upon a hill,"[36] for example, is a noble and respectable vision. But it is an explicitly Puritan vision of Christian charity drawn from the words of the Christian savior.[37] Winthrop's utopian city, with all of its ecclesiastical, political, and theological nuances,[38] is not a Jewish utopia.

Jewish morality is based on a different ethos, a different praxis, different sacred sources and texts, and a different eschatology. The good life promised by others might not be our good life. We cannot afford to defer to the visions of others. At times, we have done so, full of hope, granting obeisance to men whom we believed to have the best of intentions, and we were led to calamity. By now, we should know well the consequences of bowing to "strange gods" (Deuteronomy 32:16).

The Jewish people will never be a part of a "moral majority." The values of that group, though well intentioned, helped to lead our culture into the contentious place in which it finds itself. This morass cannot be remedied with more of the same: seed faith, abundant (Christian) living, rugged individualism, disfellowshipping of social outcasts, special revelations reserved to the elites, enforcement of fundamentalisms of belief and behavior, repression and demonization of natural human capacities and inclinations, devaluation of reason, and belief in the inherent wickedness of people and of the world. Restricted to the religious communities in which they are appreciated, these beliefs, values, ideals, and duties may be functional. Imposed on our culture and on us, they are oppressive. These are not Torah values, and they do not merit Jewish support.

I have used the words "morality" and "ethics" often in this book, as they are central to much rabbinic writing on the topic of loving God, especially in the *musar* tradition. In popular usage, these words are sometimes used interchangeably, which, strictly speaking, is not correct. Even in religious writings, these words may seem to overlap. For example, what Roman Catholic theologians term "moral theology," or application of religious teachings to human conduct, Protestant theologians generally refer to as "Christian ethics."[39]

The relationship of morality and ethics is casuistic: The former provides the general principles that underlie the latter.

Systems of morality define the rightness or wrongness of our attitudes and conduct. Ethics can be thought of as morality in action—application of moral principles for defining norms of behavior in the world. Another distinction is that morality is general, while ethics are domain-specific, such as religious ethics, medical ethics, legal ethics, business ethics, and social ethics.

We cannot act ethically, according to a gold standard of morality, unless we recognize and are familiar with such a standard. As Jews, we have our own unique code of morality. It is found in our canon, in the Torah and the Talmud, and in the writings of our rabbis and sages. It defines for us what is right and what is wrong. It tells us what we must do and what we must avoid doing. It provides us with guidance and instruction so that our actions in this post-Temple era can serve as "pleasing sacrifices to the God of Heaven" (Ezra 6:10).

The morality that we aspire to is not the morality of evangelical Christian dispensationalists, of Marxist utopians, of secular humanists, of Buddhist pacifists, or of neopagan environmentalists. Some of their beliefs and core values carry great appeal to Jews—and should: expectation of a better world to come, opposition to economic exploitation and oppression, advocacy of tolerance and human rights, adherence to nonviolence and nonattachment to worldly goods, concern about the sustainability of our natural resources. Yet these same values, *in extremis*, encompass doctrines that are antithetical, even hostile, to Jewish morality: abrogation of our worldly responsibilities in anticipation of a glorious afterlife, eradication of individual rights and liberties, disparagement of God and religion and criminalization of expressions of faith, nonresistance to evil, and elevation of nature to a moral high ground trumping basic human needs and concerns. None of these moralities is the morality of Judaism.

In our moral universe, we are the lead players in a drama of universal redemption. The endpoints are two: one personal and otherworldly, one universal and very much of this world. The *olam haba*, or world to come, refers to the eternal life that exists after we exit this physical plane. It awaits Jews who have been faithful to their covenant as well as the "righteous people among the nations of the world" (*T. Sanhedrin* 13:2).

In comparison to other religions, such as Christianity, Islam, and Buddhism, Jewish tradition has had relatively less to say about the hereafter, and there is no consensus on how it operates. For Jews, focused so completely on how to make this a better world and operating under a belief in collective and universal redemption, obsession over the fate of one's *n'shamah* after shedding the body has not occupied a large place in Jewish eschatology. We have more important things to worry about.

The more significant eschatological endpoint for Jews is known as *b'viat hamashiach*, the coming of the messiah. This phrase derives from the twelfth of Maimonides' *shloshah asar ikkarim*, or thirteen principles of faith. We are instructed to believe with perfect faith in the time of the messiah's coming. The Rambam encouraged us to remain patient and hopeful, quoting the words of the prophet, "Even if it tarries, wait for it still; for it will surely come, without delay" (Habbakuk 2:3).

The different branches of Judaism interpret this concept differently. According to traditional Jewish belief, this is to be taken literally: a male person of the Davidic line will be born and will become king, a temporal leader of a Jewish nation fully restored. This has not yet happened. For liberal Jews, *b'viat hamashiach* generally refers to a messianic age, not to the arrival of a specific person, although the Conservative movement is equivocal on this point. Regardless, all liberal branches of Judaism affirm that through our actions we can bring about the day when the moral values that we espouse as Jews will reign in the world. Jewish tradition affirms this, more or less, in that through our fulfillment of *mitzvot* we elevate the holiness of the world and ready it for the arrival of the messiah.

Whichever way it is that we conceive of *b'viat hamashiach*— literal reality or inspiring metaphor—it signals our call to action. Its presence in our future—our near future, God willing—is a challenge to every Jew. We know what we need to accomplish, and we know how we need to behave in order to reach that wonderful day when "the Lord shall be king over all the earth" (Zechariah 14:9).

The vehicle that will take us to that day is what Rabbi Sacks has called our "covenantal morality."[40] Our reciprocal relationship with God has rendered inevitable the moralization of every conceivable aspect of human life. By entrusting us with the most sacred of obligations—completing the work that He began—God has ensured that everything we may do is placed into a moral context. This speaks volumes about His faith in us and about His reliance upon us. "I know of no other vision," Rabbi Sacks concluded, "that confers on mankind so great a dignity and responsibility."[41]

In the final analysis, we will end up with the world that we deserve. We will deserve no more than what the effort we put forth merits. As Jews, we have been assigned the task of shepherding the messiah, however we interpret this, by making our world a fit abode for his presence. The longer that the messianic age is delayed, the more we should take its delay as a judgment on the strength of our commitment to "love, therefore, the Lord your God, and always keep His charge, His laws, His rules, and His commandments" (Deuteronomy 11:1). If we truly wish for this to be a better world, then we know what we must do. There are no excuses.

FOR GOD'S SAKE

Loving God and acting as His agents in the world make up our special duty as Jews. This is what it means to be a "chosen" people. God chose us for this special role, He laid out our obligations, and we accepted willingly. We thus chose Him as much as He chose us. This is the basis of our *b'rit*, our covenant with God. This covenant that we entered into and the duties to which it obliges us have brought us widespread fame and infamy.

Accordingly, we are known throughout the world as a people who "will sing of mercy and justice" (Psalms 101:1) without ceasing. Our devotion to God-ordained social change defines us, for good or ill, in the eyes of much of the world— for ill because our commitment to remaking the world according to God's specifications, as He revealed them to us, serves as a harsh judgment on "the wickedness of those nations" (Deuteronomy 9:4). Rather than accepting the truth of this judgment, the nations of the world have found it far more acceptable to seek the eradication of a people small in number who seek only universal redemption.

Many Jews have no trouble with the social agenda of Judaism, even in the face of its disparagement, yet have grave doubts about God. They may even accept that our societal obligations truly derive from a covenant executed with God and that we are bound by this covenant as much as were our ancestors who were present on Sinai with Moses. This covenant is accepted gladly, with good spirit and great courage. But the notion that each of us may come into a personal relationship with the Creator of the universe, a God Who cares dearly for each spark of His creation, is for many Jews unacceptable, implausible, and unpalatable.

As I noted in Chapter 3, I do not believe that absence of a heartfelt, loving connection with God enters into the calculus of whether or not one is a good Jew. If one is committed to carrying out God's mission for us in the world and is diligent in attending to one's moral duties, then it will be said of one, "The memory of the righteous shall be for a blessing" (Proverbs 10:7). But without the tangible and emotional support and reassurance of a loving relationship with God, we are left fragile and alone to face the onslaughts of a world that resents our intrusion and our efforts, no matter how noble our intentions.

The ability of a sincere faith in God to sustain and support us in times of challenge and trouble should not be underestimated. Rabbi Samuel E. Karff, former president of the Central Conference of American Rabbis, observed over the half century of his rabbinate "that religious faith is the most profound response to the wonders and trauma of life."[42] Belief and trust that "God is a refuge, a support are the arms everlasting" (Deuteronomy 33:27) may be a source of comfort and empowerment for us unmatched by anything that the world can offer in its place.

Some would contend, accusingly, that religious faith in this context is just a crutch. This is intended, I suppose, to belittle those who happily affirm the reality of something majestic and transcendent that gives their life meaning and purpose. Such counterclaims never make me defensive. When I am confronted with this kind of cruel skepticism, my response is typically, "Yes, thank God."

The psalmist tells us of God, "He heals their broken hearts, and binds up their wounds" (Psalms 147:3). This may be more than just metaphor or poetic imagery.

According to Professor Kenneth I. Pargament, a preeminent researcher in the field of clinical psychology and a fellow Jew, religious faith is a profound source of support that helps us to cope emotionally with the greatest of difficulties and can even assist in our recovery from illness, physical or psychological. His studies have shown that the effects of such faith-instigated coping are substantive and demonstrably functional, not merely the result of a stereotypical denial or avoidance or a reduction of tension.[43]

My own research has suggested that faith in God has many positive functions. It encourages life-promoting behavior, facilitates supportive relationships such as those nurtured in religious congregations, engenders positive emotions such as feelings of being loved and protected, affirms salutary beliefs and attitudes about who we are and how we are to live our lives, and offers hopeful messages about our destiny as individuals and as a people.[44] In my career as an academic epidemiologist, I frequently have observed, along with my colleagues such as Professor Pargament, that the benefits of a strong faith in God are capable of substantially counteracting all manner of challenging circumstances: depression, anxiety, poor health, financial difficulties, marital strains, stressful life changes, and the other traumas and tragedies that befall us in life. Our relationship with God is no magical amulet, and it does not promise a perfect "cure," but it does constitute a helpful resource that can enable us to make it through the worst of times in one piece.

In the Book of Numbers, God revealed to Moses the words of the *Birkat Kohanim*, or priestly benediction, that Moses was to pass along to Aaron and his sons. This event is of great historical significance for us. God was consecrating a human being and his successors for all time, in the form of the priesthood, to serve as His representatives in distributing His blessings to the Jewish people. This benediction thus occupies an important place in Jewish liturgy. With some variation by *nusach* or *minhag*, it is a part of daily, weekly, and yearly cycles of prayer and is pronounced at holidays, festivals, and life cycle events.[45] The words that God spoke to Moses give us a clear indication as to what God wants for our lives and how He wishes to be our Source of respite when we are troubled:

Thus shall you bless the people of Israel. Say to them: "The Lord bless you and protect you! The Lord deal kindly and graciously with you! The Lord bestow His favor upon you and grant you peace!" Thus they shall link My name with the people of Israel, and I will bless them. (Numbers 6:23–27)

The Midrash expounds at considerable length on the significance of the word "peace" in this blessing (Numbers *Rabbah* 11:7). Rabbi Elazar Hakappar stated, "Great is peace, for the seal of the whole of the Prayer is peace, and the seal of the priestly benediction is peace. . . . Great is peace, for it outweighs everything." His son, Rabbi Elazar, said, "Great is peace, for it was given to those who are repentant." Rav Meir added, "Great is peace, for the Holy One, blessed be He, has created no fairer attribute than that of peace, which has been given to the righteous. . . . Great is peace, for it was given to those who practice charity."

Additional exegeses along these lines are found in other midrashic collections, such as *Sifre* Numbers.[46] That *"shalom"* is the concluding word of the *Birkat Kohanim* is taken as profoundly meaningful by the rabbinic authors. For them, this final word represents "an opportunity to expound on the importance of peace in various contexts and makes it clear that of all God's blessings, peace is the most important."[47]

Peace, in the context of this benediction, refers both to peace among the nations and peace within each of our hearts. That this did not need to be spelled out in detail speaks to the inseparability of these two kinds of peace for the compilers and redactors of Midrash and for God. For our ancestors, both common people and rabbinic wise men, the existence of a divine being Who longs to dole out blessings, protection, kindness, graciousness, favor, and peace to every one of us was tacitly accepted. Perhaps the world was simpler then, with fewer intellectual distractions and temptations lulling us into the conceit that we are too mature and evolved for reliance upon God.

Many Jews who insist on rejecting the existence of a personal God Who is available to "grant you peace" do so with deep regret. Rabbi Karff, my childhood rabbi, poignantly described his encounters with Jews who have shared their contention that God does not exist, that life is inherently random and meaningless, and that faith is a security blanket required only by the immature.

> *In virtually all such discussions, however, I discovered that on some level my challengers wanted me to win the argument. Even if they didn't feel they could embrace the religious view of life, many wished they could. They pressed their nonbelief against my faith with an intensity that betrayed a deep longing for permission to believe.*[48]

Some of us may be embarrassed to acknowledge that we need the comfort and security that come with faith. We are too prideful to admit that we are anything but the lords of our own destiny. "What will people think?" we wonder. If by "people" one means fellow Jews, affiliated or unaffiliated, then chances are that they are wrestling and struggling with the same doubt and confusion. There are great men and women in our finest congregations and great rabbis and scholars throughout Jewish history who have experienced the same unsettling concerns and have never come to a full resolution. This need not give us pause.

In my perspective, professing doubt or degrees of disbelief yet acknowledging a quest for "permission to believe" is far more honest and hopeful a religious stance than accepting certain beliefs as so simply by default, through inertia, or on account of parental or spousal pressure or concerns about social acceptability. The latter type of faith is empty and is as unlikely to produce inner peace as it is to inspire and motivate us to work for outer peace.

The beloved Rabbi Emil G. Hirsch, one of Rabbi Karff's predecessors on the pulpit of Chicago's Sinai Congregation, expressed a sentiment that I shared earlier in this chapter. Rabbi Hirsch said, "If present conditions are not as they should be, a kingdom of God, these conditions are an accusation against us and they ought to be answered by us."[49]

This stance by an esteemed rabbi of blessed memory should hold great appeal for Jews whose religious doubt has kept them alienated from our religious tradition. It may come as a pleasant surprise to Jews who did not benefit from a formal religious education that Judaism does not require us to relinquish our stewardship over our lives or over the affairs of the world. God is sovereign, for sure, but He has empowered us to act in

His stead. By the authority that He transferred to Moses and to Aaron and their descendants, we became "a kingdom of priests and a holy nation" (Exodus 19:6). Through our actions, we can bless each other and all humankind, bestowing God's favor and granting peace. Rabbi Hirsch's comments are at once a stinging *j'accuse* and reason for great hope.

But we are not to be agents of change just for the sake of change. This leads nowhere—it is just a reshuffling of deck chairs on a sinking ship in alignment with trendy political fashions. Social change without a gold standard of morality that holds up an ideal and ennobles and enriches the lives of those working for change is destined for disaster. A look at the twentieth century is confirmation: hundreds of millions of people slaughtered or displaced and many traditional cultures annihilated by Russian Marxists, Chinese Communists, German National Socialists, European monopoly-capitalists, Protestant and Catholic imperialists, and, most recently, Islamist jihadists. Insane ideologies of the left and right have put man on a pedestal (literally "man"; I do not use the more inclusive language for an obvious reason). Worse, they have elevated some imagined *volk* or nationalist imperative to a similar position. No matter, both manifestations of this common sickness have made conquest, power, and domination their gods.

This is demonic. It is also destined to fail. Rabbi Shimon, in his *d'rash* upon the opening words of the Torah, warned, "This verse must be well laid to heart, for he who affirms that there is another god will be destroyed from the world" (*Zohar* 1:9a). These other gods are not for us. If we "follow other gods or serve them," said the prophet, then we are guilty of "wicked ways" (Jeremiah 35:15).

By contrast, Jews are called to be agents of a divine plan of justice, mercy, and lovingkindness that requires a partnership between humans and God. We are to infuse God-ness and loveness into all of the empty and broken spaces in the world—in its institutions and in the hearts of its inhabitants, who share with us life on its surface. We are to awaken the God-nature of all created things, though they may be asleep. We may be reviled for this—the whole of Jewish history shows this to be so—but we must keep our eyes on the prize. If we are faithful to our mission, then our God will always preserve us as a people. *Yasher koach.*

CHAPTER SIX
JEWISH PERSPECTIVES ON LOVING GOD

"Love that is contingent upon something else, when that something is gone, love is gone. Love that is contingent upon nothing, such a love will never end." (Pirke Avot 5:16)

Rabbi Leo Baeck once stated, "In Judaism social action is religiousness, and religiousness implies social action."[1] Rabbi Baeck, a leader in the cause of Progressive Judaism following World War II, articulated a belief that has been my working thesis in writing this book. Fulfillment of the *mitzvot ben adam l'chavero*, the horizontal or ethical commandments, is a *sine qua non* of Jewish religious observance. Our acts of *tz'dakah* and *chesed*, of justice and mercy, are the moral center of our covenant with God. They are where the rubber hits the road, so to speak. All of our Torah learning, our prayer and worship, our strongest and purest *kavannah*—these are empty gestures and close to worthless if they do not lead to ethical behavior undertaken for the benefit of other human beings.

Action undertaken in pursuit of social justice or mercy or kindness, as I have asserted throughout this book, is essential in Judaism—a foundation and its purest form of practice. Nothing could be more consonant with Jewish religious tradition than a concerted effort "to reject the bad and choose the good" (Isaiah 7:15) and "let all thine actions be for the sake of heaven" (*Pirke Avot* 2:12). Anything less than that will not suffice.

It has long been a stereotypical complaint from within certain quarters that elevating acts of social justice or lovingkindness to the moral center of Jewish observance is a dereliction of an idealized orthodoxy of Jewish belief and practice. By this reasoning, celebration of our commitment to *tikkun olam* and *g'milut chasadim* in our religion is a mere accommodation of liberal Judaism and a distraction from other more essential and historically settled imperatives.

Such as what?

This book has shown, I hope, that affirming morally grounded ethical action as the most valid marker of Jewish observance is not any kind of abrogation but rather is central to normative Judaism. Our enshrinement of good deeds as a hallmark of Jewish religious practice defines our covenant with God and our unique mission as a people. If we are to love God—and the consensus of Jewish tradition says that we are—then this is how best to do it.

Often, rabbis and Jewish organizations that endorse the principle of *tikkun olam* are criticized for allowing their social agendas to trump their religious fealty. This position presupposes that such Jews have permitted their social or political agendas to override their devotion to Jewish tradition. Too often, this devolves into old, familiar arguments over the nature and authority of *halakhah*—whether eternally binding and unalterable or malleable, in whole or in part, in order to address the unanticipated contingencies of the present day. The nuances and potency of this debate and subsequent responses have been seminal for all modern branches of our religion—Reform, Modern Orthodox, Conservative, Reconstructionist, Renewal, and Traditional (Conservadox) Judaism—that have emerged in North America over the past two centuries.

That Jews who emphasize social justice and social action should be criticized as inherently lax toward Jewish observance strikes me as misguided at best. It is as if devotion to *tz'dakah* and *chesed* is a sinister development that must be nipped in the bud before it spreads and does real damage to some imagined religious purity. I suspect that it is the critics of such socially conscious Jews who are allowing their politics to trump all else. It is far easier to condemn what we imagine to be motivating others than to acknowledge those same motives in ourselves.

Worse, in impugning ethical observance, we are joining a battle that has no place in Jewish theology. It revisits the disputes of a century ago in American Protestantism over a social gospel that elevated the ethical call to follow in the footsteps of the Christian savior above a commitment to traditional beliefs and practices emphasizing individual salvation that were indeed being deemphasized in relation to a social and political agenda. This movement was resisted by some Christians as overtly heterodox, in much the same way that the early Classical Reform movement was understandably condemned for casting aside Jewish tradition.

But unlike the situation in the mainline Protestant churches, which still have not recovered from the surrender of ever larger portions of their market share to evangelical and fundamentalist churches, Classical Reform effectively disappeared in North America over three decades ago. There is thus no major branch of Judaism that is overtly hostile to or dismissive of Jewish tradition or Jewish law, although the different Jewish movements vary considerably in their understanding and acceptance of the continued authority and moral value of *halakhah*.

Still, the response of many liberal Jews to criticism that their emphasis on social consciousness is misplaced and antithetical to Jewish law is to defensively restate centuries-old platforms affirming, for example, that the spirit of the law must prevail over the letter, an argument borrowed from another religion. This conciliation is unnecessary. I believe that liberal Judaism does not have to make excuses for its ethical commitments, nor must it feel obliged to justify itself only by slighting the authority of our *halakhic* tradition.

Reform Judaism tries to distance itself from *halakhah* or at least from its strict interpretation, as this represents too stringent a standard for the complexities of the modern world and does not sufficiently accommodate personal autonomy. This stance implies that Jewish law is static and unchanging, cast in stone in codes redacted by the sages. This also implies that efforts to adapt to the modern world must entail a liberalization or relaxation of the law.

According to Rabbi Moshe Zemer, a modern-day leader of Progressive Judaism in Israel, these tacit understandings of Jewish law are themselves not *halakhic*. In *Evolving Halakhah*, he found a way to reconcile liberal Judaism with Jewish law, and vice versa, in a way that preserved the historical and moral integrity of both.[2] Jewish law, he contended, and thus Jewish tradition are founded on an understanding of *halakhah* as constantly evolving and developing "to confront the changing reality in every generation";[3] as pluralistic and thus "diverse in nature and certainly far from monolithic";[4] as ethical and thus subject to "the claims of individual conscience";[5] and as holy and thus "not an end in [itself] but a means by which one may be sanctified and draw closer to God."[6] Liberal Judaism, in its various forms and movements, thus need not feel compelled to apologize for its *responsa* and ethical stances; nor should it feel compelled to distance itself from Jewish law and thus risk defining itself outside of normative (traditional) Judaism. Rabbi David Ellenson, chancellor of Hebrew Union College, also has noted that, even among the Orthodox, "the halakhic system is a pluralistic one."[7]

For me, there is an irony present. A rethinking of Jewish law along the lines of Rabbi Zemer's insightful book is not necessary as an apologia for the idea that we love God best by loving and serving and helping others. Socially progressive members of the rabbinate, exemplified in modern times by Rabbi Heschel and his followers, are in accord with the most exalted principles of Jewish observance. I would assert that choosing every day to consecrate our waking hours toward achieving justice and mercy for all beings constitutes the height of *halakhic* allegiance and is thus a model for Jewish religious observance.

Let me restate this as plainly as I can: affirming our covenant with God through performing *g'milut chasadim* and *tz'dakah* in any of their myriad forms is not a detour from traditional Jewish religious observance. It *is* traditional observance. It is rabbinic Judaism in fullest flower.

The Talmud records the words of one of our sages: "The whole world is sustained by [God's] charity (*b'tz'dakah*), and [the righteous] are sustained by their own force" (*B'rakhot* 17b). It is charity, which comes from God, that alone has the power to sustain. If there are those among us who are sustained by our own doing, then it is only on account of our charitableness, which implies that we have walked in the footsteps of God.

The Talmud also tells of a rabbinic discussion of the circumstances under which a divine decree is annulled (*Y'vamot* 105a). The starting point for this conversation is "the iniquity of the house of Eli" (I Samuel 3:14) on account of the sacrilege of his sons, who defiled the sacrifices of the priest and were described as "scoundrels" (I Samuel 2:12). Rav Shmuel bar Ami said that the text of the Torah has made clear that the iniquity "will never be expiated by sacrifice or offering" (I Samuel 3:14). Rabbah agreed but said "it will be expiated with the words of Torah" (Y'vamot 105a). Abaye also agreed but said that "it will be expiated with the practice of lovingkindness (b'g'milut chasadim)" (Y'vamot 105a).

In Chapter 1, I discussed the dilemma of being commanded to love God. This is paradoxical only if loving God is conceived of solely as the experience of warm, fuzzy feelings. But this was never the Jewish perspective. True, the command is real. For example, in Sefer HaMitzvot HaKatzar, the Chofetz Chaim's compilation of the commandments that are applicable for post-Temple Judaism, he stated, "It is a positive commandment to love the blessed God with all one's heart, spirit and might,"[8] a mitzvah that "a person has a duty to observe at every occasion and every moment."[9] This understanding of loving God as a positive commandment goes back to the Rambam's own Sefer HaMitzvot,[10] one of the earliest, and the most authoritative, of such compilations.

The Chofetz Chaim's inclusion of this commandment in his enumeration of positive mitzvot makes sense only if we agree that, in loving God, the word "loving" implies something much broader and more inclusive of our capabilities and actions than it does in common English parlance. Indeed, he noted, "Included in this mitzvah [is the obligation] to bring human beings closer to His service and worship (blessed is He), and to make Him beloved by His human beings, as Abraham our father did (peace abide with him)."[11] By loving God, then, we are to understand our duty as no less than to emulate our great patriarch whose acts of lovingkindness were legion and whose reputation thus endures.

THREE WAYS OF LOVING GOD

My study and exploration over many years have led me to identify three distinct ways in which all people of faith tend to love God, to engage the divine, regardless of their respective religion. These ways of loving God are almost identical to a generic reading of the three-legged stool of Pirke Avot. There is much that is unique about Judaism, but valuing each of the constituent elements of "these three things" is not among them.

Besides Judaism, major religions tend to define observance or piety according to a threefold path corresponding to the three respective human psychological functions, as described by psychologists. These are cognition, affect, and behavior—or, in simpler terms, thinking, feeling, and doing. In an earlier book, I spoke of the "triune nature of human beings"[12]—an observation that we are hard-wired to experience and interact with the world in all three ways. This fact lies at the core of how important religious and wisdom traditions idealize the spiritual quest of their followers.

Implicit in traditions as diverse as Protestant theology, Yoga, Theosophy, and Islam is acknowledgment of this three-fold dimensionality of the human psyche. Each of these respective belief systems distinguishes among godly pursuits dependent upon engagement of body, mind, and spirit and provides pathways for spiritual growth or healing—of self and of the world—that emphasize one or another of these paths.

For example, Protestant theologian Paul Tillich defined faith as "ultimate concern," or a centered act of the whole person directed toward another being or toward a transcendent end. In his classic text *Dynamics of Faith*, Professor Tillich asserted that the most effective way to achieve such ends is by a balance of our intellectual, devotional, and physical actions, which he termed "reason," "emotion," and "will."[13]

In the philosophy of Yoga, three disciplines or pathways to union (*yoga*) with God are distinguished. These emphasize the familiar three domains or aspects of our personhood—mind, spirit or heart, and body—and give rise to respective systems of yogic practice. The disciplines of *karma yoga*, *jñāna yoga*, and *bhakti yoga* denote the respective paths of ethical behavior, learning of sacred teachings, and devotion and surrender to God.[14]

The triune nature of human beings and of idealized human lives is also found within Western esoteric traditions, notably Theosophy. As described in works beginning with *The Secret Doctrine*,[15] humans are said to comprise a series of overlapping, interpenetrating bodies or sheaths. These include our physical and etheric or energy bodies, our astral or emotional body, and our mental body. These subtle bodies in turn are manifest in respective subtle realms or dimensions, such as the "mental plane" consisting of "thought forms," where that particular aspect of our being works out its *karma* and advances the progress of the ego or self on its way along "the great path."[16]

Islam has its own unique tradition of the threefold path. A *hadith*, or account of the teachings of the Prophet Muhammad, attributed to him the wise words, "O people! Worship Allah, the Beneficent, feed His bondsmen, and spread Salaam [peace] much, and you will reach Heaven in safety."[17] A noted commentary states, "Upon these three things, the Prophet, *sallallahu alayhi wasallam* [Allah bless him and give him peace], has given the assurance that whoever will observe them will safely attain the goal of paradise."[18] The fate of one's soul is contingent upon whether one has successfully labored in the cause of peace.

Part of the great genius of *Pirke Avot* and of the traditions of our Oral Torah, Midrash, and later rabbinic writings is the widespread applicability of its principal moral and ethical tenets to a world that extends beyond the Jewish people. While providing specific guidance for Jewish observance and ethical living, the wise recommendations of our sages are universal to all of our brothers and sisters of every faith who "appoint mercy and truth, that they may preserve him" (Psalms 61:8). The rewards of obedience are not just preservation but "honor" (*Midrash T'hillim* 61:3). Moreover, they accrue to all people, regardless of religion, who "pray for the peace of Jerusalem" (Psalms 122:6) and thus "make peace abound in the world" (*Midrash T'hillim* 122:7).

We should not be surprised to see our most important moral principles enshrined in the sacred writings and teachings of other great traditions. All of the great theistic religious faiths ideally seek to strengthen the bond between the faithful and their Creator. All of us, Jew and gentile, seek to increase our knowledge and wisdom by studying God's truths in order that we may be consecrated to righteousness. All of us seek to express our praise for God and our devotion to Him by way of heartfelt prayer and worship. All of us seek to externalize our love of God through service to others in the form of acts of mercy, justice, and lovingkindness.

Over the years, I have observed that individual Jews, like the observant of other faiths, typically feel most comfortable expressing their love of God predominantly in one of these three ways. Granted, most of us who explicitly follow a particular faith tradition measure our spiritual progress to some extent according to our efforts at all of "these three things." I have yet to meet a single practicing Jew whose spiritual journey was confined exclusively, without exception, to only one of these paths. The most dedicated scholars that I have known are among the most pious and generous people; the most spirited geniuses of prayer among the most committed to learning and service; the most socially conscious and industrious among the most engaged in our teachings and traditions.

Still, we tend to emphasize or gravitate to a particular path. Only the greatest saints or *tzaddikim* among us can truthfully say that they maximize their efforts along all three paths. Tillich's definition of faith as a perfect balance of reason, emotion, and will is an ideal—as much for us as for the Christian audience for whom he wrote. Likewise, we may aspire to love God "with all your heart and with all your soul and with all your might" (Deuteronomy 6:5), but most of us are too human to attain perfect and enduring success.

Our preferences, too, can change over the course of our life. My own journey exemplifies this point.

As a small child, growing up across the street from our synagogue, I loved the rituals of worship, the rhythm of our prayers and liturgy, and the way that I felt inside while chanting and praying with other children, led by our young rabbi. I also relished opportunities to celebrate rituals of observance and pray with my beloved grandparents, with whom we lived. As an older child and teenager, I was too distracted and alienated from Jewish tradition to engage Judaism or God in any meaningful way. As a young adult, I became enchanted with the scholarly study of religion and later was attracted to a deep exploration of meditation and Jewish mystical experience. Upon entering my academic teaching career, I felt called to the systematic study of sacred texts and more consistent involvement in communal worship. Over the past couple of decades, I have been drawn to more traditional forms of learning, worship, and observance as well as to participation in activities related to charity and social justice, both privately with my wife, Lea, and communally as a part of our synagogue.

This personal trajectory has seen my interest in esoteric Judaism wax and then wane, supplanted by more traditional and satisfying forms of Jewish observance. At the same time, I have gained a greater respect for markedly radical expressions of Jewish ethical behavior, even on the part of those who do not share my own more centrist religious preferences and my political views. Becoming cognizant of the prophetic element in *musar* has been instrumental to my understanding of the indivisibility of personal morality and social consciousness in Judaism. It is from this point on my own Jewish growth curve that I have written this book.

For me, this entire journey has been about learning to become adept at "loving the Lord your God, heeding His commands, and holding fast to Him" (Deuteronomy 30:20). The way in which I loved God as a child, naturally, is not the same way in which I loved God as a young adult or the way in which I express my love for God today. Nor, I imagine, will it be the same for me in, God willing, my old age. For one, my Jewish learning continues and will continue to deepen, please God, as will my Jewish wisdom and insight. With the passage of time, my familiarity with the myriad cycles and rhythms of worship and liturgy and my appreciation of them also have grown. Finally, I have learned that, for me, nothing that I experience in my Jewish life brings greater *nachus* to my heart than when Lea or I am privileged to do a *chesed* for another being, whether face to face, through supporting a worthy cause or organization, or through our own creative efforts (such as Lea's research on sick veterans or my writing of this book).

These observations are a revelation to me. Reflection upon one's journey toward a deeper engagement with God and Judaism can help to crystallize the direction in which one is headed and to identify and clarify one's core values. My own adventure of over fifty years has led me—steadily, I can now recognize—toward both greater traditional observance and greater social consciousness. These two destinations, I can attest, are not mutually exclusive.

My own experiences, of course, have shaped the words that I have written here. Yet when I talk with Jews who also have taken the time to reflect on their own life's journeys, I am struck by how familiar their stories are to me. While we are all unique beings with unique spiritual histories, I believe that there is a common Jewish thread.

For so many Jews that I have known, awakening of a spirit of commitment to *tz'dakah* and *chesed*, to *tikkun olam* and *g'milut chasadim*, is rarely about acting on purely political or ideological predispositions. Rather, this seems to me to be a consistent fruit or grace of the deepening of the relationship between individual Jews and their God, as Jacob testified, "who answered me when I was in distress and who has been with me wherever I have gone" (Genesis 35:3). Regardless of our starting point and regardless of which branches of Judaism we do (or do not) affiliate with, I believe that an earnest effort to "follow the Lord your God" (I Samuel 12:14) could lead any Jew to conclusions similar to mine.

GOD, LOVE, AND RELIGION

To love God, to act according to the moral code implied in our covenant with Him, is a voluntary act of our will. For Jews, loving God implies following God and does not require an absolute orthodoxy of belief. We need only agree that the moral and ethical traditions passed down to us from our ancestors are the best hope of ensuring that we continue to exist, just as the prophet said of God, "His righteousness, it sustained Him" (Isaiah 59:16). Doubt or equivocation about God's existence and nature are acceptable; hesitation or moderation in following Him, and thus fulfilling our obligations, are not.

This kind of love is not all about warm emotional feelings of attachment, as I have noted, but rather is about a desire to accept God's moral authority and to follow His guidance. Love does not mean much if it is all about "me" and "my feelings." True love is expressed by compassionately accommodating the other's needs. This is as true for our relationship with God as it is for our relationships with our spouse, our family, our friends, and our synagogue. "In Judaism," according to Rabbi Baeck, "there is no yearning without duty."[19]

Our love of God is not just about trying to experience the wonderful feelings that we hope are evoked by getting close to God but also about imagining how fulfilling our commitments to God will make Him feel. The biggest problem with viewing the love of God through an emotional lens is not in defining love in terms of feelings. The problem arises in focusing on our own feelings rather than on God's.

This is not dissimilar to what other religions have to say about loving God.

Granted, among the major faith traditions, a conception of God as a single, indivisible, and divine Being, as in Judaism, is not the norm. Christianity, depending upon the particular branch, believes in one God who is really three-divine-persons-in-one, which it refers to as a divine mystery. In Buddhism, there is no god as we conceive of in the Western monotheistic traditions, as Creator of the universe and God of history. Hinduism endorses a hierarchy of many gods. In Shinto, the cultic *mythos* is centered on a human emperor-god.

Only Islam, among the major world religions, comes close to sharing our conception of the oneness and indivisibility of God, Who is both Creator of the universe and a personal deity Who "loves the charitable."[20] God's instructions to the Prophet, words to be conveyed to the (future) Muslim people, are reminiscent of similar words spoken to Moses on our own behalf on many occasions: "Say, 'If you love Allah follow me. Allah will love you and forgive you your sins. Allah is forgiving and merciful.'"[21]

The close similarity in how Judaism and Islam characterize an ideal relationship with God—expressing love of God as following Him and thus acting charitably to others—should be no surprise to us. After all, Ishmael and Isaac were brothers, sons of the same Abraham whose covenant with the one God gives purpose and meaning to Jewish lives.

In *Parashat Lekh-Lekha*, Abram pleaded with God, "O that Ishmael might live by Your favor!" (Genesis 17:18). God replied:

As for Ishmael, I have heeded you. I hereby bless him. I will make him fertile and exceedingly numerous. He shall be the father of twelve chieftains, and I will make of him a great nation. (Genesis 17:20)

God later reaffirmed that His special covenant was solely with Isaac (Genesis 17:21). But these verses make clear that His blessings extend to Ishmael, something that is all too easily forgotten by contemporary Jews and Christians.

Similarly to Judaism and Islam, Christianity identifies a singular God Who, in His specific identity as Father, is both Creator of the universe and Lord of all creation. This Creator is identified with love, as in the Apostle John's inspiring words, "God is love, and he who abides in love abides in God, and God abides in him."[22] But Christian dogma defines the ideal relationship between humans and this Being in ways distinctly alien to Judaism. This relationship is grounded in several important concepts, including original sin, personal salvation, justification by faith, and vicarious atonement. These doctrines are foundational for how Christians encounter God and how they understand human nature, the purpose of life, and the significance of confession and redemption. But none of these are Torah doctrines.

Hinduism, at first glance, would appear to have little in common with Judaism. But along with Judaism and Shinto, it is the other major world religion based on national identity. There is thus a similar emphasis on peoplehood. One of its greatest apostles to the West was Paramahansa Yogananda. A dialogue with one of his students elucidates a nondualistic understanding of loving God that should resonate with Jews:

> *"Master, I love everyone," a disciple said.*
>
> *"You should love only God," Paramahansaji replied.*
>
> *The disciple met the Guru a few weeks later. He asked her, "Do you love others?"*
>
> *"I keep my love only for God," the devotee answered.*
>
> *"You should love all with that same love."*
>
> *The baffled disciple said, "Sir, what is your meaning? First you say that to love all is wrong; then you say that to exclude anyone is wrong."*
>
> *"You are attracted to the personality of people; that leads to limiting attachments," the Master explained. "When you truly love God you will see Him in each face, and will know what it means to love all. It is not forms and egos we should adore, but the indwelling Lord in everyone. He alone informs His creatures with life, charm, and individuality."*[23]

For an ordained teacher of the Swami Order, Yogananda could have passed as a pretty decent rabbi. This insightful *d'rash* on God, love, the *Sh'khinah*, and our obligations to the stranger is worthy of a *tzaddik* or a Zen *roshi*.

Although these other traditions do exhibit points of convergence with Judaism, especially where it comes to an imperative to love God, the points of divergence outweigh them for us. It is important that we recognize that God has something uniquely wonderful—and right and fitting—for us as Jews that we cannot find anywhere else.

As I have stated many times already, our tradition is unique. It views life as a steady progression of clear-cut ethical decisions to be made by a people who was created with free will. Our choices are stark, with little grey area, but we are entirely free to follow the right path or the wrong path. Every day, many times over, we are confronted with ethical choices. There is the *mitzvah* way or the way of inertia (or ignorance or convenience or selfishness or rebellion). No divine power or being controls us like a puppet and forces our actions. We get to choose.

Accordingly, God urges us, "Choose life—if you and your offspring would live" (Deuteronomy 30:19). The way in which we choose life, God explains, is "by loving the Lord your God, heeding His commands, and holding fast to Him" (Deuteronomy 30:20). The rabbis taught that while God has laid out a clear choice, He is forgiving and respectful of our best efforts. According to Rav Chaggai, what God really meant was "And what is more, not only have I set two paths before you, but I have not dealt with you according to the strict letter of the law" (Deuteronomy *Rabbah* 4:3).

I believe that there is a voice inside of each Jewish *n'shamah* that tells us which is the correct way to act in any given situation. If we pause to listen with our hearts, it will tell us how to proceed. This is the voice of the *Sh'khinah*. For some of us, this whisper of the Divine Presence may be drowned out by other voices that overwhelm our hearts, and we are unable to hear it clearly. So we are led astray.

Just as the choices that we make are more clear-cut than we may be willing to admit, so too the consequences are stark and leave little room for equivocation. Shimon bar Abba taught that God showed Abraham four things: hell, foreign kingdoms, the revelation (*matan torah*; literally "gift of Torah"), and the Temple. God made clear to Abraham, "As long as thy children occupy themselves with the latter two, they will be saved from the former two; if they neglect the latter two they will be punished by the former two" (Genesis *Rabbah* 44:21). In other words, our faithfulness to the truths that God revealed to us and to our duty to obey and love Him is what preserves us from hell and subjugation to our enemies.

This is certainly a serious charge and, ignored, may become an unbearable burden. What then is each of us to do?

To begin, we need to be clear about our intentions. I have stated several times that I believe that in Judaism it is our actions that are paramount. Even the most unwholesome of motives cannot disqualify the good that accrues to the beneficiary of an act of *chesed* or *tz'dakah*. The danger of selfish or unclear intentions is not that they override a good act on our part. Rather, the danger is that they prevent such acts.

If we manage to do good despite base motivations, then the recipients of our good should count themselves fortunate. The merit that we earn is far less than it could have been, but at least someone benefited. But if we make a habit of self-serving acts of pretend kindness, then we run the risk that soon enough, the acts will dry up and only the selfishness will remain. Rabbis Byron L. Sherwin and Seymour J. Cohen noted:

> True love of God must not only be love, but it must also be true. It cannot be self-love masquerading as love of God, self-interest pretending to be altruism. Nor can it be a passing fancy disguising itself as a life-long commitment.[24]

Only a lifelong commitment to honor the Creator and Sustainer of our people by choosing "to love the Lord your God and to walk in His ways at all times" (Deuteronomy 19:9) will mold us into people for whom righteousness becomes second nature. This takes repetition and requires learning, but a great reward of self-transformation is promised: "And one who loves [God] cannot despise [His commandments]" (*Y. B'rakhot* 9:5). Where true love of God resides, hate cannot flourish.

Despite these assured explanations, the uneasiness that some of us feel in contemplating what is expected of us can too easily leave us cowed and confused. Knowing what we are to do and why still may not be enough to start us on our way. Even the gentle advice to look inward or "carefully listen to the voice of the Lord your God" (Deuteronomy 15:5) may not be enough to calm our fears. For some of us, the thought that our Creator may have included a part of Himself within us, to Whom we may turn for guidance, is a thought that cannot be countenanced. It is too much of a reproof of the alien worldviews that we have adopted as our own—the materialism, rationalism, individualism, secularism, positivism, and moral relativism that we have allowed to define us and our values and life's purpose and to create a gulf of distance between us and God.

That first step toward God and out of our addictive morass is thus too painful for many of us to contemplate. For the fortunate among us, pain or embarrassment or skepticism is not a barrier. The biggest challenge is overcoming our lingering doubts about whether we are truly capable of feeling God's tug on us and then responding to the call.

Rabbi Zalman Schachter-Shalomi articulated this doubt when he posed the question "How do I know whether it is God stirring in me, or if whether that which stirs is merely my own ego program, my inclination for evil, my search for comfort?"[25] In other words, can we really trust our feelings, our perceptions, when it comes to something that we cannot see or taste or touch, something transcendent?

That is a difficult question to answer. Unless we were blessed to be born into a state of fully realized spirituality—and I do not believe that this is possible—then we all must grow into our relationship with God. At some point during our lives, we must take the initial step of faith, of trusting, of moving out of our comfort zone and into a space in which all that we can cling to are the promises of One unseen and the testimonies of our ancestors. God's challenge to us is not unlike that of the bramble that said to the trees, "Come and take shelter in my shade" (Judges 9:15).

If we are able to answer yes to God, then God will answer in kind, "Fear not, for I am with you, be not frightened, for I am your God; I strengthen you and I help you, I uphold you with My victorious right hand" (Isaiah 41:10). The history of our people testifies to the veracity of God's promise. God believes us capable of trusting in Him and capable of following His guidance for our lives. Whether we are able to trust in God's call to us perhaps says less about our faith in Him than about our faith in ourselves. The first step in our journey to God is a baby step of courage. Professor Tillich astutely called this the "courage to be,"[26] the courage to believe in ourselves, to accept ourselves and God's acceptance of us, though we may believe ourselves unacceptable.

For those of us who are overwhelmed by what lies before us and filled with feelings of uncertainty and unworthiness, the rabbinic sages had a terrific idea. It is worth revisiting.

The Netziv taught that the sages (e.g., in *Y. Kiddushin* 1:9) recommended that each one of us adopt a single *mitzvah* as our own, one that we can do consistently, with passion and *kavannah*, above all others.[27] This is not to say, of course, that we should fulfill only this one commandment and no others. All of our other covenantal obligations remain. But we should choose one thing and do it perfectly, mastering its every nuance, rather than offering up a middling effort at everything. Not only will we then become adept at redeeming our little corner of God's creation, but we will gain the confidence and courage to live a productive Jewish life. Some of our rabbinic sages apparently were as enlightened in human psychology as in theology and *musar*.

We can apply this idea about the *mitzvot* to our relationship with God. Few of us are capable of fulfilling every commandment related to each of "these three things" completely and in every situation that presents itself. But all of us can select one particular *mitzvah* that attracts us, one specific way of "loving the Lord your God and serving Him with all your heart and soul" (Deuteronomy 11:13). If each of us adopts one special way of expressing our gratitude to God, then we can offer it up as our own special gift to the world. Not only would this be for a blessing, but it would surely open us up to other ways of loving God that we could feel comfortable growing into once our confidence expands and our spirituality deepens.

The answer, then, for those who do not know how to begin to love God is just to begin. God said to Abram, "Go forth" (Genesis 12:1). This is what we are to do too: Go forth. From whatever point in our lives that we start to "search there for the Lord your God, you will find Him, if only you seek Him with all your heart and soul" (Deuteronomy 4:29).

These are the same words found in the *Sh'ma*, the same words that describe how we are to accomplish "these three things," as discussed in the first chapter of this book. We thus have come full circle. By tapping into the core of our being, our heart and our soul, and earnestly and diligently making the effort to "turn to Him" (Psalms 24:6), to emulate God's ways, we will learn to love God, and the world will continue to stand.

THE JEWISH WAY OF LOVING GOD

Jews are not the only people who profess to love God. Nor are we the only people whose spiritual growth is measured by a combination of learning, worship, and good deeds. When we abide by the moral heritage bequeathed to us by our ancestors and sages, we are no better than any others among the observant of the great religions of the world. But as our tradition emphasizes, our special way of loving God fulfills a charge that is uniquely ours and that blesses the world in a way that is like none other.

What makes the Jewish way of loving God Jewish?

Our way of loving God is different because of several elements that distinctively come together. Alone, these features of our relationship with God are not unique to us. In combination, they define how it is that we become "privileged to enter on the path of life" (*Zohar* 1:82a).

First, the Jewish way of loving God emphasizes our deeds over our words or sentiments. Our actions are what matter most, specifically actions in service to others. Acts of justice or mercy or kindness constitute the greatest of all *mitzvot*, and our performance of these acts is more pleasing to God than "the multitude of your sacrifices to Me" (Isaiah 1:11).

Second, the Jewish way of loving God values learning and worship as mighty means of attaining two kinds of wisdom: wisdom of the mind, as in "learning wisdom and discipline" (Proverbs 1:2), and "wisdom of heart" (*chach'mat-lev*) (Exodus 35:35). But their greatest value lies in their instrumentality—their strengthening us to follow God's ethical mandate for us. When we have both knowledge and heart wisdom, we are unlikely to copy the ways of the "evil," "wicked," "crooked," "devious," or those who forget their covenant with God (Proverbs 2:12–17).

Third, the Jewish way of loving God is based foremost on a covenantal relationship with our Creator. When we agreed to "hold fast to Him" (Deuteronomy 13:5), we agreed to special obligations that require us to represent a particular set of values among the people of the world. God expects us to translate those values into actions that serve, elevate, and redeem. God promises us rewards parallel to our obligations. If we demonstrate that our love of God is sincere by pursuing *tz'dakah* and acts of *chesed*, then likewise He will "[show] kindness to the thousandth generation of those who love Me" (Exodus 20:6).

Fourth, the Jewish way of loving God derives from a view of redemption as a collective and ongoing process, contingent upon our fulfilling our covenantal commitments. Each Jew must take responsibility for his or her fellow Jew, and together we must serve as "a light of nations, that My salvation may reach the ends of the earth" (Isaiah 49:6). Although we may be "despised of men" and "abhorred of nations" (Isaiah 49:7), by our actions we infuse the world with holiness and merit God's promise, "I will preserve you" (Isaiah 49:8).

Fifth, the Jewish way of loving God acknowledges a God-given moral standard as the basis for our actions. There is right and there is wrong, and, no matter the cost, we are to act in accordance with eternal standards of righteousness. This is pleasing to God, for "the Lord is righteous; He loves righteous deeds" (Psalms 11:7). He wishes that we emulate Him and His morality, accepting His guidance as a gold standard for our behavior.

Sixth, the Jewish way of loving God makes no explicit distinction between Jew and "other" in our ethical relationships with humans. Because we "were strangers in the land of Egypt" (Deuteronomy 10:19), we must love and befriend the stranger. This commandment, in Deuteronomy, sits directly in the middle of a series of verses in which God reminds us that He "shows no favor" (Deuteronomy 10:17), "upholds the cause" of the orphan and widow and clothes and feeds the needy stranger (Deuteronomy 10:18), and requires us to revere and worship Him (Deuteronomy 10:20). These are among the most important and essential directives that God has ever given to our people. The commandment to love the stranger is thus conspicuous in its placement, and the seriousness of God's dictate to us is obvious.

Seventh, the Jewish way of loving God is not defined by a spiritual practice or technique that produces some sort of warm feeling of imagined "inner oneness" with God. It is about responding to God's call to each of us, saying yes, we will "walk in His ways and revere Him" (Deuteronomy 8:6). Loving God is expressed by joining with our fellow Jews to accept our place in the grand Jewish moral tradition. Loving God means that we gladly enter our names alongside those of our courageous ancestors who sanctified God's name by laboring to spread holiness throughout the world, often at great personal cost.

To understand why our unique Jewish way of loving God is a perfect fit for us, we need to understand a few pertinent facts about our magnificent religious tradition. At first glance, these characteristics may appear to be contradictory, but a more careful look proves otherwise.

Specifically, Judaism is a faith that is at once conservative and progressive, tribal and universal, judgmental and tolerant.

Judaism conserves and preserves a moral standard that is unchanging and eternal. The covenant to which we agreed is binding, and it dictates behavior consistent with the highest possible standards, as descriptive of God Himself. It can never be compromised. We are to take after "the steadfast God who keeps His covenant faithfully to the thousandth generation of those who love Him" (Deuteronomy 7:9). In other words, we are to do the same.

This ultraconservative standard demands of us an attitude toward social change and cultural transformation that is undeniably progressive. God has no concern for the perpetuation of enduring social structures that are unjust, unmerciful, or exploitative. In response to excessive violence among the people during the time of Noah, God announced His intention "to destroy them with the earth" (Genesis 6:13). In response to callous acts of inhospitality during the time of Abraham, actions that God considered an "outrage" and "grave" (Genesis 18:20), He "annihilated the cities where Lot dwelt" (Genesis 19:29). In response to Pharaoh's cruel oppression of our people during the time of Moses, God punished Egypt, humiliated Pharaoh, and finally decimated the entire Egyptian army (Exodus 7–14).

Our covenant, our repentance, and our renewal and re-demption are enacted or experienced communally. All of our efforts for good in this world are performed collectively, and their merit is attributed to us as a whole people. Our tribe is "a people distinct and separate from others"[28] on account of our religious and moral obligations. We have our own ways—our own beliefs and rituals—that we do not expect others to adopt.

Our tribal outlook is realized in a world vision that is uni-versal and hopeful. We believe that through our actions and through similar actions undertaken by others, all humans may be redeemed. Moreover, we choose to believe that all humans *will* be redeemed. This will be so regardless of their religion or of the life path that they travel, so long as they pursue justice and mercy, for "the righteous people among the nations of the world . . . do have a portion in the world to come" (*T. Sanhedrin* 13:2).

Our continued existence and our continued persecution constitute a harsh judgment on the brokenness of the world. Our moral code is stringent and unyielding. Because we gave the world the gift of ethical monotheism, we are abhorred. Our greatest religious innovation is a God-given philosophy that proclaims "the wrong place is not as the right place" (*Z'vachim* 27a). These words of Rabbi Yochanan were spoken regarding the ritual purity of the Temple altar, but they are just as applicable to our actions that today substitute for the sacrifice. Every moment and every situation present us with choices to be made. Judaism demands that we choose wisely and act accordingly, eschewing what is wrong and affirming what is right.

We apply our judgment to no people as stringently as to ourselves. Because we understand the weight of judgment and the burden of being held to such lofty standards, we are toler-ant of others. Because "You were a forgiving God for [us]" (Psalms 99:8), we are forgiving of others. We are accepting and generous because we know what it is like to experience intolerance, still to this day. We side with the underdog, the oppressed, the victimized, the despised. We even defend the legal rights of those who hate us, not necessarily because we expect to change their minds but because it is the right thing to do. We side with those in their struggles who would never side with us in ours.

Throughout the millennia, the Jewish people have persisted and survived because we have been able to see through these seeming dichotomies. For us, there is nothing impossible about being both conservative and progressive, both tribal and universal, both judgmental and tolerant. Our success in negotiating our way through these dualities exemplifies our good fortune in executing a covenant with a God Who will faithfully grant our request for "discernment in dispensing justice" (I Kings 3:11), just as He did with Solomon. In return for our faithfulness and gratitude to God, we are reminded again and again that "He guards the lives of His loyal ones, saving them from the hand of the wicked" (Psalms 97:10).

Whether we Jews continue to love God, as we have been directed, will determine the fate of the world. Whether the world continues to exist or instead slides into oblivion is up to us. Every day, we renew our faith in God by pursuit of Torah learning, by *avodah* and *t'fillah*, and by *g'milut chasadim*—myriad acts that promote *tz'dakah*, *chesed*, and *tikkun olam*. On account of our great love, expressed through actions of our minds, hearts, and bodies, Rabbi Shimon assured us that "the world stands" (*Pirke Avot* 1:2). Through applying the lessons that we learn from the Torah and from sharing with others the love aroused in us by our worship of God, our good deeds will redeem the world.

NOTES

PREFACE

1. Jeff Levin, *God, Faith, and Health: Exploring the Spirituality-Healing Connection* (New York: John Wiley & Sons, 2001).

2. Jeff Levin, "The Power of Love" [interview], *Alternative Therapies in Health and Medicine* 5, 4 (1999), 78–86; quotation on p. 80.

3. Jeffrey S. Levin, "Esoteric vs. Exoteric Explanations for Findings Linking Spirituality and Health," *Advances: The Journal of Mind-Body Health* 9, 4 (1993), 54–56; quotation on p. 56.

4. Jeff Levin and Lea Steele, "The Transcendent Experience: Conceptual, Theoretical, and Epidemiologic Perspectives," *EXPLORE: The Journal of Science and Healing* 1 (2005), 89–101.

5. Paul Tillich, *Dynamics of Faith* (New York: Harper Colophon Books, 1957).

6. Jeff Levin and Stephen G. Post, Eds., *Divine Love: Perspectives from the World's Religious Traditions* (Conshohocken, PA: Templeton Foundation Press, 2010).

CHAPTER 1: THREE THINGS, MANY QUESTIONS

1. Rami M. Shapiro, *Wisdom of the Jewish Sages: A Modern Reading of Pirke Avot* (New York: Bell Tower, 1993), p. 3.

2. Jonah ben Abraham Gerondi, paraphrased in Judah Goldin, Trans., *The Living Talmud: The Wisdom of the Fathers, and Its Classical Commentaries* (New York: Heritage Press, 1960), p. 7.

3. Yehuda Leib Alter, *S'fas Emes*, p. 63, paraphrased in Victor Cohen, *The Soul of the Torah: Insights of the Hasidic Masters on the Weekly Torah Portions* (Northvale, NJ: Jason Aronson, 2000), p. 388.

4. Yisrael Meir Kagan, *Sefer Ahavas Chesed* 2:12, paraphrased in Fishel Schachter with Chana Nestlebaum, *Chofetz Chaim: Loving Kindness: Daily Lessons in the Power of Giving* (Brooklyn, NY: Mesorah Publications, 2003), p. 116.

5. Nathan Sternharz, "Letter # 5," *Healing Leaves (Alim LiTerufah): Prescriptions for Inner Strength, Meaning and Hope: From the Letters of Reb Noson of Breslov* [1896], compiled by Yitzchok Leib Bell, adapted

from the translation of Yaakov Gabel (Deerfield Beach, FL: Simcha Press, 1999), p. 5.

6. Kagan, *Sefer Ahavas Chesed* 2:13, paraphrased in Schachter with Nestlebaum, *Chofetz Chaim*, p. 139.

7. *The Complete ArtScroll Machzor (Machzor Yikhron Yosef): Yom Kippur*, translated and anthologized by Nosson Scherman, co-edited by Meir Zlotowitz and Avie Gold (Brooklyn, NY: Mesorah Publications, 1986), pp. 532–533.

8. For Orthodox, Conservative, and Reform examples, respectively: *The Complete ArtScroll Machzor; Mahzor Lev Shalom for Rosh Hashanah and Yom Kippur* (New York: Rabbinical Assembly, 2010), p. 143; *Gates of Repentance (Shaarei T'shuvah): The New Union High Holiday Prayer Book*, edited by Chaim Stern (New York: Central Conference of American Rabbis, 1978), p. 313.

9. Abba Hillel Silver, *Where Judaism Differs: An Inquiry into the Distinctiveness of Judaism* [1956] (New York: Collier Books, 1987), pp. 158–181.

10. A fundamental concept of Lurianic *kabbalah*. See, e.g., Lawrence Fine, *Safed Spirituality: Rules of Mystical Piety, The Beginning of Wisdom* (Mahwah, NJ: Paulist Press, 1984), pp. 61–63.

11. Kagan, *Sefer Ahavat Chesed* 2:12, paraphrased in Schachter with Nestlebaum, *Chofetz Chaim*, p. 117.

12. Kagan, *Sefer Ahavat Chesed* 2:4, paraphrased in Schachter with Nestlebaum, *Chofetz Chaim*, p. 42.

13. Kagan, *Sefer Ahavat Chesed* 2:17 footnotes, paraphrased in Schachter with Nestlebaum, *Chofetz Chaim*, p. 197.

14. Silver, *Where Judaism Differs*, p. 143.

15. Ibid., p. 177.

16. Pinhas ha Lévi of Barcelona, *Séfer haHinnuch: The Book of (Mitzvah) Education, Vol. IV: Numbers, & Deuteronomy, Part I* [1523], translated by Charles Wengrov (Jerusalem/New York: Feldheim Publishers, 1992), pp. 252–255.

17. Ibid., p. 255.

18. Ovadia ben Yaacov Sforno, *Sforno: Commentary on the Torah* [1567], translated with explanatory notes by Raphael Pelcovitz (Brooklyn, NY: Mesorah Publications, 1997), p. 864.

19. Ibid., p. 884.

20. Moses Maimonides, *Mishneh Torah: The Book of Knowledge* [1180], edited and translated by Moses Hyamson (Jerusalem/New York: Feldheim Publishers, 1981), pp. 66a–68b.

21. Robert N. Bellah, "Civil Religion in America," *Daedalus* 96 (1967), 1–21.

22. Schneur Zalman, *Tanya, Vol. 2*, paraphrased in Cohen, *The Soul of the Torah*, p. 342.

23. Ibid., p. 341.

24. Menachem Mendel Schneerson, *In the Garden of the Torah: Insights of the Lubavitcher Rebbe Rabbi Menachem M. Schneerson on the Weekly Torah Readings, Vol. 2* (Brooklyn, NY: Sichos in English, 1994), p. 3.

25. Menachem Mendel Schneerson, *Toward a Meaningful Life: The Wisdom of the Rebbe*, adapted by Simon Jacobson (New York: William Morrow and Company, 1995), pp. 59, 158–159.

26. Shlomo Josef Zevin, Ed., *Encyclopedia Talmudica: A Digest of Halachic Literature and Jewish Law from the Tannaitic Period to the Present Time Alphabetically Arranged, Vol. 1*, English translation edited by Isidore Epstein and Harry Freedman (Jerusalem: Talmudic Encyclopedia Institute, 1969), p. 268.

27. Ibid., pp. 268–269.

28. Ibid., p. 269.

29. Moshe Chaim Luzzatto, *Derech Hashem (The Way of God)* [c. 1734], 6th extensively revised edition, translated and annotated by Aryeh Kaplan (Jerusalem/New York: Feldheim Publishers, 1997), p. 267.

30. Ibid., p. 269.

31. Samson Raphael Hirsch, *T'rumath Tzvi. The Pentateuch with a Translation by Samson Raphael Hirsch and Excerpts from The Hirsch Commentary* [1867], edited by Ephraim Oratz, English translation by Gertrude Hirschler (New York: The Judaica Press, 1997), p. 680.

32. Ibid., pp. 680–681.

33. Leo Jung, *Knowledge and Love in Rabbinic Lore* (New York: Yeshiva University, 1963), p. 40.

34. Martin Buber, *Ten Rungs: Collected Hasidic Sayings*, p. 82, quoted in *Gates of Prayer (Shaarei T'fillah): The New Union Prayerbook* (New York: Central Conference of American Rabbis, 1975), p. 9.

35. David L. Lieber, Ed., *Etz Hayim: Torah and Commentary* (New York: The Rabbinical Assembly and the United Synagogue of Conservative Judaism, 2001), p. 1025.

36. Ibid.

37. Rifat Sonsino and Daniel B. Syme, *Finding God: Ten Jewish Responses* (Northvale, NJ: Jason Aronson, 1986).

38. Heidi M. Ravven and Lenn E. Goodman, "Introduction," in *Jewish Themes in Spinoza's Philosophy*, edited by Heidi M. Ravven and Lenn E. Goodman (Albany, NY: SUNY Press, 2002), pp. 3–16; Lee C. Rice, "Love and God in Spinoza," in Ravven and Goodman, *Jewish Themes in Spinoza's Philosophy*, pp. 93–106.

39. An alternative explanation is also possible: "It could be that *'b'chol l'vav'kha'* corresponds not to emotions but to cognition (as in the ancient Near East tradition to view the heart as the seat of the mind) and *'uv'chol nafsh'kha'* corresponds not to higher mind but to spirit. Accordingly, it would be the spirit (*nefesh*), in turn, that engages in *avodah* and achieves *shalom* and the mind (i.e., heart: *leivav*) that pursues *torah* and realizes *emet*. But, no matter, the general scheme holds—three psychological functions of mind, emotions, and behavior as highlighted in the *V'ahavta*—as well as the exegetical application of the Mishnaic passages to the *pasukim* in Deuteronomy" (from Jeff Levin, "Jewish Ethical Themes That Should Inform the National Healthcare Discussion: A Prolegomenon," in *Judaism and Health: A Handbook of Practical, Professional and Scholarly Resources*, edited by Jeff Levin and Michele F. Prince [Woodstock, VT: Jewish Lights, 2013], pp. 336–351, 394–397; quotation on p. 396). Thanks to Rabbi Gordon Fuller for this additional insight.

40. Samson Raphael Hirsch, *The Hirsch Siddur [Sidur Tefilot Yisra'el]: The Order of Prayers for the Whole Year* [1895] (Jerusalem/New York: Feldheim Publishers, 1997), p. 419.

CHAPTER 2: WHAT DOES IT MEAN TO LOVE GOD?

1. David de Sola Pool, Ed. and Trans., *The Traditional Prayer Book for Sabbath and Festivals (Siddur l'Shabbat v'Yom Tov)*, revised edition (New York: Behrman House, 1960), pp. 327–328.

2. Hirsch, *T'rumath Tzvi*, p. 88.

3. Nachmanides quoted in A. Cohen, Ed., *The Soncino Chumash: The Five Books of Moses with Haphtaroth* [1947], second edition (London: The Soncino Press, 1983), p. 86.

4. Macy Nulman, *The Encyclopedia of Jewish Prayer: Ashkenazic and Sephardic Rites* (Northvale, NJ: Jason Aronson, 1993), pp. 71–73.

5. de Sola Pool, *The Traditional Prayer Book for Sabbath and Festivals*.

6. Van A. Harvey, *A Handbook of Theological Terms* (New York: Touchstone, 1992), pp. 127–128, 242–243.

7. Solomon Schechter, *Aspects of Rabbinic Theology* [1909] (Woodstock, VT: Jewish Lights Publishing, 1993), p. 25.

8. Ibid., p. 29.

9. Ibid., p. 33.

10. Nulman, *The Encyclopedia of Jewish Prayer*, pp. 375–376.

11. Jordan Lee Wagner, *The Synagogue Survival Kit* (Northvale, NJ: Jason Aronson, 1997), pp. 275–277.

12. For Orthodox, Conservative, and Reform examples, respectively: de Sola Pool, *The Traditional Prayer Book for Sabbath and Festivals*, pp. 103–106; Jules Harlow, Ed., *Siddur Sim Shalom: A Prayerbook for Shabbat, Festivals, and Weekdays* (New York: The Rabbinical Assem-

bly/The United Synagogue of Conservative Judaism, 1985), pp. 326–327; and Elyse D. Frishman, *Mishkan T'filah: A Reform Siddur* (New York: Central Conference of American Rabbis, 2007), pp. 628–629.

13. Ronald H. Isaacs and Kerry M. Olitzky, Eds., *Critical Documents of Jewish History: A Sourcebook* (Northvale, NJ: Jason Aronson, 1995), pp. 179–180.

14. Isidore Epstein, *The Faith of Judaism: An Interpretation for Our Times* (London: Soncino Press, 1954), pp. 229–250.

15. Ibid., p. 236.

16. Bachya ibn Pakuda, *The Duties of the Heart* [1040], translated by Yaakov Feldman (Northvale, NJ: Jason Aronson, 1996).

17. Ibid., p. 443.

18. Ibid., p. 445.

19. Ibid., p. 442.

20. Ibid., p. 441.

21. Martin Buber, *Good and Evil: Two Interpretations* (New York: Charles Scribner's Sons, 1953), pp. 51–60.

22. Ibid., p. 59.

23. Ibid., pp. 54–55.

24. Ibid., p. 57.

25. Ibid., p. 58.

26. Ibid., p. 57.

27. Tzadok HaKohen, *Fun di ChasidisheOtsros*, p. 335, paraphrased in Cohen, *The Soul of the Torah*, p. 251.

28. A. Alan Steinbach, *Faith and Love* (New York: Philosophical Library, 1959), p. 4.

29. Ibid.

30. Ibid.

31. Bachya, *The Duties of the Heart*, p. 453.

32. Irving Singer, *The Nature of Love: 1. Plato to Luther* [1966], second edition (Chicago: The University of Chicago Press, 1984), p. 344.

33. Abraham Isaac Kook, *Abraham Isaac Kook—The Lights of Penitence, The Moral Principles, Lights of Holiness, Essay, Letters, and Poems*, translated by Ben Zion Bokser (Mahwah, NJ: Paulist Press, 1978).

34. Ibid., p. 135.

35. Ibid.

36. Ibid., p. 136.

37. Ibid., p. 137.

38. David Hartman, *A Living Covenant: The Innovative Spirit in Traditional Judaism* (Woodstock, NY: Jewish Lights Publishing, 1997), p. 148.

39. Ibid.

40. Joseph B. Soloveitchik, *The Lonely Man of Faith* (New York: Doubleday, 1965).

41. Silver, *Where Judaism Differs*, pp. 272–273.

42. Aryeh Kaplan, *Sefer Yetzirah—The Book of Creation: In Theory and Practice* (York Beach, ME: Samuel Weiser, 1990), pp. 25–26, 68–69.

CHAPTER 3: HOW DO WE LOVE GOD?

1. Elijah Benamozegh, *Israel and Humanity* [1914], translated and edited by Maxwell Luria (New York: Paulist Press, 1995), pp. 190–204.

2. Ibid., p. 195.

3. Ibid., p. 197.

4. Ibid., p. 192.

5. Neil Gillman, *The Way into Encountering God in Judaism* (Woodstock, VT: Jewish Lights Publishing, 2000), pp. 176.

6. Ibid., p. 179.

7. Levi Yitzchak of Berditchev, quoted in David R. Blumenthal, *God at the Center: Meditations on Jewish Spirituality* (Northvale NJ: Jason Aronson, 1994), p. 43.

8. Elliot N. Dorff, *Knowing God: Jewish Journeys to the Unknowable* (Northvale, NJ: Jason Aronson, 1992).

9. Ibid., p. 251.

10. Aryeh Kaplan, *Jewish Meditation: A Practical Guide* (New York: Schocken Books, 1985), p. 142.

11. Schneerson, *In the Garden of the Torah, Vol. 2*, p. 57.

12. Quoted in Robert Scheer, "*Playboy* Interview: Jimmy Carter," *Playboy* 23, 11 (1976, November), 63–64, 66, 69–71, 74, 77, 81, 84, 86; quotation on p. 86.

13. Luzzatto, *Derech Hashem*, p. 95.

14. Ibid., pp. 95, 97.

15. Yudit Kornberg Greenberg, "Love," in *The Cambridge Dictionary of Judaism and Jewish Culture*, edited by Judith R. Baskin (New York: Cambridge University Press, 2011), pp. 404–406, quotation on p. 404; and Yudit Kornberg Greenberg, "Commandments to Love," in *Encyclopedia of Love in World Religions, Vol. I: A–I*, edited by Yudit Kornberg Greenberg (Santa Barbara, CA: ABC/CLIO, 2008), pp. 118–119, quotation on p. 118. See also F. Brown, S. Driver, and C. Briggs, *The Brown-Driver-Briggs Hebrew and English Lexicon* [1906] (Peabody,

MA: Hendrickson Publishers, 1996), pp. 12–13, in which the root *ahv* includes denotations of "love to neighbor," "to individual men," and "to righteousness."

16. Byron L. Sherwin and Seymour J. Cohen, *How to Be a Jew: Ethical Teachings of Judaism* (Northvale, NJ: Jason Aronson, 1992), p. 32.

17. Sherwin and Cohen, *How to Be a Jew*.

18. Moshe Chaim Luzzatto, *Mesillas Yesharim (Path of the Just)* [1740], translated by Shraga Silverstein (Jerusalem/New York: Feldheim Publishers, 1980).

19. David A. Cooper, *God Is a Verb: Kabbalah and the Practice of Mystical Judaism* (New York: Riverhead Books, 1997).

20. Ibid., pp. 184–185.

21. Ibid., pp. 230–231.

22. Jacob Neusner, *Invitation to the Talmud: A Teaching Book*, revised and expanded edition (New York: HarperSanFrancisco, 1984), p. 273.

23. Ibid., p. 275.

24. Ibid., p. 282.

25. Moses Maimonides, *The Guide for the Perplexed* [1190], second revised edition, translated by M. Friedlander (New York: Dover Publications, 1956), p. 314.

26. Ibid.

27. Maharal of Prague, *Nesivos Olam: Nesiv HaTorah: An Appreciation of Torah Study* [1596], translated and adapted by Eliakim Willner (Brooklyn, NY: Mesorah Publications, 1994), p. 153.

28. Rifat Sonsino, *6 Jewish Spiritual Paths: A Rationalist Looks at Spirituality* (Woodstock, VT: Jewish Lights Publishing, 2000), p. 71.

29. Shapiro, *Wisdom of the Jewish Sages*, p. 29.

30. Moses Mielziner, *Introduction to the Talmud* [1894], fourth edition (New York: Bloch Publishing Company, 1968), p. 272.

31. Silver, *Where Judaism Differs*, p. 120.

32. Ismar Schorsch, *Canon Without Closure: Torah Commentaries* (New York: Aviv Press, 2007), p. 285.

33. Abraham Cohen, *Everyman's Talmud: The Major Teachings of the Rabbinic Sages* (New York: Schocken Books, 1949), pp. 121–158.

34. Ibid., p. 149.

35. Ibid.

36. Ibid.

37. Abraham Joshua Heschel, *Man's Quest for God: Studies in Prayer and Symbolism* [1954] (Santa Fe, NM: Aurora Press, 1998), p. 5.

38. Soloveitchik, *The Lonely Man of Faith*, p. 56.

39. Abraham Joshua Heschel, *God in Search of Man: A Philosophy of Judaism* (New York: Farrar, Straus & Cudahy, 1955).

40. Jeff Levin, "Prayer, Love, and Transcendence: An Epidemiologic Perspective," in *Religious Influences on Health and Well-Being in the Elderly*, edited by K. Warner Schaie, Neal Krause, and Alan Booth (New York: Springer, 2004), pp. 69–95.

41. Ibid., p. 72.

42. Jeffrey S. Levin and Robert Joseph Taylor, "Age Differences in Patterns and Correlates of the Frequency of Prayer," *The Gerontologist* 37 (1997), 75–88.

43. Ibid., p. 85.

44. Nulman, *The Encyclopedia of Jewish Prayer*.

45. Jeffrey S. Levin, "How Prayer Heals: A Theoretical Model," *Alternative Therapies in Health and Medicine* 2, 1 (1996), 66–73.

46. Larry VandeCreek, Ed., *Scientific and Pastoral Perspectives on Intercessory Prayer: An Exchange Between Larry Dossey, M.D. and Health Care Chaplains* (New York: Haworth Pastoral Press, 1988).

47. Seth Kadish, *Kavvana: Directing the Heart in Jewish Prayer* (Northvale, NJ: Jason Aronson, 1997), pp. 45–60.

48. Nulman, *The Encyclopedia of Jewish Prayer*, pp. 243–245.

49. Brother Lawrence, *The Practice of the Presence of God* [1692], translated by Robert J. Edmonson; edited by Hal H. Helms (Orleans, MA: Paraclete Press, 1985).

50. Gershom Scholem, *Kabbalah* (New York: Meridian, 1974).

51. Moshe D. Sherman, *Orthodox Judaism in America: A Biographical Dictionary and Sourcebook* (Westport, CT: Greenwood Press, 1996), pp. 133–134.

52. Zalman Schachter-Shalomi, *Paradigm Shift: From the Jewish Renewal Teachings of Reb Zalman Schachter-Shalomi*, edited by Ellen Singer (Northvale, NJ: Jason Aronson, 1993), p. 22.

53. Aryeh Kaplan, *Jewish Meditation*; Aryeh Kaplan, *Meditation and the Bible* (York Beach, ME: Samuel Weiser, 1978); and Aryeh Kaplan, *Meditation and Kabbalah* (York Beach, ME: Samuel Weiser, 1981).

54. Rodger Kamenetz, *The Jew and the Lotus: A Poet's Rediscovery of Jewish Identity in Buddhist India* (New York: HarperSanFrancisco, 1994); and *Stalking Elijah: Adventures with Today's Jewish Mystical Masters* (New York: HarperSanFrancisco, 1997).

55. Schachter-Shalomi, *Paradigm Shift*, p. 19.

56. Kaplan, *Meditation and the Bible*, p. 152.

57. *Schulchan Aruch, Orach Chayyim* 162.

58. Yaakov Baal HaTurim, *Baal Haturim Chumash: The Torah: With the Baal Haturim's Classic Commentary Translated, Annotated, and Elucidated* [1544], translated by Eliyahu Touger; edited, elucidated, and annotated by Avi Gold (Brooklyn, NY: Mesorah Publications Ltd., 2004), p. 663.

59. Emil L. Fackenheim, "Apologia for a Confirmation Text," *Commentary* 31 (May 1961), 401–410; quotation from p. 409.

60. Elie Munk, *The Call of the Torah (Kol HaTorah): An Anthology of Interpretation and Commentary on the Five Books of Moses, Vol. 5: Devarim* [1975], translated by E. S. Mazer; edited by Yitzchok Kirzner (Brooklyn, NY: Mesorah Publications, 1995), p. 67.

61. Elie Munk, *The Call of the Torah (Kol HaTorah): An Anthology of Interpretation and Commentary on the Five Books of Moses, Vol. 2: Shemos* [1975], translated by E. S. Mazer; edited by Yitzchok Kirzner (Brooklyn, NY: Mesorah Publications, 1994), p. 198.

62. *The Ways of the Tzaddikim (Orchot Tzaddikim)* [1430, as *Sefer ha-Middot*], edited by Gavriel Zaloshinksy; translated by Shraga Silverstein (Jerusalem/New York: Feldheim Publishers, 1995), p. 131.

63. *Tanna Debe Eliyyahu: The Lore of the School of Elijah*, translated by William G. Braude and Israel J. Kapstein (Philadelphia: Jewish Publication Society of America, 1981), *Eliyyahu Rabbah*, 140, p. 306.

64. Schorsch, *Canon Without Closure*, p. 29.

65. Ibid., p. 152.

66. Naftali Rothenberg, "Love of Neighbor in Judaism," in *Encyclopedia of Love in World Religions, Volume 2: J–Z*, edited by Yudit Kornberg Greenberg (Santa Barbara, CA: ABC-CLIO, 2008), pp. 384–385; quotation on p. 384.

67. Seymour Rossel, *The Torah Portion-by-Portion* (Los Angeles: Torah Aura Publications, 2007), p. 337.

68. Shai Held, "Compassion in Judaism," in Greenberg, *Encyclopedia of Love in World Religions, Volume 1: A–I*, pp. 132–133; quotation on p. 133.

69. Sarah Pessin, "Divine Love in Judaism," in Greenberg, *Encyclopedia of Love in World Religions, Volume 1: A–I*, pp. 166–167; quotation on p. 167.

70. Jacob Neusner, "Rabbinic Judaism," in Greenberg, *Encyclopedia of Love in World Religions, Volume 2: J–Z*, pp. 497–501; quotation on p. 499.

71. Lawrence H. Schiffman, "Commandment or Emotion?: Love of God, Family, and Humanity in Classical Judaism," in *Love—Ideal and Real—in the Jewish Tradition from the Hebrew Bible to Modern Times*, edited by Leonard J. Greenspoon, Ronald A. Simkins, and Jean A.

Cahan (Omaha, NE: Creighton University Press, 2008), pp. 1–19; quotation on p. 4.

72. Ibid.

73. Schachter with Nestlebaum, *Chofetz Chaim.*

74. Samson Raphael Hirsch, *The Hirsch Siddur [Sidur Tefilot Yisra'el]: The Order of Prayers for the Whole Year* [1895] (Jerusalem/New York: Feldheim Publishers, 1997), p. 420.

75. Charles Poncé, *Kabbalah: An Introduction and Illumination for the World Today* (Wheaton, IL: Quest Books, 1973), p. 125.

76. Note 40 to *Sukkah* 49b, in Isidore Epstein, Trans. and Ed., *The Babylonian Talmud* (London: Soncino Press, 1961).

77. Joseph ben Abraham Gikatilla, *Gates of Light (Sha'are Orah)* [c. 1293], translated by Avi Weinstein (New York: HarperCollins, 1994), pp. 106–108.

78. Rashi on Genesis 47:29, in Nosson Scherman, *The Chumash: The Torah: Haftaros and Five Megillos with a Commentary Anthologized from the Rabbinic Writings, The Stone Edition* (Brooklyn, NY: Mesorah Publications, 1993), p. 269.

79. Silver, *Where Judaism Differs,* p. 231.

80. Ibid., p. 236.

81. Paul Johnson, *A History of the Jews* (New York: HarperPerennial, 1987), p. 155.

82. Isaacs and Olitzky, *Critical Documents of Jewish History,* pp. 79–82.

83. Elliot N. Dorff, *The Way into Tikkun Olam (Repairing the World)* (Woodstock, VT: Jewish Lights Publishing, 2005), p. 19.

84. Ibid., p. 13.

85. Ibid., p. 19.

86. Michael Lerner, *The Politics of Meaning: Restoring Hope and Possibility in an Age of Cynicism* (New York: Addison-Wesley, 1996).

87. Michael Lerner, *The Socialism of Fools: Anti-Semitism on the Left* (Oakland, CA: Institute for Labor and Mental Health, 1992).

88. Arthur Waskow, *These Holy Sparks: The Rebirth of the Jewish People* (San Francisco: Harper & Row, 1983).

89. Elliott Abrams, *Faith or Fear: How Jews Can Survive in a Christian America* (New York: The Free Press, 1997).

Chapter 4: How Does Loving God Affect Our Lives?

1. Moses Maimonides, *Mishneh Torah: Sefer HaMadda: Hilchot Teshuvah,* p. 93a, quoted in Shalom Noach Berezovsky, *Jewish Pathways of Equa-*

nimity (Netivot Shalom): A Compendium of Spiritual Guidance from a Contemporary Hassidic Master, Rabbi Shalom Noach Berezovsky Z"L, Rebbe of Slonim, translated by Jonathan Glass (http:// www.geocities.ws/ravjglass/netivotshalom.htm).

2. Luzzatto, *Derech Hashem*, p. 67.

3. Luzzatto, *Mesillas Yesharim*, p. 176.

4. Ibid., p. 177.

5. Ibid., pp. 177–178.

6. Nulman, *The Encyclopedia of Jewish Prayer*, pp. 42–43.

7. For Orthodox, Conservative, and Reform examples, respectively: de Sola Pool, *The Traditional Prayer Book for Sabbath and Festivals*, pp. 3–6; Harlow, *Siddur Sim Shalom*, pp. 420–423; and Frishman, *Mishkan T'filah*, pp. 215–217.

8. de Sola Pool, *The Traditional Prayer Book for Sabbath and Festivals*, p. 6.

9. Luzzatto, *Mesillas Yesharim*, p. 12.

10. David J. Wolpe, *The Healer of Shattered Hearts* (New York: Penguin Books, 1990), p. 20.

11. Joseph Telushkin, "Preface," in Dennis Prager and Joseph Telushkin, *The Nine Questions People Ask About Judaism* (New York: Touchstone, 1981), p. 16.

12. Bradley Shavit Artson, *The Bedside Torah: Wisdom, Visions, and Dreams*, edited by Miriyam Glazer (Chicago: Contemporary Books, 2001).

13. Ibid., p. 295.

14. Ibid.

15. Ibid., p. 296.

16. Ibid.

17. Ibid.

18. S. Angus, *The Mystery-Religions* [1925] (New York: Dover Publications, 1975), pp. 95–100.

19. Harvey, *A Handbook of Theological Terms*, pp. 33–35.

20. Simon Glustrom, *The Language of Judaism* (Northvale, NJ: Jason Aronson, 1988), pp. 171–172.

21. Emil Fackenheim, *To Mend the World: Foundations of Future Jewish Thought* (New York: Schocken Books, 1982), p. 10.

22. Dan Cohn-Sherbok, *The Crucified Jew: Twenty Centuries of Christian Anti-Semitism* (Grand Rapids, MI: William B. Eerdmans, 1992), p. 232.

23. Yosef Dov Ber Soloveitchik, "Shemos," in *Beis Halevi: Shemos* [1884], translated by Yisrael Isser Zvi Herczeg (Southfield, MI: Targum/ Spring Valley, NY: Feldheim, 1991), pp. 9–39; quotation on p. 14.

The consequence, as paraphrased by a contemporary Orthodox rabbi, is that our otherness will be reinforced and "the Jewish people will remain a people apart" (Avi Shafran, "Shedding Light on Anti-Semitism," Reflections on Jews, Judaism, Media and Life (2010) (http://rabbiavishafran.com/shedding-light-anti-semitism/).

24. Rami M. Shapiro, quoted in *Being a Blessing: 54 Ways You Can Help People Living with AIDS*, edited by Harris R. Goldstein (Los Angeles: Alef Design Group, 1994), p. 82.

25. de Sola Pool, *The Traditional Prayer Book for Sabbath and Festivals*, pp. 55–56.

26. Ibid., pp. 187–188.

27. Maimonides, *Mishneh Torah*, p. 82b.

28. Adin Steinsaltz, *The Thirteen Petalled Rose: A Discourse on the Essence of Jewish Existence and Belief* (New York: Basic Books, 1980), p. 127.

29. Ibid., p. 131.

30. Ibid., p. 130.

31. Ibid., pp. 131–132.

32. Ibid., p. 134.

33. Ibid., p. 133.

34. Luzzatto, *Mesillas Yesharim*.

35. Buber, *Ten Rungs*, p. 7.

36. John Suler, "It Will Pass," in *Zen Stories to Tell Your Neighbors* (1997) (http://truecenterpublishing.com/zenstory/willpass.html).

37. Huston Smith, *Why Religion Matters: The State of the Human Spirit in an Age of Disbelief* (New York: HarperSanFrancisco, 2001), pp. 255–256.

38. Levin, *God, Faith, and Health*, pp. 9–10.

39. Ibid., p. 10.

40. Shmuel Shmayeh Ostrovitzer, *Milei D'Chasida*, p. 176, paraphrased in Cohen, *The Soul of the Torah*, p. 170.

41. Silver, *Where Judaism Differs*, p. 195.

42. Kook, *Abraham Isaac Kook*, p. 50.

43. Ibid., p. 88.

44. Ibid., p. 95.

45. Ibid., p. 84.

46. Ibid., p. 85.

47. Ibid., p. 93.

48. Ibid., p. 362.

49. Schneerson, *Toward a Meaningful Life*, p. 280.

50. Ibid., p. 281.

CHAPTER 5: HOW DOES LOVING GOD AFFECT OUR WORLD?

1. For Orthodox, Conservative, and Reform examples, respectively: de Sola Pool, *The Traditional Prayer Book for Sabbath and Festivals*, pp. 107–110; Harlow, *Siddur Sim Shalom*, pp. 10–11; and Frishman, *Mishkan T'filah*, pp. 36–38.

2. Buber, *Ten Rungs*, p. 7.

3. Jonathan Sacks, *A Letter in the Scroll: Understanding Our Jewish Identity and Exploring the Legacy of the World's Oldest Religion* (New York: Free Press, 2000), p. 42.

4. Ibid.

5. Ibid., p. 44.

6. Ibid., p. 47.

7. Ibid.

8. Neusner, *Invitation to the Talmud*, p. 26.

9. Ibid., p. 38.

10. Ibid., p. 232.

11. Ibid., pp. 221–222.

12. J. H. Hertz, Ed., *The Pentateuch and Haftorahs: Hebrew Text, English Translation and Commentary* [1936], second edition (London: Soncino Press, 1992), p. 14.

13. Lieber, *Etz Hayim*, p. 13.

14. Ibid.

15. W. Gunter Plaut, Ed., *The Torah: A Modern Commentary*, revised edition (New York: Union for Reform Judaism, 2005), p. 41.

16. Hirsch, *T'rumath Tzvi*, p. 23.

17. Ibid.

18. Ibid.

19. Plaut, *The Torah*.

20. C. S. Lewis, *The Abolition of Man, or Reflections on Education with Special Reference to the Teaching of English in the Upper Forms of Schools* [1941] (New York: HarperSanFrancisco, 1974), pp. 83–101.

21. Sacks, *A Letter in the Scroll*, p. 154.

22. Dorff, *The Way into Tikkun Olam*, pp. 226–249.

23. Yonah ben Avraham of Gerona, *The Gates of Repentance (Shaarei Teshuvah)* [1505], translated by Shraga Silverstein (Jerusalem/New York: Feldheim Publishers, 1967), pp. 186–187.

24. Jonathan Sacks, *The Dignity of Difference: How to Avoid the Clash of Civilizations*, second edition (London: Continuum, 2003), p. 192.

25. Ibid., pp. 192–209.

26. Simeon ben Zemah Duran, paraphrased in Judah Goldin, Trans., *The Living Talmud: The Wisdom of the Fathers, and Its Classical Commentaries* (New York: Heritage Press, 1960), p. 24.

27. Ibid.

28. Cooper, *God Is a Verb*, p. 179.

29. Ibid., pp. 179–180.

30. Wayne Dosick, *Living Judaism: The Complete Guide to Jewish Belief, Tradition, and Practice* (New York: HarperSanFrancisco, 1995), p. 38.

31. Jacob Neusner and Alan J. Avery-Peck, "Altruism in Classical Judaism," in *Altruism in World Religions*, edited by Jacob Neusner and Bruce D. Chilton (Washington, DC: Georgetown University Press, 2005), pp. 31–52.

32. Nachman of Breslov, *The Aleph-Bet Book (Sefer HaMiddot) (The Book of Attributes): Rabbi Nachman's Aphorisms on Jewish Living* [1811], translated by Moshe Mykoff (Jerusalem: Breslov Research Institute, 1986).

33. Ben Zion Bokser, "A Note on the Text," in Kook, *Abraham Isaac Kook*, p. 132.

34. Kook, *Abraham Isaac Kook*, pp. 135–185.

35. Abraham Isaac Kook, *Iggerot ha-Re'iyah* I, 45–46, cited in Michael Z. Nehorai, "Halakhah, Metahalakhah, and the Redemption of Israel: Reflections on the Rabbinic Rulings of Rav Kook," in *Rabbi Abraham Isaac Kook and Jewish Spirituality*, edited by Lawrence J. Kaplan and David Shatz (New York: New York University Press, 1995), pp. 120–156, quotation on p. 149.

36. John Winthrop, "A Modell of Christian Charity" [1630], in *Collections of the Massachusetts Historical Society. Vol. VII: Of the Third Series* (Boston: Charles C. Little and James Brown, 1838), pp. 31–48; quotation on p. 47.

37. Matthew 5:14–16.

38. Sydney E. Ahlstrom, *A Religious History of the American People* [1972], second edition (New Haven, CT: Yale University Press, 2004), pp. 144–150.

39. Harvey, *A Handbook of Theological Terms*, p. 155.

40. Sacks, *A Letter in the Scroll*, pp. 77–90.

41. Ibid., p. 84.

42. Samuel E. Karff, *Permission to Believe: Finding Faith in Troubled Times* (Nashville: Abingdon Press, 2005), p. ix.

43. Kenneth I. Pargament, *The Psychology of Religion and Coping: Theory, Research, Practice* (New York: Guilford Press, 1997).

44. Levin, *God, Faith, and Health.*

45. Nulman, *The Encyclopedia of Jewish Prayer*, pp. 109–112.

46. Reuven Hammer, Trans., *The Classic Midrash: Tannaitic Commentaries on the Bible* (New York: Paulist Press, 1995), pp. 222–233.

47. Ibid., p. 233.

48. Karff, *Permission to Believe*, p. vii.

49. Emil G. Hirsch, *My Religion*, compiled by Gerson B. Levi (New York: Macmillan, 1925), pp. 76–77.

CHAPTER 6: JEWISH PERSPECTIVES ON LOVING GOD

1. Leo Baeck, *The Essence of Judaism* [1905], translated by Victor Grubwieser and Leonard Pearl (New York: Macmillan, 1936), p. 197.

2. Moshe Zemer, *Evolving Halakhah: A Progressive Approach to Traditional Jewish Law*, translated by Yehuda Hanegbi (Woodstock, VT: Jewish Lights Publishing, 1999).

3. Ibid., p. 46.

4. Ibid.

5. Ibid., p. 49.

6. Ibid., p. 50.

7. David Ellenson, *Tradition in Transition: Orthodoxy, Halakhah, and the Boundaries of Modern Jewish Identity* (Lanham, MD: University Press of America, 1989), p. 3.

8. Yisrael Meir Kagan, *The Concise Book of Mitzvoth (Sefer haMitzvoth haKatzar): The Commandments Which Can Be Observed Today* [1931], translated by Charles Wengov (Jerusalem: Feldheim Publishers, 1990), pp. 14–15.

9. Ibid.

10. Moses Maimonides, *The Commandments: Sefer Ha-Mitzvoth of Maimonides* [a. 1204], translated by Charles B. Chavel (London: Soncino Press, 1967).

11. Kagan, *The Concise Book of Mitzvoth.*

12. Levin, *God, Faith, and Health*, pp. 208–215.

13. Tillich, *Dynamics of Faith.*

14. Huston Smith, *The Religions of Man* (New York: Harper & Row, 1958), pp. 36–51; and Heinrich Zimmer, *Philosophies of India*, edited by Joseph Campbell (Princeton, NJ: Princeton University Press, 1951), pp. 294–305.

15. H. P. Blavatsky, *The Secret Doctrine: The Synthesis of Science, Religion, and Philosophy* [1888] (Pasadena, CA: Theosophical University Press, 1970).

16. Robert Ellwood, *Theosophy: A Modern Expression of the Wisdom of the Ages* (Wheaton, IL: Theosophical Publishing House, 1986), pp. 118–144.

17. Hadith of Tirmizi, 1490/125, quoted in Maulana Muhammad Manzoor No'mani, *Meaning and Message of the Traditions (Ma'ariful Hadith), Vol. Three, Part VI* [1975], translated by Mohammad Asif Kidwai; completed and revised by Rafiq Abdur Rehman (Karachi, Pakistan: Darul-Ishaat, 2002), p. 437.

18. No'mani, *Meaning and Message of the Traditions*, p. 437.

19. Baeck, *The Essence of Judaism*, p. 191.

20. *Qur'an* 5:93, in *The Koran*, fourth revised edition, translated by N. J. Dawood (Harmondsworth, Middlesex, England: Penguin Classics, 1974), p. 397.

21. *Qur'an* 3:31, in Ibid., p. 410.

22. I John 4:16 (RSV).

23. Paramahansa Yogananda, *Sayings of Paramahansa Yogananda* [1952], fourth edition (Los Angeles: Self-Realization Fellowship, 1980), pp. 84–85.

24. Sherwin and Cohen, *How to Be a Jew*, p. 29.

25. Schachter-Shalomi, *Paradigm Shift*, p. 144.

26. Paul Tillich, *The Courage to Be* (New Haven, CT: Yale University Press, 1952).

27. *Ha'amek Davar: The Netziv's Classic Work Translated and Explained* [1879–1880], translated by Yaacov Deutsch (Bet Shemesh, Israel: Machon Ohr Olam, n.d.), commentary on Numbers 24:6.

28. Note 34 to *Sanhedrin* 56a, in Epstein, *The Babylonian Talmud*.

INDEX OF VERSES

To minimize use of notes, all biblical and canonical rabbinic references are given parenthetically in the text. English-language passages are quoted from the following sources. Biblical verses are taken from the 1985 New Jewish Publication Society (NJPS) translation, as published in revised form by the Jewish Publication Society (JPS) in its 1999 *Hebrew-English Tanakh,*[1] except in instances where the older 1917 JPS translation (a.k.a. the American Jewish Version), or another translation, such as the Koren Tenakh, is more familiar. Talmudic passages are from Epstein's Soncino version,[2] as are passages from the Mishnah, except where Neusner's new literal translation is used.[3] Neusner is also the source for the Tosefta[4] and the Yerushalmi.[5] Midrashic passages come from various sources: passages from *Midrash Rabbah* are from Freedman and Simon's Soncino text,[6] *Sifre* are from Hammer,[7] *Midrash T'hillim* are from Braude,[8] and *Midrash Tanchuma* are from Berman.[9] Passages from *Zohar* are from Sperling and Simon's 1984 edition of the Soncino version.[10] Quotations from *Pirke Avot* are variously from Soncino, Neusner, Goldin,[11] and Shapiro's poetic version;[12] those from *Avot d'Rabbi Natan* are also taken from Goldin.[13] Occasionally, I have made minor cosmetic changes to cited passages with respect to punctuation, proper names, or bracketed material to ensure greater uniformity throughout the book.

---

1. *JPS Hebrew-English Tanakh: The Traditional Hebrew Text and the New JPS Translation* [1985], second edition (Philadelphia: Jewish Publication Society, 1999).

2. Epstein, Isidore, Trans. and Ed., *The Babylonian Talmud* (London: Soncino Press, 1961).

3. Jacob Neusner, Trans., *The Mishnah: A New Translation* (New Haven, CT: Yale University Press, 1988).

4. Jacob Neusner, Trans., *The Tosefta* (Peabody, MA: Hendrickson Publishers, 2002).

5. Jacob Neusner, Trans., *The Talmud of the Land of Israel: An Academic Commentary to the Second, Third, and Fourth Divisions* (Atlanta: Scholars Press, 1998).

6. H. Freedman and Maurice Simon, Trans. and Ed., *Midrash Rabbah* [1939] (London: Soncino Press, 1977).

7. Reuven Hammer, Trans., *Sifre: A Tannaitic Commentary on the Book of Deuteronomy* (New Haven, CT: Yale University Press, 1986).

8. William G. Braude, Trans., *The Midrash on Psalms* (New Haven, CT: Yale University Press, 1987).

9. Samuel A. Berman, Trans., *Midrash Tanhuma-Yelammendenu: An English Translation of Genesis and Exodus from the Printed Version of Tanhuma-Yelammendenu with an Introduction, Notes, and Indexes* (Hoboken, NJ: KTAV Publishing, 1996).

10. Harry Sperling and Maurice Simon, Trans., *The Zohar* [1934], second edition (London: Soncino Press, 1984).

11. Judah Goldin, Trans., *The Living Talmud: The Wisdom of the Fathers, and Its Classical Commentaries* (New York: Heritage Press, 1960).

12. Rami M. Shapiro, *Wisdom of the Jewish Sages: A Modern Reading of Pirke Avot* (New York: Bell Tower, 1993).

13. Judah Goldin, Trans., *The Fathers According to Rabbi Nathan* (New Haven, CT: Yale University Press, 1954).

TANAKH

Genesis

1:26	97
1:27	23
1:31	8
3:17	129
3:21	138
4:8–9	129
4:11	129
4:12	129
4:17–22	132
5:1–31	132
6:13	173
9:6	23
9:16	19
11:6	59
12:1	8, 47, 119, 170
17:1	30
17:3	30
17:4–22	30
17:18	165
17:20	165
17:21	165
18:1	30, 138
18:20	173
19:29	173
24:27	80
25:11	138
32:31	13
35:3	164

Exodus

3:4	28
3:6	28
3:7	28
3:8	28
3:10	28
3:11	28
3:12	28
3:13	29
3:14	26, 29
3:15	29
7-14	173
8:6	101
12:49	84
14:15	76
15:26	11
19:5	53
19:6	152
19:8	21
20:6	172
21:30	120
22:21	83
22:22–23	83
23:2	127
23:9	136
23:12	84
24:7	49
32:29	20
34:6–7	26, 35
35:35	171
40:38	138

Leviticus

10:1	102
18:5	54
19:18	78, 133
19:19	133
19:34	92
24:22	84

Numbers

6:23–27	150
6:24	20
15:16	84
23:9	101

Deuteronomy

4:24	138
4:29	170
5:2	26
6:4	32
6:5	3, 14, 17, 18, 20, 25, 42, 53, 64, 78, 95, 142, 162
7:6	59, 104
7:9	173
7:9–10	27
8:6	172
9:4	148
10:12	15
10:17	172
10:18	172
10:19	172
10:20	7, 172
11:1	148
11:13	95, 170
11:22	13
11:27	21
13:5	36, 137, 171
15:5	168
16:20	xiii, 9, 79
19:9	95, 168
23:8	44
28:9	118
29:8	12
30:6	3
30:14	5
30:16	25, 95
30:19	45, 47, 167
30:20	53, 163, 167
31:23	106
32:16	16, 102, 145
32:20	41
33:27	149
34:6	138

INDEX

Jeff Levin, PhD, MPH, an epidemiologist by training, holds a distinguished chair at Baylor University, where he is University Professor of Epidemiology and Population Health, Professor of Medical Humanities, and Director of the Program on Religion and Population Health at the Institute for Studies of Religion. He also serves as Adjunct Professor of Psychiatry and Behavioral Sciences at Duke University School of Medicine. Dr. Levin lives with his wife, Dr. Lea Steele Levin, in Texas.